VISUAL FACTFINDER

SCIENCE

First published by Bardfield Press in 2004
Copyright © Miles Kelly Publishing 2004

Bardfield Press is an imprint of
Miles Kelly Publishing Ltd,
Bardfield Centre, Great Bardfield, Essex, CM7 4SL

2 4 6 8 10 9 7 5 3

Publishing Director: Anne Marshall

Editors: Stuart Cooper, Belinda Gallagher

Editorial Assistant: Rosalind McGuire

Designer: Debbie Meekcoms

Design Assistant: Tom Slemmings

Production Manager: Estela Boulton

Indexer: Charlotte Marshall

British Library Cataloguing-in-Publication Data
A catalogue record for this book is available from the British Library

ISBN 1-84236-381-6

Printed in China

www.mileskelly.net
info@mileskelly.net

VISUAL FACTFINDER

SCIENCE

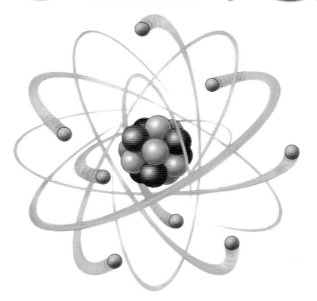

John Farndon
Consultants: Steve Parker
Brian Williams

**BARDFIELD
PRESS**

Contents

——— ◆ ◆ ◆ ———

Electricity, magnetism and radiation

——— ◆ ◆ ◆ ———

Technology

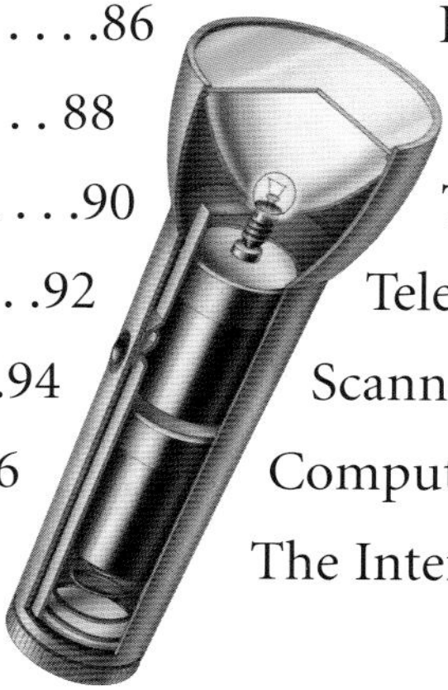

———— ◆ ◆ ◆ ————

Energy, force and motion

———— ◆ ◆ ◆ ————

The frontiers of science

Skeleton and muscle

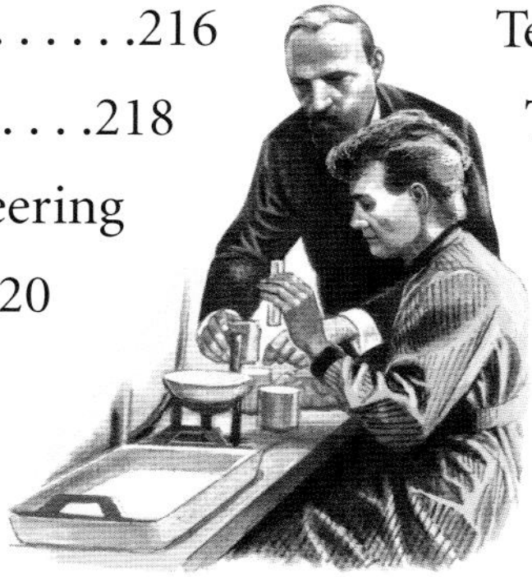

—— ◆ ◆ ◆ ——

Breathing and blood

—— ◆ ◆ ◆ ——

The digestive system

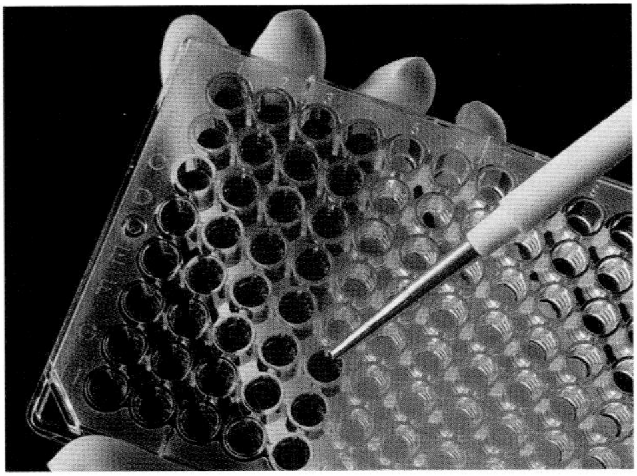

──── ◆ ◆ ◆ ────

Health and disease

──── ◆ ◆ ◆ ────

Transport

—— ◆ ◆ ◆ ——

Engineering

SCIENCE

How fast is the speed of light?

Is time travel really possible?

What is the largest internal organ of the body?

The answers to these and many other questions can be found in this amazing book of almost 2500 facts. The branches of science have been split into sections, each dealing with core subjects such as matter, chemicals and materials through to electricity, energy, force and motion.

The second part of the book takes a closer look at human biology. As well as covering main body systems, there are hundreds of facts on subjects such as mind and senses and health and disease. The final section of the book introduces transport and engineering in the form of record-breaking vehicles and stunning architecture.

Elements

- **Elements** are the basic chemicals of the Universe. Each element is made from only one kind of atom, with a certain number of sub atomic particles and its own unique character.

- **More than 115** elements have so far been identified.

- **Each element** is listed in the periodic table.

- **At least 20** of the most recently identified elements were created entirely by scientists and do not exist naturally.

- **All the most recently discovered elements** have very large, heavy atoms.

- **The lightest atom** is hydrogen.

- **The densest naturally occurring element** is osmium.

- **When different elements combine** they make chemical compounds (see chemical compounds).

- **New elements** get their name from their atomic number (see the Periodic Table). So the new element with atomic number 116 is called ununhexium. *Un* is the Latin word for one; *hex* is Latin for six.

▲ *Very few elements occur naturally by themselves. Most occur in combination with others in compounds. Gold is one of the few elements found as a pure 'native' element.*

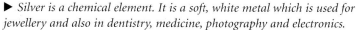

▶ *Silver is a chemical element. It is a soft, white metal which is used for jewellery and also in dentistry, medicine, photography and electronics.*

▲ *As the demand for aluminium grows each year with more and more uses being found for it, so recycling becomes ever more important.*

▲ *Aluminium is used to make drink cans since it is a light weight metal that does not rust and resists wear from weather or chemicals.*

Atoms

- **Atoms are** tiny particles which build together to make every substance. An atom is the tiniest bit of any pure substance or chemical element.

- **You could fit** two billion atoms on the full stop after this sentence.

- **The number of atoms** in the Universe is about 10 followed by 80 zeros.

- **Atoms are mostly** empty space dotted with a few even tinier particles called subatomic particles.

- **In the centre** of each atom is a dense core, or nucleus, made from two kinds of particle: protons and neutrons. Protons have a positive electrical charge, and neutrons none. Both protons and neutrons are made from different combinations of quarks (see quarks).

- **If an atom** were the size of a sports arena, its nucleus would be just the size of a pea.

- **Around the nucleus** whizz even tinier, negatively-charged particles called electrons (see electrons).

- **Atoms can be split** but they are usually held together by three forces: the electrical attraction between positive protons and negative electrons, and the strong and weak 'nuclear' forces that hold the nucleus together.

- **Every element** is made from atoms with a certain number of protons in the nucleus. An iron atom has 26 protons, gold has 79. The number of protons is the atomic number.

- **Atoms with the same number** of protons but a different number of neutrons are called isotopes.

▶ *The nucleus of an atom is made up of two kinds of particle: protons (red) and neutrons (green). Protons have a positive electric charge while neutrons have none. Tiny electrons (blue) whizz around the nucleus.*

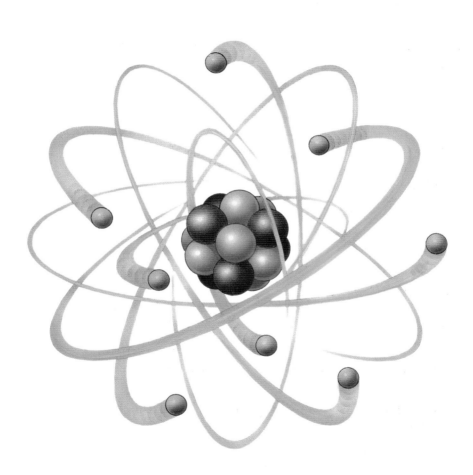

Electrons

- **Electrons** are by far the smallest of the three main, stable parts of every atom; the other two parts are protons and neutrons (see atoms). In a normal atom there are the same number of electrons as protons.

- **Electrons** are 1836 times as small as protons and have a mass of just 9.109×10^{-31} kg. 10^{-31} means there are 30 zeros after the decimal point. So they weigh almost nothing.

- **Electrons were discovered** by English physicist Joseph John Thomson in 1897 as he studied the glow in a cathode-ray tube (see television). This was the first time anyone realized that the atom is not just one solid ball.

▼ *Each atom has a different number of electrons. Its chemical character depends on the number of electrons in its outer shell. Atoms with only one electron in their outer shell, such as lithium, sodium and potassium, have many properties in common. The electron shell structures for five common atoms are shown here.*

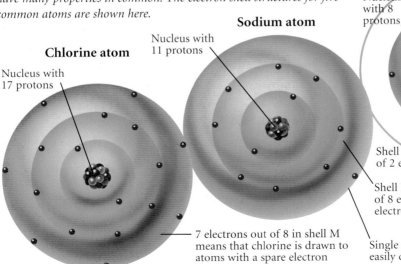

Oxygen atom

Nucleus with 8 protons

Sodium atom

Nucleus with 11 protons

Chlorine atom

Nucleus with 17 protons

Shell K holds a maximum of 2 electrons

Shell L holds a maximum of 8 electrons, so the next electron goes in shell M

7 electrons out of 8 in shell M means that chlorine is drawn to atoms with a spare electron

Single electron in shell M is easily drawn to other atoms

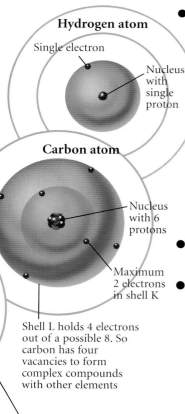

Hydrogen atom

Single electron

Nucleus with single proton

Carbon atom

Nucleus with 6 protons

Maximum 2 electrons in shell K

Shell L holds 4 electrons out of a possible 8. So carbon has four vacancies to form complex compounds with other elements

Shell L holds 6 electrons out of a possible 8. So oxygen has 2 'missing' electrons and is very reactive

- **Electrons are** packets of energy. They can be thought of either as a tiny vibration or wave, or as a ball-like particle. They travel as waves and arrive as particles.

  - **You can never be sure** just where an electron is. It is better to think of an electron circling the nucleus not as a planet circling the Sun but as a cloud wrapped around it. Electron clouds near the nucleus are round, but those farther out are other shapes.

  - **Electrons** have a negative electrical charge. This means they are attracted to positive electrical charges and pushed away by negative charges.

- **Electrons cling** to the nucleus because protons have a positive charge equal to the electron's negative charge.

- **Electrons have so much energy** that they whizz round too fast to fall into the nucleus. Instead they circle the nucleus in shells (layers) at different distances, or energy levels, depending on how much energy they have. The more energetic an electron, the farther from the nucleus it is. There is room for only one other electron at each energy level, and it must be spinning in the opposite way. This is called Pauli's exclusion principle.

- **Electrons are** stacked around the nucleus in shells. Each shell is labelled with a letter and can hold up to a particular number of electrons. Shell K can hold up to 2, L 8, M 18, N 32, O about 50, and P about 72.

19

Molecules

- **A molecule** is two or more atoms bonded together. It is normally the smallest bit of a substance that exists independently.

- **Hydrogen atoms** exist only in pairs, or joined with atoms of other elements. A linked pair of hydrogen atoms is a hydrogen molecule.

- **The atoms in a molecule** are held together by chemical bonds (see chemical bonds).

- **The shape of a molecule** depends on the arrangement of bonds that hold its atoms together.

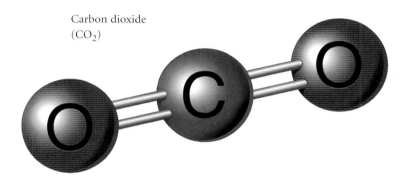

Carbon dioxide
(CO₂)

◄ *A carbon dioxide molecule consists of one carbon atom and two oxygen atoms, and has the chemical formula CO_2.*

- **Ammonia molecules** are pyramid shaped; some protein molecules are long spirals.

- **Compounds** only exist as molecules. If the atoms in the molecule of a compound were separated, the compound would cease to exist.

- **Chemical formulas** show the atoms in a molecule.

- **The formula for ammonia,** a kind of gas, is NH_3 – one nitrogen atom and three hydrogen.

- **The mass of a molecule** is called the molecular mass. It is worked out by adding the mass of all the atoms in it.

◄ *A crystal such as this is built from billions of identical molecules.*

```
...FASCINATING FACT...
If the DNA molecule in every human
body cell were as thick as a hair, it would
be eight km long.
```

Chemical bonds

- **Chemical bonds** link together atoms to make molecules (see molecules).

- **Atoms can bond** in three main ways: ionic bonds, covalent bonds and metallic bonds.

- **In ionic bonds** electrons are transferred between atoms.

- **Ionic bonds** occur when atoms with just a few electrons in their outer shell give the electrons to atoms with just a few missing from their outer shell.

- **An atom** that loses an electron becomes positively charged; an atom that gains an electron becomes negatively charged so the two atoms are drawn together by the electrical attraction of opposites.

- **Sodium** loses an electron and chlorine gains one to form the ionic bond of sodium chloride (table salt) molecules.

- **In covalent bonding,** the atoms in a molecule share electrons.

- **Because they are negatively** charged, the shared electrons are drawn equally to the positive nucleus of both atoms involved. The atoms are held together by the attraction between each nucleus and the shared electrons.

- **In metallic bonds** huge numbers of atoms lose their electrons. They are held together in a lattice by the attraction between 'free' electrons and positive nuclei.

. . . FASCINATING FACT . . .
Seven elements, including hydrogen, are
found in nature only as two atoms
covalently bonded.

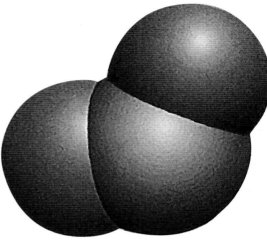

▶ *In this carbon dioxide molecule the carbon is held to two oxygen atoms by covalent bonds.*

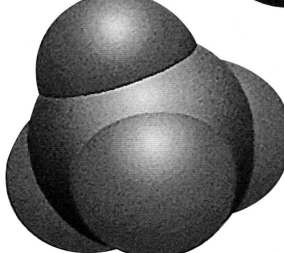

◀ *Each of the four hydrogen atoms in methane (CH_4) shares its electron with the central carbon atom to create strong covalent bonds.*

23

Crystals

- **Crystals** are particular kinds of solids that are made from a regular arrangement, or lattice, of atoms. Most rocks and metals are crystals, so are snowflakes and salt.

- **Most crystals** have regular, geometrical shapes with smooth faces and sharp corners.

- **Most crystals** grow in dense masses, as in metals. Some crystals grow separately, like grains of sugar.

- **Some crystals** are shiny and clear to look at. Crystals got their name from the chunks of quartz that the ancient Greeks called krystallos. They believed the chunks were unmeltable ice.

- **Crystals** form by a process called crystallization. As liquid evaporates or molten solids cool, the chemicals dissolved in them solidify.

- **Crystals** grow gradually as more and more atoms attach themselves to the lattice, just as icicles grow as water freezes onto them.

- **The smallest crystals** are microscopically small. Occasionally crystals of a mineral such as beryl may grow to the size of telegraph poles.

- **A liquid crystal** is a crystal that can flow like a liquid but has a regular pattern of atoms.

- **A liquid crystal** may change colour or go dark when the alignment of its atoms is disrupted by electricity or heat. Liquid crystal displays (LCDs) use a tiny electric current to make crystals affect light.

- **X-ray crystallography** uses x-rays to study the structure of atoms in a crystal. This is how we know the structure of many important life substances such as DNA.

▲ *Crystals such as these grow naturally as minerals and are deposited from hot mineral-rich liquids underground.*

Organic chemistry

◀ *All living things are made basically of carbon compounds.*

- **Organic chemistry** is the study of compounds that contain carbon atoms.
- **Over 90%** of all chemical compounds are organic.
- **Organic chemicals** are the basis of most life processes.
- **Scientists once thought** carbon compounds could only be made by living things. However, in 1828 Friedrich Wöhler made the compound urea in his laboratory.
- **By far the largest** group of carbon compounds are the hydrocarbons (see oil).
- **Aliphatic organic compounds** are formed from long or branching chains of carbon atoms. They include ethane, propane and paraffin, and the alkenes from which many polymers are made (see oil compounds).

- **Cyclic organic compounds** are formed from closed rings of carbon atoms.

- **Aromatics** are made from a ring of six atoms (mostly carbon), with hydrogen atoms attached. They get their name from the strong aroma (smell) of benzene.

- **Benzene** is the most important aromatic. Friedrich Kekuleé von Stradowitz discovered benzene's six-carbon ring structure in 1865, after dreaming about a snake biting its own tail.

- **Isomers** are compounds with the same atoms but different properties. Butane and 2-methyl propane in bottled gas are isomers.

▲ *A giant container containing butane, a colourless, flammable gas used for fuel.*

Acids and alkalis

- **Mild acids,** such as acetic acid in vinegar, taste sour.

- **Strong acids,** such as sulphuric acid, are highly corrosive. They can dissolve metals.

- **Acids** are solutions that are made when certain substances containing hydrogen dissolve in water.

- **Hydrogen atoms** have a single electron. When acid-making substances dissolve in water, the hydrogen atoms lose their electron and become positively charged ions. Ions are atoms that have gained or lost electrons.

- **The strength of an acid** depends on how many hydrogen ions form.

▲ *Citrus fruits such as oranges, lemons and limes have a tart taste because they contain a mild acid, called citric acid. It has a pH of 3.*

- **The opposite of an acid** is a base. Weak bases such as baking powder taste bitter and feel soapy. Strong bases such as caustic soda are corrosive.

- **A base that dissolves** in water is called an alkali. Alkalis contain negatively charged ions – typically ions of hydrogen and oxygen, called hydroxide ions.

- **When you add an acid** to an alkali, both are neutralized. The acid and alkali react together forming water and a salt.

- **Chemists** use indicators such as litmus paper to test for acidity. Acids turn litmus paper red. Alkalis turn it blue. The strength of an acid may be measured on the pH scale. The strong acid (laboratory hydrochloric) has a pH of 1. The strongest alkali has a pH of 14. Pure water has a pH of about 7 and is neutral – neither acid nor alkali.

▲ *Water, with its neutral pH of 7, is safe for people to drink or wash with.*

◀ *Some batteries are made from alkaline cells. These contain a strong alkali solution such as potassium hydroxide which conducts electricity very effectively, making such batteries a strong source of energy.*

...**FASCINATING FACT**...
Hydrochloric acid in the stomach (with a pH of 1 to 2) is essential for digestion.

Soaps

- **Some soaps** are natural; all detergents are synthetic.
- **All soaps and detergents** clean with a 'surfactant'.
- **Surfactants** are molecules that attach themselves to particles of dirt on dirty surfaces and lift them away.
- **Surfactants** work because one part of them is hydrophilic (attracted to water) and the other is hydrophobic (repelled by water).
- **The hydrophobic tail** of a surfactant digs its way into the dirt; the other tail is drawn into the water.

▼ *Surfactant molecules in soap lift dirt off dirty surfaces.*

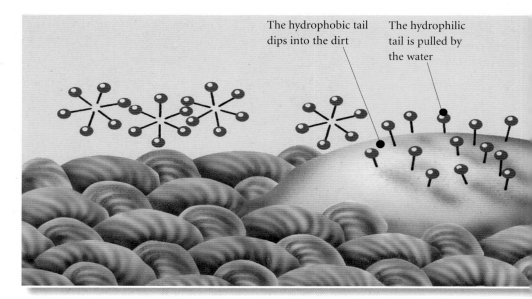

The hydrophobic tail dips into the dirt

The hydrophilic tail is pulled by the water

- **Soaps** increase water's ability to make things wet by reducing the surface tension of the water.

- **Soap** is made from animal fats or vegetable oil combined with chemicals called alkalis, such as sodium or potassium hydroxide.

- **Most soaps** include perfumes, colours and germicides (germ-killers) as well as a surfactant.

- **The Romans used** soap over 2000 years ago.

- **Detergents** were invented in 1916 by German chemist, Fritz Gunther.

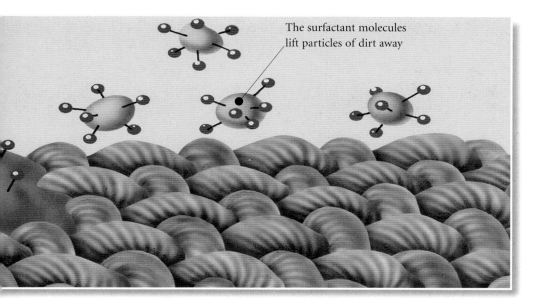

The surfactant molecules lift particles of dirt away

Chemical compounds

- **Compounds** are substances that are made when the atoms of two or more different elements join together.

- **The properties of a compound** are usually very different from those of the elements which it is made of.

- **Compounds** are different from mixtures because the elements are joined together chemically. They can only be separated by a chemical reaction.

- **Every molecule** of a compound is exactly the same combination of atoms.

- **The scientific name** of a compound is usually a combination of the elements involved, although it might have a different common name.

- **Table salt** is the chemical compound sodium chloride. Each molecule has one sodium and one chlorine atom.

- **The chemical formula** of a compound summarizes which atoms a molecule is made of. The chemical formula for water is H_2O because each water molecule has two hydrogen (H) atoms and one oxygen (O) atom.

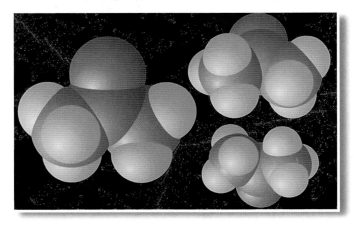

◄ The molecules of a compound are identical combinations of atoms.

▲ *Table salt, or sodium chloride, forms when sodium hydroxide neutralizes hydrocloric acid.*

- **There only 100 or so elements** but they can combine in different ways to form many millions of compounds.

- **The same combination of elements,** such as carbon and hydrogen, can form many different compounds.

- **Compounds** are either organic (see organic chemistry), which means they contain carbon atoms, or inorganic.

Chemical reactions

- **A candle burning,** a nail rusting, a cake cooking – all involve chemical reactions.

- **A chemical reaction** is when two or more elements or compounds meet and interact to form new compounds or separate out some of the elements.

- **The chemicals** involved in a chemical reaction are called the reactants. The results are called the products.

- **The products** contain exactly the same atoms as the reactants but in different combinations.

- **The products** have exactly the same total mass as the reactants. This is called conservation of mass.

- **Some reactions** are reversible, which means the products can be changed back to the original reactants. Others, such as making toast, are irreversible.

- **Effervescence** is a reaction in which gas bubbles form in a liquid, turning it fizzy.

- **A catalyst** is a substance that speeds up, slows down, or enables a chemical reaction to happen but remains unchanged at the end.

- **Nearly all reactions** involve energy. Some involve light or electricity. Most involve heat. Reactions that give out heat are called exothermic. Those that draw in heat are called endothermic.

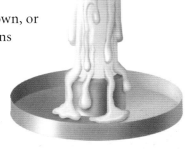

▼ *Candle wax contains a mixture of carbon and hydrogen. When lit, the melted wax is drawn up the wick and burns, using oxygen in the air.*

- **Oxidation** is a reaction in which oxygen combines with a substance. Burning is oxidation; as the fuel burns it combines with oxygen in the air. Reduction is a reaction in which a substance loses its oxygen.

▲ *Burning is an oxidation reaction. Carbon in the trees combines with oxygen in the air to form carbon dioxide.*

Solutions

◄ *A cup of tea is made up of the solvent, water, and a number of solutes: the tea, milk and perhaps sugar. A highly saturated solution produces strong, sweet tea. A poorly saturated solution produces weak tea.*

● **Tap water** is rarely pure water; it usually contains invisible traces of other substances. This makes it a solution.

● **A solution** is a liquid that has a solid dissolved within it.

● **When a solid dissolves,** its molecules separate and mix completely with the molecules of the liquid.

● **The liquid** in a solution is called the solvent.

● **The solid** dissolved in a solution is the solute.

● **The more of a solid that dissolves,** the stronger the solution becomes until at last it is saturated and no more will dissolve. There is literally no more room in the liquid.

● **If a saturated** solution is heated the liquid expands, making room for more solute to dissolve.

- **If a saturated** solution cools or is left to evaporate there is less room for solute, so the solute is precipitated (comes out of the solution).

- **Precipitated solute** molecules often link together to form solid crystals.

▲ *Sea water is a solution containing a huge range of dissolved substances. They include simple salt (sodium chloride) and magnesium chloride, but most are in very tiny amounts.*

...FASCINATING FACT...
Ancient alchemists searched for a universal solvent in which all substances would dissolve.

Solids, liquids and gases

- **Most substances** can exist in three states – solid, liquid or gas. These are the states of matter.

- **Substances** change from one state to another at particular temperatures and pressures.

- **As temperature rises,** solids melt to become liquids. As it rises further, liquids evaporate to become gases.

- **The temperature** at which a solid melts is its melting point.

- **The maximum temperature** a liquid can reach before turning to gas is called its boiling point.

- **Every solid has strength** and a definite shape as its molecules are firmly bonded in a rigid structure.

- **A liquid has a fixed volume** and flows to take up the shape of any solid container into which it is poured.

- **A liquid flows** because although bonds hold molecules together, they are loose enough to move over each other, rather like dry sand.

- **A gas** such as air does not have any shape, strength or fixed volume. This is because its molecules are moving too quickly for any bonds to hold them together.

- **When a gas cools,** its molecules slow down until bonds form between them to create drops of liquid. This process is called condensation.

▲ *The grains of sand in this egg timer act like a liquid, taking on the shape of the glass as they flow from top to bottom.*

▲ *A giant iceberg floats on the sea. Although ice is lighter than water and looks so different, chemically it is exactly the same.*

Radioactivity

- **Radioactivity** is when a certain kind of atom disintegrates spontaneously and sends out little bursts of radiation from its nucleus (centre).

- **Isotopes** are slightly different versions of an atom, with either more or less neutrons (see atoms). With stable elements, such as carbon, only certain isotopes called radio-isotopes are radioactive.

- **Some large atoms,** such as radium and uranium, are so unstable that all their isotopes are radio-isotopes.

- **Radioactive isotopes** emit three kinds of radiation: alpha, beta and gamma rays.

- **When the nucleus** of an atom emits alpha or beta rays it changes and becomes the atom of a different element. This is called radioactive decay.

- **Alpha rays** are streams of alpha particles. These are made from two protons and two neutrons – basically the nucleus of a helium atom. They travel only a few centimetres and can be stopped by a sheet of paper.

- **Beta rays** are beta particles. Beta particles are electrons (or their opposite, positrons) emitted as a neutron decays into a proton. They can travel up to 1 m and can penetrate aluminium foil.

- **Gamma rays** are an energetic, short-wave form of electromagnetic radiation (see electromagnetic spectrum). They penetrate most materials but not lead.

- **The half-life** of a radioactive substance is the time it takes for its radioactivity to drop by half. This is much easier to assess than the time for the radioactivity to disappear altogether.

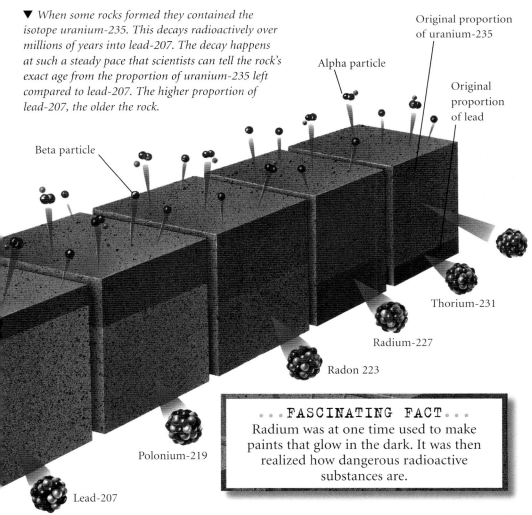

▼ *When some rocks formed they contained the isotope uranium-235. This decays radioactively over millions of years into lead-207. The decay happens at such a steady pace that scientists can tell the rock's exact age from the proportion of uranium-235 left compared to lead-207. The higher proportion of lead-207, the older the rock.*

Original proportion of uranium-235

Alpha particle

Original proportion of lead

Beta particle

Thorium-231

Radium-227

Radon 223

Polonium-219

Lead-207

...FASCINATING FACT...
Radium was at one time used to make paints that glow in the dark. It was then realized how dangerous radioactive substances are.

Moving particles

- **The tiny atoms and molecules** from which every substance is made are constantly moving.

- **The speed** at which molecules move depends on temperature.

- **Heat gives atoms and molecules** extra energy, making them move faster.

- **In 1827** Scottish botanist Robert Brown saw through a microscope that pollen grains in water were constantly dancing. They are buffeted by moving molecules that are too small to be seen. The effect is called Brownian motion.

- **In a gas,** the atoms and molecules are so far apart that they are able to zoom about freely in all directions.

▲ As liquids boil, the atoms and molecules move around more and more energetically until some break away altogether and turn to gas. This is called evaporation.

▼ *Air is made up of tiny, freely-moving particles. They push on any surface they come in contact with - you can see their power by looking at how they push clouds along on a windy day.*

● **Smells spread** quickly because the smell molecules move about very quickly.

● **In a liquid,** molecules are closely packed and move like dancers in a nightclub. If molecules stopped moving in liquids we would all die, because this movement is what moves materials in and out of human cells.

● **In a solid,** atoms and molecules are bound together and vibrate on the spot.

● **Air and water pressure** is simply bombardment by billions of moving molecules.

● **At –273.15°C,** which is called absolute zero, the movement of atoms and molecules slows down to a complete standstill.

The Periodic Table

- **The Periodic Table** is a chart of all the 100-plus different chemical elements.

- **The Periodic Table** was devised by Russian Dmitri Mendeleyev. He realized that each element is part of a complete set, and so he predicted the existence of three then unknown elements – gallium, scandium and germanium.

- **The Periodic Table** arranges the elements according to their Atomic Number, which is the number of protons in their atoms (see atoms). The table lists the elements in order of Atomic Number, starting with hydrogen at 1.

- **Atoms** usually have the same number of electrons as protons. So the Atomic Number also indicates the normal number of electrons an atom has.

- **Atomic mass** is the average weight of an atom of an element and corresponds to the average number of protons and neutrons in the nucleus. The number of neutrons varies in some atoms so the atomic mass is never a round number.

- **Columns** in the Periodic Table are called Groups. Rows are called Periods.

- **The number** of electron layers (shells) in the atoms of an element increases by one down each Group. The elements in each Period have the same number of electron shells.

- **The electrons** in the atom's outer shell increases by one across each Period.

- **Each Group** is made up of elements with a certain number of electrons in their outer shell. This is what largely determines the element's character. All the elements in each Group have similar properties. Many of the Groups have a name as well as a number, as shown opposite.

- **Each Period** starts on the left with a highly reactive alkali metal of Group 1, such as sodium. Each atom of elements in Group 1 has an electron in its outer shell. Each Period ends on the right with a 'noble' gas of Group 0, such as argon. These elements have the full number of electrons in their outer shell and do not react.

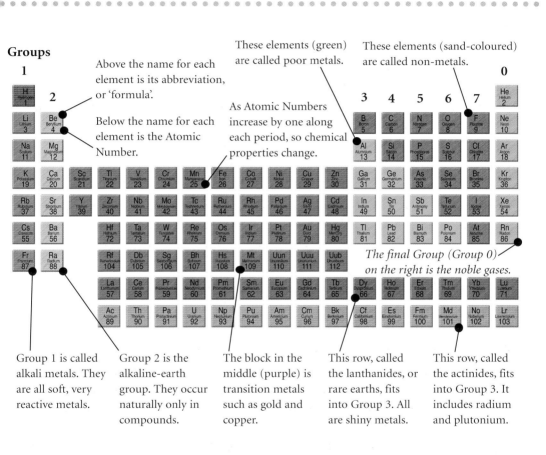

Groups

These elements (green) are called poor metals.

These elements (sand-coloured) are called non-metals.

Above the name for each element is its abbreviation, or 'formula'.

Below the name for each element is the Atomic Number.

As Atomic Numbers increase by one along each period, so chemical properties change.

The final Group (Group 0) on the right is the noble gases.

Group 1 is called alkali metals. They are all soft, very reactive metals.

Group 2 is the alkaline-earth group. They occur naturally only in compounds.

The block in the middle (purple) is transition metals such as gold and copper.

This row, called the lanthanides, or rare earths, fits into Group 3. All are shiny metals.

This row, called the actinides, fits into Group 3. It includes radium and plutonium.

▲ *There are eight columns, or Groups, across in the Periodic Table and seven rows, or Periods, down. The block of transition metals in the middle fits into Group 3. Each element has three electrons in its outer shell, but different numbers in the inner shells.*

Hydrogen

- **Hydrogen** is the lightest of all gases and of all elements. A large swimming pool full of hydrogen would weigh just 1 kg.

- **Hydrogen** is the smallest and simplest of all atoms, with just one proton and one electron.

- **Hydrogen** is the first element in the Periodic Table. It has an Atomic Number of 1 and an atomic mass of 1.00794.

- **One in every 6000** hydrogen atoms has a neutron as well as a proton in its nucleus, making it twice as heavy. This heavy hydrogen atom is called deuterium.

- **Very rare** hydrogen atoms have two neutrons as well as the proton, making them three times as heavy. These are called tritium.

- **Hydrogen** is the most common substance in the Universe, making up over 90% of the Universe's weight.

◀ *Hydrogen's combination with oxygen in water makes it one of the most important elements on the Earth.*

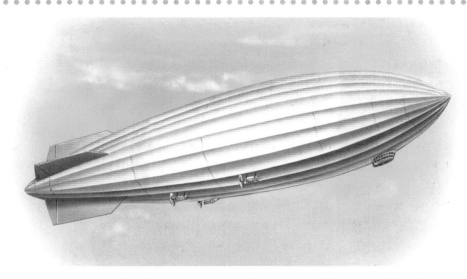

▲ *In 1937, the hydrogen used to lift the airship* Hindenburg *ignited, killing many of the ship's passengers. Eventually, non-flammable helium was used in airships.*

- **Hydrogen** was the first element to form, soon after the Universe began. It was billions of years before any other element formed.

- **Most hydrogen** on Earth occurs in combination with other elements, such as oxygen in water. Pure hydrogen occurs naturally in only a few places, such as small underground pockets and as tiny traces in the air.

- **Hydrogen** is one of the most reactive gases. It bursts easily and often explosively into flames.

- **Under extreme pressure** hydrogen becomes a metal – the most electrically conductive metal of all.

47

Nitrogen

- **Nitrogen** is a colourless, tasteless, odourless, inert (unreactive) gas, yet it is vital to life.

- **Nitrogen is** 78.08% of the air.

- **Nitrogen** turns liquid at −196°C and freezes at −210°C.

- **Liquid nitrogen** is so cold that it can freeze organic substances so quickly they suffer little damage.

- **Food such as cheesecakes** and raspberries are preserved by being sprayed with liquid nitrogen.

▲ *On average 100 kg of nitrate fertilizer are used on every hectare of farmland in the world to replace nitrogen taken from the soil by crops.*

- **Compounds of nitrogen** and oxygen are called nitrates.

- **Nitrogen and oxygen** compounds are an essential ingredient of the proteins and nucleic acids from which all living cells are made.

- **Lightning makes** 250,000 tonnes of nitric acid a day. It joins nitrogen and oxygen in the air to make nitrogen oxide.

- **On a long sea dive,** the pressure in a diver's lungs makes extra nitrogen dissolve in the blood. If the diver surfaces too quickly the nitrogen forms bubbles, giving 'the bends', which can be painful or even fatal.

▲ *Nitrogen-frozen raspberries. Although expensive, this method freezes food faster and better than air-blast and indirect-contact methods.*

...FASCINATING FACT...
When they die, some people have their bodies frozen with liquid nitrogen in the hope that medical science will one day bring them back to life.

49

Oxygen

- **Oxygen** is the second most plentiful element on Earth, making up 46% of the Earth's crust. Air is 20.94% oxygen.

- **Oxygen** is one of the most reactive elements. This is why oxygen in the Earth's crust is usually found joined with other chemicals in compounds.

- **Oxygen has an atomic number** of 8 and an atomic weight of 15.9994.

- **Oxygen molecules** in the air are made from two oxygen atoms; three oxygen atoms make the gas ozone.

- **Oxygen turns to a pale blue liquid** at −182.962°C. It freezes at −218.4°C.

- **Most life depends on oxygen** because it joins with other chemicals in living cells to give the energy needed for life processes. The process of using oxygen in living cells is called cellular respiration.

- **Liquid oxygen,** or LOX, is combined with fuels such as kerosene to provide rocket fuel.

- **Oxygen** was discovered independently by Carl Scheele and Joseph Priestley during the 1770s.

- **The name** 'oxygen' means acid-forming. It was given to the gas in 1779 by Antoine Lavoisier (see Lavoisier).

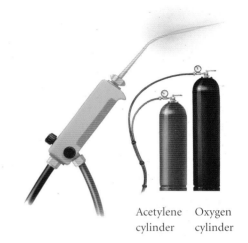

Acetylene cylinder   Oxygen cylinder

▲ *Oxyacetylene torches produce an extremely hot flame for welding and cutting materials. By combining oxygen and acetylene the torch can produce a flame of around 3300°C.*

▲ *Oxygen is needed for combustion to take place. Substances like wood give off heat with a flame when they burn, while others, such as charcoal, give off heat with a faint glow.*

...FASCINATING FACT...
The oxygen in the air on which your life depends was produced mainly by algae.

51

Air

- **The air** is a mixture of gases, dust and moisture.

- **The gas nitrogen** makes up 78.08% of the air. Nitrogen is largely unreactive, but it sometimes reacts with oxygen to form oxides of nitrogen.

- **Nitrogen** is continually recycled by the bacteria that consume plant and animal waste.

- **Oxygen** makes up 20.94% of the air. Animals breathe in oxygen. Plants give it out as they take their energy from sunlight in photosynthesis.

- **Carbon dioxide** makes up 0.03% of the air. Carbon dioxide is continually recycled as it is breathed out by animals and taken in by plants in photosynthesis.

- **The air contains** other, inert (unreactive) gases: 0.93% is argon; 0.0018% is neon; 0.0005% is helium.

- **There are tiny traces** of krypton and xenon which are also inert.

- **Ozone makes up** 0.00006% of the air. It is created when sunlight breaks up oxygen.

- **Hydrogen makes up** 0.00005% of the air. This gas is continually drifting off into space.

▶ *People often think that air is largely made up of oxygen. In fact, only 21% of air is oxygen, while 78% of it is nitrogen.*

> ...FASCINATING FACT...
> Air is a unique mixture that exists on Earth and nowhere else in the Solar System.

▶ *Air is the mixture of gases that surrounds the Earth and is contained in the atmosphere. Clouds form when large masses of moist air rise and cool.*

Nitrogen 78.08%

Oxygen 20.94%

Carbon dioxide 0.03%

Argon and other gases 0.97%

Carbon

▶ *The extraordinary hardness of diamonds comes from the incredibly strong tetrahedron (pyramid shape) that carbon atoms form.*

- **Pure carbon** occurs in four forms: diamond, graphite, amorphous carbon and fullerenes.

- **Fullerenes** are made mostly artificially, but all four forms of carbon can be made artificially.

- **Diamond** is the world's hardest natural substance.

- **Natural diamonds** were created deep in the Earth billions of years ago. They were formed by huge pressures as the Earth's crust moved, and then brought nearer the surface by volcanic activity.

- **Graphite** is the soft black carbon used in pencils. It is soft because it is made from sheets of atoms that slide over each other.

- **Amorphous carbon** is the black soot left behind when candles and other objects burn.

▲ *The pencil is the most widely used writing instrument in the world. Astronauts use pencils in space because they are not affected by gravity or pressure.*

- **Fullerenes** are big molecules made of 60 or more carbon atoms linked together in a tight cylinder or ball. The first was made in 1985.

- **Fullerenes** are named after the architect Buckminster Fuller who designed a geodesic (Earth-shaped) dome.

- **Carbon forms** over one million compounds which are the basis of organic chemistry. It does not react chemically at room temperature. Carbon has the chemical formula C and the atomic number 6. Neither diamond nor graphite will melt at normal pressures.

▲ *Diamonds are crystals made up almost entirely of carbon. They occur in various shapes and sizes, and were formed under great heat and pressure.*

...FASCINATING FACT...
All living things are based on carbon, yet it makes up just 0.032% of the Earth's crust.

Water

- **Water is the only substance** that is solid, liquid and gas within the natural range of Earth temperatures. It melts at 0°C and boils at 100°C.

- **Water is at its densest** at 4°C.

- **Ice is much less dense** than water, which is why ice forms on the surface of ponds and why icebergs float.

- **Water is one of the few substances** that expands as it freezes, which is why pipes burst during cold winter weather.

- **Water has a unique capacity** for making mild solutions with other substances.

- **Water is a compound** made of two hydrogen atoms and one oxygen atom. It has the chemical formula H_2O.

- **A water molecule** is shaped like a flattened V, with the two hydrogen atoms on each tip.

▲ A water molecule has two hydrogen atoms and one oxygen atom in a shallow V-shape.

▲ Water is found in liquid form in many places, such as rivers, and as a gas in the atmosphere.

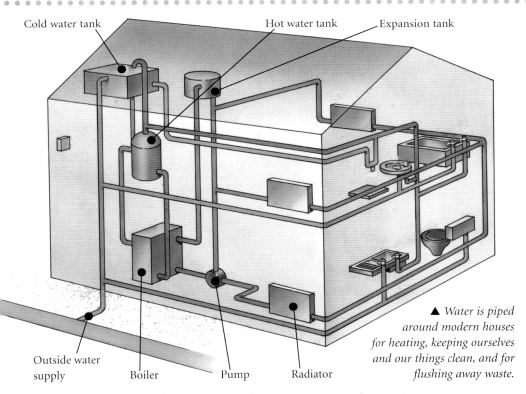

Cold water tank

Hot water tank

Expansion tank

▲ *Water is piped
around modern houses
for heating, keeping ourselves
and our things clean, and for
flushing away waste.*

Outside water
supply

Boiler

Pump

Radiator

- **A water molecule** is said to be polar because the oxygen end is more negatively charged electrically.

- **Similar substances** such as ammonia (NH_3) are gases to below 0°C.

- **Water stays liquid** until 100°C because pairs of its polar molecules make strong bonds, as the positively charged end of one molecule is drawn to the negatively charged end of another.

57

Oil

- **Oils** are liquids that do not dissolve in water and burn easily.
- **Oils are usually made** from long chains of carbon and hydrogen atoms.
- **There are three main kinds of oil:** essential, fixed and mineral oils.
- **Essential oils** are thin, perfumed oils from plants. They are used in flavouring and aromatherapy.
- **Fixed oils** are made by plants and animals from fatty acids. They include fish oils and nut and seed oils.
- **Mineral oils** come from petroleum formed underground over millions of years from the remains of micro-organisms.
- **Petroleum,** or crude oil, is made mainly of hydrocarbons. These are compounds made only of hydrogen and carbon, such as methane (see oil compounds).
- **Hydrocarbons** in petroleum are mixed with oxygen, sulphur, nitrogen and other elements.
- **Petroleum** is separated by distillation into various substances such as aviation fuel, petrol or gasoline and paraffin. As oil is heated in a distillation column, a mixture of gases evaporates. Each gas cools and condenses at different heights to a liquid, or fraction, which is then drawn off.

▶ *Oil from underground and undersea sediments provides over half the world's energy needs.*

Petroleum is used to make products
from aspirins and toothpaste to CDs, as
well as gasoline, or petrol.

▲ *From oil comes petrol and other
fuels, which can be burned to
release their fossil energy. The oil
has to go through a processing
stage before it can be used.*

59

Oil compounds

- **Hydrocarbons** are compounds made only of carbon and hydrogen atoms. Most oil products are hydrocarbons.

- **The simplest hydrocarbon** is methane, the main gas in natural gas (and flatulence from cows!). Methane molecules are one carbon atom and four hydrogen atoms.

- **Alkanes or paraffins** are a family of hydrocarbons in which the number of hydrogen atoms is two more than twice the number of carbon atoms.

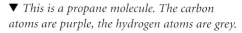

This is a propane molecule. The carbon atoms are purple, the hydrogen atoms are grey.

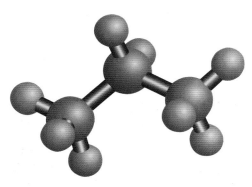

- **Lighter alkanes** are gases such as methane and propane which make good fuels.

- **Candles** contain a mixture of alkanes.

- **Alkenes or olefins** are a family of hydrocarbons in which there are twice as many hydrogen atoms as carbon atoms.

◀ *PVC is a vinyl plastic used for making raincoats. It is a hydrocarbon with chlorine atoms added.*

- **The simplest alkene** is ethene, also called ethylene (C_2H_4) which is used to make polythene and other plastics such as PVC.

- **Green bananas and tomatoes** are often ripened rapidly in ripening rooms filled with ethene.

- **Ethene** is the basis of many paint strippers.

- **Ethene** can be used to make ethanol, the alcohol in alcoholic drinks.

▲ *In an oil refinery, crude oil is broken down into an enormous range of different hydrocarbons.*

Metals

▲ *Mercury, sometimes known as quicksilver, expands by a relatively large amount when warmed, and so is widely used to measure temperature.*

- **75% of all known elements** are metals.

- **Most metals** ring when hit. A typical metal is hard but malleable, which means it can be hammered into thin sheets.

- **Metals** are usually shiny. They conduct both heat and electricity very well.

- **Metals** do not form separate molecules. Instead atoms of metal knit together with metallic bonds (see chemical bonds) to form lattice structures.

- **The electron shells of all metals** are less than half-full. In a chemical reaction metals give up their electrons to a non-metal.

- **Most metals** occur naturally in the ground only in rocks called ores.

- **Gold, copper,** mercury, platinum, silver and a few other rare metals occur naturally in their pure form.

- **Mercury** is the only metal that is liquid at normal temperatures. It melts at −38.87°C.

- **A few atoms** of the new metal ununquadium (atomic number 114) were made in January 1999.

▲ *Metals are very tough but can be easily shaped. They are used for an enormous variety of things, from chains to cars.*

▶ *Molten gold is poured into moulds at a smelting plant. When the bullion cools, it forms bars that are about 99.99% pure. These are stored in strong vaults.*

```
. . . FASCINATING FACT . . .
At 3410°C, tungsten has the highest
melting point of any metal.
```

Calcium

- **Calcium** is a soft, silvery white metal. It doesn't occur naturally in pure form.

- **In compounds,** calcium is the fifth most abundant element on the Earth.

- **Calcium** is one of six alkaline-earth metals.

- **Most calcium compounds** are white solids called limes. They include chalk, porcelain, tooth enamel, cement, seashells, the limescale on taps.

- **The word 'lime'** comes from the Latin word for 'slime'.

- **Quicklime** is calcium oxide. It is called 'quick' (Old English for 'living') because when water drips on it, it twists and swells as if it is alive.

▲ *Calcium is one of the basic building materials of living things. It is one of the crucial ingredients in shell, such as those on crabs, and bone, which is why they are typically white.*

- **Slaked lime** is calcium hydroxide. It may be called 'slaked' because it slakes (quenches) a plant's thirst for lime in acid soils.

- **Calcium has** an atomic number of 20. It has a melting point of 839°C and a boiling point of 1484°C.

- **Limelight** was the bright light used by theatres in the days before electricity. It was made by applying a mix of oxygen and hydrogen to pellets of calcium.

- **Calcium adds rigidity** to bones and teeth and helps to control muscles. Your body gets it from milk and cheese.

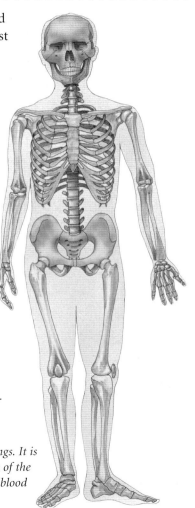

◀▲ *Milk and its products, such as butter and cheese, are key sources of calcium. Green vegetables are another important source.*

▶ *Calcium is essential to human beings. It is vital for the growth and maintenance of the bones and teeth, and it also helps the blood to clot and the muscles to contract.*

65

Iron and steel

- **Iron** is the most common element in the world. It makes up 35% of the Earth, but most of it is in the Earth's core.

- **Iron is never found** in its pure form in the Earth's crust. Instead it is found in iron ores, which must be heated in a blast furnace to extract the iron.

- **The chemical symbol** for iron is Fe from *ferrum*, the Latin word for iron. Iron compounds are called either ferrous or ferric.

- **Iron has** an atomic number of 26 and an atomic weight of 55.85.

- **Iron melts** at 1535°C and boils at 3000°C. It conducts heat and electricity quite well and dissolves in water very slowly. Iron is easily magnetized. It also loses its magnetism easily, but steel can be permanently magnetic.

- Iron combines readily with oxygen to form iron oxide, especially in the presence of moisture. This is rusting.

◀ *Pouring molten iron into a steelmaking furnace in a steel mill. The temperature of the liquid metal is about 1500°C.*

▶ *A solid-state laser can cut through carbon steel like butter even though steel is incredibly tough.*

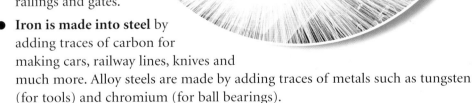

- **Cast iron** is iron with 2 to 4% carbon and 1 to 3% silicon. It is suitable for pouring into sand moulds. Wrought iron is almost pure iron with carbon removed to make it easy to bend and shape for railings and gates.

- **Iron is made into steel** by adding traces of carbon for making cars, railway lines, knives and much more. Alloy steels are made by adding traces of metals such as tungsten (for tools) and chromium (for ball bearings).

- **60% of steel** is made by the basic oxygen process in which oxygen is blasted over molten iron to burn out impurities.

- **Special alloy steels** such as chromium steels can be made from scrap iron (which is low in impurities) in an electric arc furnace.

Aluminium

- **Aluminium** is by far the most common metal on the Earth's surface. It makes up 8% of the Earth's crust.

- **Aluminium** never occurs naturally in its pure form; in the ground it is combined with other chemicals as minerals in ore rocks.

- **The major source** of aluminium is layers of soft ore called bauxite, which is mostly aluminium hydroxide.

▶ *Half of the soft drinks cans in the USA are made from recycled aluminium.*

- **Alum powders** made from aluminium compounds were used 5000 years ago for dyeing. Pure aluminium was first made in 1825 by the Danish scientist Hans Oersted.

- **Aluminium** production was the first industrial process to use hydroelectric power when Paul Héroult set up a plant on the river Rhine in 1887.

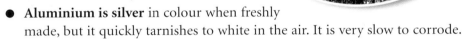

- **Aluminium is silver** in colour when freshly made, but it quickly tarnishes to white in the air. It is very slow to corrode.

- **Aluminium** is one of the lightest of all metals. It weighs just one-third as much as steel.

- **Aluminium oxide** can crystallize into one of the hardest minerals, corundum, which is used to sharpen knives.

- **Aluminium** melts at 650°C and boils at 2450°C.

- **Each year 21 million tonnes** of aluminium are made, mostly from bauxite dug up in Brazil and New Guinea.

◀ *Although aluminium is common in the ground, it is worth recycling because extracting it from bauxite uses a lot of energy.*

69

Copper

▲ *The high conductivity of copper makes it a perfect material for the core of electrical cables.*

- **Copper** was one of the first metals used by humans over 10,000 years ago.

- **Copper** is one of the few metals that occur naturally in a pure form.

- **Most of the copper** that we use today comes from ores such as cuprite and chalcopyrite.

- **The world's biggest deposits** of pure copper are in volcanic lavas in the Andes Mountains in Chile.

- **Copper has** the atomic number 29, an atomic mass of 63.546 and melts at 1083°C.

- **Copper is** by far the best low-cost conductor of electricity, so it is widely used for electrical cables.

- **Copper is also** a good conductor of heat, which is why it is used to make the bases of saucepans and heating pipes.

- **Copper is so ductile** (easily stretched) that a copper rod as thick as a finger can be stretched out thinner than a human hair.

- **After being in the air** for some time, copper gets a thin green coating of copper carbonate called verdigris. '*Verdigris*' means green of Greece.

▲ *Copper utensils on sale. Copper not only withstands heat but is an attractive material to have in people's homes.*

... **FASCINATING FACT** ...
Copper is mixed with tin to make bronze, the oldest of all alloys dating back more than 5000 years.

Halogens

- **Halogens** are the chemical elements fluorine, chlorine, bromine, iodine and astatine.

- **The word 'halogen'** means salt-forming. All halogens easily form salt compounds.

- **Many of the salts in the sea** are compounds of a halogen and a metal, such as sodium chloride and magnesium chloride.

- **The halogens** all have a strong, often nasty, smell.

- **Fluorine** is a pale yellow gas, chlorine a greenish gas, bromine a red liquid, and iodine a black solid.

- **Astatine** is an unstable element that survives by itself only briefly. It is usually made artificially.

◄ *Chlorine salts are often added to the water in swimming pools to kill bacteria, giving the water a greenish-blue tinge.*

▼ *Halogen lights floodlight a stadium at night, allowing large audiences to watch. Halogens are non-metals and make up part of the seventh main Group in the Periodic Table.*

- **The halogens** together form Group 7 of the Periodic Table, elements with 7 electrons in the outer shells.

- **Because halogens have** one electron missing, they form negative ions and are highly reactive.

- **The iodine and bromine** in a halogen lightbulb make it burn brighter and longer than a normal electric lightbulb.

. . . . **FASCINATING FACT** . . .
Fluorides (fluorine compounds) are often added to drinking water to prevent tooth decay.

Glass

- **Glass** is made mainly from ordinary sand (composed of silica), from soda ash (sodium carbonate) and from limestone (calcium carbonate).

- **Glass** can be made from silica alone. However, silica has a very high melting point (1700°C), so soda ash is added to lower its melting point.

- **Adding a lot of soda ash** makes glass too soluble in water, so limestone is added to reduce its solubility.

- **To make sheets of glass,** 6% lime and 4% magnesia (magnesium oxide) are added to the basic mix.

▲ *Glass is one of the most versatile of all materials – transparent, easily moulded and resistant to the weather. This is why it is used in modern buildings such as this extension to the Louvre in Paris.*

- **To make glass for bottles,** 2% alumina (aluminium oxide) is added to the basic mix.

- **Very cheap glass** is green because it contains small impurities of iron.

- **Metallic oxides** are added to make different colours.

- **Unlike most solids,** glass is not made of crystals and does not have the same rigid structure. It is called an amorphous solid.

- **When glass is very warm** it flows slowly like a very thick liquid.

...**FASCINATING FACT**...
The person who controls the fires and loads the glass into the furnace is called a teaser.

▲ *Certain oxides are added to glass to colour it. One part of nickel oxide in 50,000 produces a tint ranging from yellow to purple. One part of cobalt oxide in 10,000 gives an intense blue. Red glasses are made with gold, copper or selenium oxides.*

New materials

- **Synthetic materials** are materials created by humans, such as plastics.

- **Many synthetic materials** are polymers. These are substances with chains of organic molecules made up from identical smaller molecules, monomers.

- **Some polymers** are natural, such a the plant fibre cellulose.

- **The first synthetic polymer** was Parkesine, invented by Alexander Parkes in 1862. The first successful synthetic polymer was celluloid, invented by John Hyatt in 1869 and soon used for photographic film.

- **Nylon** was the first completely synthetic fibre. It is a polymer created by Wallace Carothers of Du Pont in the 1930s.

◀ *This phone was made from Bakelite, one of the earliest types of plastic.*

▲ *Snowboards are made from composites such as Kevlar, which combine lightness with strength.*

- **PVC** is polyvinyl chloride, a synthetic polymer developed in the 1920s.

- **Composites** are new, strong, light materials created by combining a polymer with another material.

- **Carbon-reinforced plastic** consists of tough carbon fibres set within a polymer.

- **Kevlar** is a composite developed by Du Pont in 1971. It is made from nylon-like fibres set within a polymer.

· · · **FASCINATING FACT** · · ·
New 'smart' materials might change their properties in response to conditions.

77

Plastics

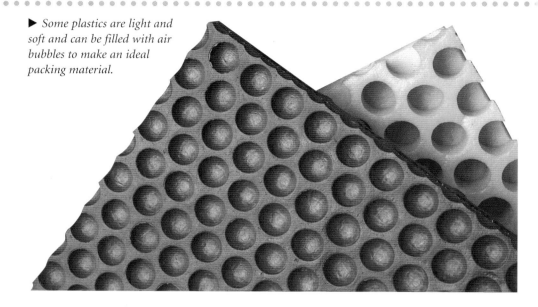

▶ *Some plastics are light and soft and can be filled with air bubbles to make an ideal packing material.*

- **Plastics are synthetic** (man-made) materials that can be easily shaped and moulded.

- **Most plastics are polymers** (see new materials). The structure of polymer molecules gives different plastics different properties.

- **Long chains of molecules** that slide over each other easily make highly flexible plastics such as polythene. Tangled chains make rigid plastics such as melamine.

- **Typically** plastics are made by joining carbon and hydrogen atoms. These form ethene molecules, which can be joined to make a plastic called polythene.

- **Many plastics** are made from liquids and gases that are extracted from crude oil.

● **Thermoplastics** are soft and easily moulded when warm but set solid when cool. They are used to make bottles and drainpipes and can be melted again.

● **Thermoset plastics,** which cannot be remelted once set, are used to make telephones and pan handles.

● **Blow moulding** involves using compressed air to push a tube of plastic into a mould.

● **Vacuum moulding** involves using a vacuum to suck a sheet of plastic into a mould.

● **Extrusion moulding** involves heating plastic pellets and forcing them through a nozzle to give the required shape.

Plastic pellets

◀ *Extrusion moulding is used to produce continuous shapes such as pipes.*

Plastic pellets

Heating element

Plastic tube

Heating element

▶ *Injection moulding is used to produce non-continuous forms such as bowls.*

Plastic bowl

79

Radiation

- **Radiation** is an atom's way of getting rid of its excess energy.

- **There are two main kinds** of radiation: electromagnetic and particulate.

- **Electromagnetic radiation** is pure energy. It comes from electrons (see electrons).

- **Particulate radiation** is tiny bits of matter thrown out by the nuclei of atoms.

- **Particulate** radiation comes mainly from radioactive substances (see radioactivity) such as radium, uranium and other heavy elements as they break down.

- **Radiation is measured** in curies and becquerels (radiation released), röntgens (victim's exposure), rads and grays (dose absorbed), rems and sieverts (amount of radiation in the body).

- **Bacteria can stand** a radiation dose 10,000 times greater than the dose that would kill a human.

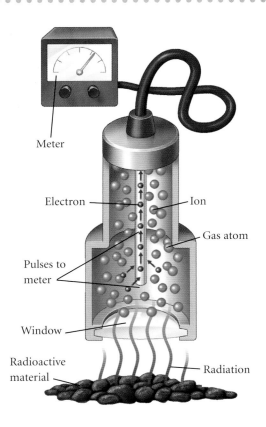

Meter

Electron

Ion

Gas atom

Pulses to meter

Window

Radioactive material

Radiation

▲ *Radiation entering a Geiger counter tube hits the gas atoms there, causing them to ionise. The electrons that are freed by this process spread along the wire, creating electrical pulses, which are counted by a meter.*

- **The Chernobyl nuclear accident** released 50 million curies of radiation. A 20 kilotonne nuclear bomb releases 10,000 times more radiation.

- **The natural radioactivity** of a brazil nut is about six becquerels (one ten-millionth of a curie), which means six atoms break up every second.

- **The natural background** radiation you receive over a year is about 100 times what you receive from a single chest X-ray.

▼ *An X-ray image made by passing electromagnetic radiation through someone's chest. It shows this person has been fitted with a pacemaker.*

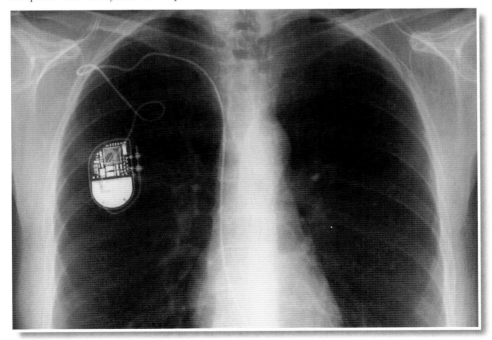

Spectrum

- **A spectrum** is a range of different wavelengths of electromagnetic radiation.

- **The white light of sunlight** can be broken up into its full spectrum of colours with a triangular block of glass called a prism. The prism is set in a dark room and lit only by a shaft of sunlight or similar white light.

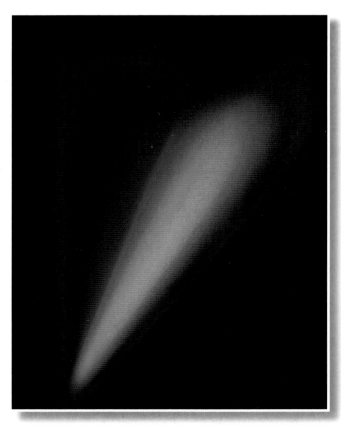

- **The prism refracts (bends)** short wavelengths of light more than longer wavelengths, so the light fans out in bands ranging from violet to red.

- **The order of colours** in a spectrum is always the same: red, orange, yellow, green, blue, indigo, violet.

◄ *Isaac Newton first discovered that sunlight is made of all colours mixed together. It can be broken down into the seven main constituent colours since each colour has a different wavelength.*

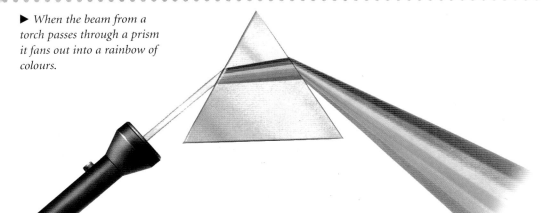

▶ *When the beam from a torch passes through a prism it fans out into a rainbow of colours.*

- **Scientists** remember the order of the colours with the first letter of each word in this ancient phrase: 'Richard Of York Gained Battles In Vain'.

- **Infrared** is red light made of waves that are too long for human eyes to see.

- **Ultraviolet** is violet light made of waves that are too short for our eyes to see.

- **Spectroscopy,** or spectral analysis, is the study of the spectrum created when a solid, liquid or gas glows.

- **Every substance** produces its own unique spectrum, so spectroscopy helps to identify substances.

> ...FASCINATING FACT...
> Spectral analysis can reveal what anything
> from a distant galaxy to a drug is made of.

Light

- **Light is a form of energy.** It is one of the forms of energy sent out by atoms when they become excited.

- **Light is just one** of the forms of electromagnetic radiation (see electromagnetic spectrum). It is the only form we can see.

- **Although we are surrounded** by light during the day, very few things give out light. The Sun and other stars and electric lights are light sources, but we see most things only because they reflect light. If something does not send out or reflect light, we cannot see it.

▶ *This straw is not a light source, so we see it by reflected light. As the light rays reflected from the straw leave the water, they are bent, or refracted, as they emerge from the water and speed up. So the straw looks broken even though it remains intact.*

- **Light beams** are made of billions of tiny packets of energy called photons (see moving light). Together, the photons behave like waves on a pond. But the waves are tiny – 2000 would fit on a pinhead.

- **Light travels** in straight lines. The direction can be changed when light bounces off something or passes through it, but it is always straight. The straight path of light is called a ray.

- **When the path of a light ray** is blocked altogether, it forms a shadow. Most shadows have two regions: the umbra and penumbra. The umbra is the dark part where light rays are blocked altogether. The penumbra is the lighter rim where some rays reach.

- **When light rays** hit something, they bounce off, are soaked up or pass through. Anything that lets light through, such as glass, is transparent. If it mixes the light on the way through, as does frosted glass, it is translucent. If it stops light altogether, it is opaque.

- **When light strikes a surface,** some or all of it is reflected. Most surfaces scatter light in all directions, and all you see is the surface. But mirrors and other shiny surfaces reflect light in exactly the same pattern in which it arrived, so you see a mirror image.

- **When light passes** into transparent things such as water, rays are bent, or refracted. This happens because light travels more slowly in glass or water, and the rays swing round like the wheels of a car running onto sand.

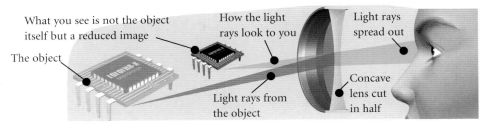

What you see is not the object itself but a reduced image

The object

How the light rays look to you

Light rays spread out

Light rays from the object

Concave lens cut in half

▲ *Glass lenses are shaped to refract light rays in particular ways. Concave lenses are dish-shaped lenses – thin in the middle and fat at the edges. As light rays pass through a concave lens they are bent outwards, so they spread out. The result is that when you see an object through a concave lens, it looks smaller than it really is.*

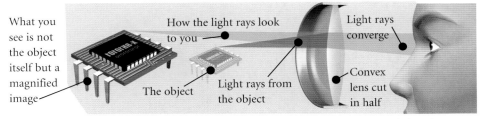

What you see is not the object itself but a magnified image

How the light rays look to you

Light rays converge

The object

Light rays from the object

Convex lens cut in half

▲ *Convex lenses bulge outwards. They are fatter in the middle and thin around the edges. As light rays pass through a convex lens they are bent inwards, so they come together, or converge. When you see an object through a convex lens, it looks magnified.*

85

Light and atoms

- **All light comes** from atoms. They give out light when they gain energy – by absorbing light or other electromagnetic waves when hit by other particles.

- **Atoms** are normally in a 'ground' state. Their electrons circle close to the nucleus where their energy is at its lowest ebb.

- **An atom emits light** when 'excited' by taking in energy. Excitement boosts an electron's energy so it jumps further out from the nucleus.

- **An atom** only stays excited a fraction of second before the electron drops back towards the nucleus.

▲ *Spectroscopy is used to analyse the colour of light from distant stars and galaxies. It allows scientists to identify what the stars are made of.*

- **As the electron** drops back inwards, it lets go the energy it gained as a tiny packet of electromagnetic radiation called a photon.

- **Electrons** do not drop in towards the nucleus steadily like a ball rolling down a hill, but in steps, like a ball bouncing down stairs.

- **Since each step** the electron drops in has a particular energy level, so the energy of the photon depends precisely on how big the steps are. Big steps send out higher-energy short-wave photons like X-rays.

- **The colour of light** an atom sends out depends on the size of the steps its electrons jump down.

- **Each kind of atom** has its own range of electron energy steps, so each sends out particular colours of light. The range of colours each kind of atom sends out is called its emission spectrum (see spectrum). For gases, this acts like a colour signature to identify in a process called spectroscopy.

- **Just as an atom** only emits certain colours, so it can only absorb certain colours. This is its absorption spectrum.

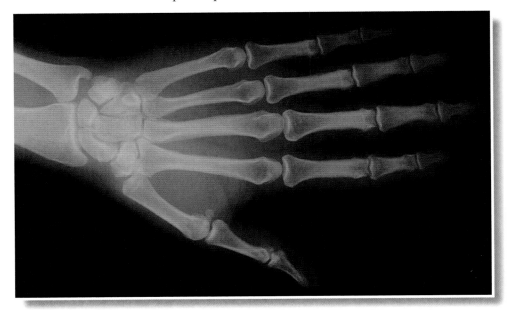

▲ *While X-rays are high-energy enough to pass through most body tissue, they cannot pass through bones. As a result, these show up as white areas on an X-ray image.*

Moving light

- **Light is the fastest thing** in the Universe.

- **The speed of light** is 299,792,458 metres per second.

- **Scientists remember** light's speed from the number of letters in each word of this sentence: 'We guarantee certainty, clearly referring to this light mnemonic'.

- **Isaac Newton** suggested in 1666 that light is made up of streams of tiny particles, or corpuscles.

- **The Dutch scientist** Christiaan Huygens (1629–1695) said in 1678: no, light is waves or vibrations instead.

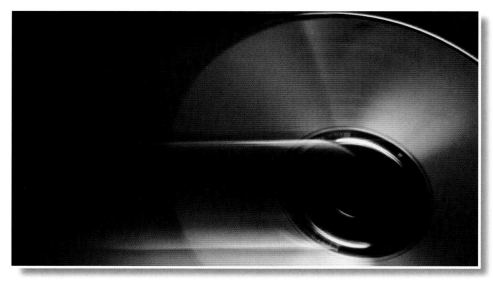

▲ *The shimmering colours on a CD are caused by interfering light waves, where different wave lengths cancel out their peaks and troughs.*

- **In 1804 Thomas Young** showed that light is waves in a famous experiment with two narrow slits in a light beam. Light coming through each slit creates bands of shadow that must be caused by waves interfering with each other.

- **James Clerk Maxwell** suggested in the 1860s that light is electromagnetic waves.

- **Albert Einstein** showed with the photoelectric effect that light must also be particles called photons.

- **Light sometimes** looks like photons, sometimes like waves. Weirdly, in a way scientists can't explain, a single photon can interfere with itself in Young's slit experiment.

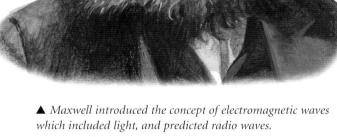

▲ *Maxwell introduced the concept of electromagnetic waves which included light, and predicted radio waves.*

FASCINATING FACT
On a sunny day one thousand billion photons fall on a pinhead every second.

89

Light sources

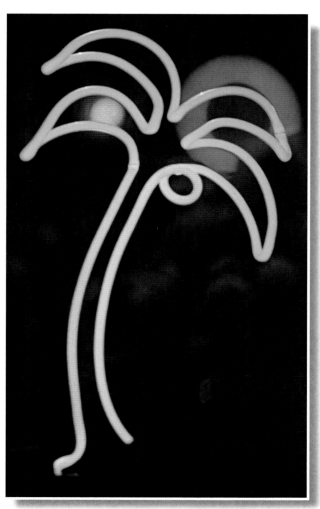

- **Our main sources of natural light** are the Sun and the stars. The hot gases on their surface glow fiercely.

- **The brightness** of a light source is measured in candelas (cd); one candela is about as bright as a small candle.

- **For 0.1 millisecond** an atom bomb flashes out 2000 billion candelas for every square metre (m^2).

- **The Sun's surface** pumps out 23 billion candela per m^2. Laser lights are even brighter, but very small.

◄ *The fluorescent coating on the inside of a gas-filled tube produces white light when the electricity is switched on.*

- **The light falling** on a surface is measured in lux. One lux is how brightly lit something is by a light of one candela 1 m away. You need 500 lux to read by.

◀ Electrical resistance makes the thin filament in a bulb glow.

- **Electric lightbulbs** are incandescent, which means that their light comes from a thin tungsten wire, or filament, that glows when heated by an electric current.

- **Lightbulbs** are filled with an inert (unreactive) gas, such as argon, to save the filament from burning out.

- **Electric lights** were invented independently in 1878 by Englishman Sir Joseph Swan and Americans Thomas Alva Edison and Hiram Maxim.

- **Fluorescent lights** have a glass tube coated on the inside with powders called phosphors. When electricity excites the gases in the tube to send out invisible UV rays, the rays hit the phosphors and make them glow, or fluoresce.

- **In neon lights,** a huge electric current makes the gas inside a tube electrically charged and so it glows.

▲ Gas mixtures in neon lights glow different colours. Pure neon glows red.

Colour

- **Colour is the way** our eyes see different wavelengths of light (see electromagnetic spectrum).

- **Red light** has the longest waves – about 700 nanometres, or nm (billionths of a metre).

- **Violet light** has the shortest waves – about 400 nm.

- **Light that is a mixture** of every colour, such as sunlight and the light from torches and ordinary lightbulbs, is called white light (see mixing colours).

- **Things are different colours** because molecules in their surface reflect and absorb certain wavelengths of light.

- **Deep-blue printers' inks** and bright-red blood are vividly coloured because both have molecules shaped like four-petalled flowers, with a metal atom at the centre.

- **Iridescence** is the shimmering rainbow colours you see flashing every now and then on a peacock's feathers, a fly's wings, oil on the water's surface or a CD.

◀ *The macaw gets its brilliant colours because pigment molecules in its feathers soak up certain wavelengths of light and reflect others, including reds, yellows and blues, very strongly.*

- **Iridescence** can be caused by the way a surface breaks the light into colours like a prism does (see spectrum).

- **Iridescence** can also be caused by interference when an object has a thin, transparent surface layer. Light waves reflected from the top surface are slightly out of step with waves reflected from the inner surface, and they interfere.

▲ *Iridescence on a CD is a result of light waves reflecting from both the top surface and the inner surface. This causes the spectrum of light which is sometimes visible.*

▲ *The surface skin of water on some spilt oil interferes with the vibrations of light causing it to be split up into the colours of the spectrum.*

Mixing colours

- **White light** such as sunlight contains all the colours of the rainbow: red, orange, yellow, green, blue, indigo and violet – and all the colours in between.

- **There are three basic,** or primary colours of light – red, green and blue. They can be mixed in various proportions to make any other colour.

- **The primary colours** of light are called additive primaries, because they are added together to make different colours.

- **Each additive primary** is one third of the full spectrum of white light, so adding all three together makes white.

▲ *These circles are the primary colours of light: red, green and blue. Where two colours overlap, you see the three subtractive primaries: magenta, cyan and yellow.*

- **When two additive primaries** are added together they make a third colour, called a subtractive primary.

- **The three subtractive primaries are:** magenta (red plus blue), cyan (blue plus green) and yellow (green plus red). They too can be mixed in various proportions to make other colours.

- **Coloured surfaces** such as painted walls and pictures get their colour from the light falling on them. They soak up some colours of white light and reflect the rest. The colour you see is the colour reflected.

- **With reflected colours,** each subtractive primary soaks up one third of the spectrum of white light and reflects two-thirds of it. Mixing two subtractive primaries soaks up two-thirds of the spectrum. Mixing all three subtractive primaries soaks up all the spectrum, making black.

- **Two subtractive primaries** mixed make an additive primary.

- **Cyan and magenta** make blue; yellow and cyan make green; yellow and magenta make red.

▶ *When raindrops fall through sunlight they act as prisms. The seven main colours shine out of each raindrop in narrow bands, forming a rainbow.*

95

Sound

- **Most sounds** you hear, from the whisper of the wind to the roar of a jet, are simply moving air. When any sound is made it makes the air vibrate, and these vibrations carry the sound to your ears.

- **The vibrations** that carry sound through the air are called sound waves.

- **Sound waves** move by alternately squeezing air molecules together and then stretching them apart like a spring.

- **The parts of the air** that are squeezed are called condensations; the parts of the air that are stretched are called rarefactions.

- **Sound waves** travel faster through liquids and solids than through air because the molecules are more closely packed together in liquids and solids.

- **In a vacuum** such as space there is complete silence because there are no molecules to carry the sound.

▲ *When you sing, talk or shout, you are actually vibrating the vocal cords in your throat. These set up sound waves in the air you push up from your lungs.*

- **Sound travels** at about 344 m per second in air at 20°C.

- **Sound travels** faster in warm air, reaching 386 m per second at 100°C.

- **Sound travels** at 1500 m per second in pure water and at about 6000 m per second in solid steel.

- **Sound travels a million times** slower than light, which is why you hear thunder well after you see a flash of lightning, even though they both happen at the same time.

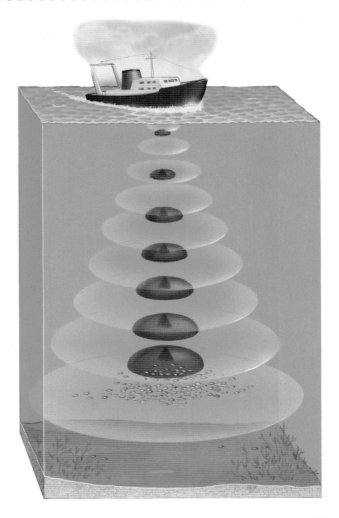

▶ *This fishing boat is using sonar to find out the depth of an object. It bounces sound waves off the object and measures how long they take to be reflected back to the boat.*

97

Sound measurement

- **The loudness of a sound** is usually measured in units called decibels (dB).

- **One decibel** is one tenth of a bel, the unit of sound named after Scots-born inventor Alexander Graham Bell.

- **Decibels** were originally used to measure sound intensity. Now they are used to compare electronic power output and voltages too.

- **Every ten points up** on the decibel scale means that a sound has increased by ten times.

- **One dB** is the smallest change the human ear can hear.

- **The quietest sound** that people can hear is 10 dB.

> **FASCINATING FACT**
> Sounds over 130 dB are painful;
> sounds between 90–100 dB for long
> periods cause deafness.

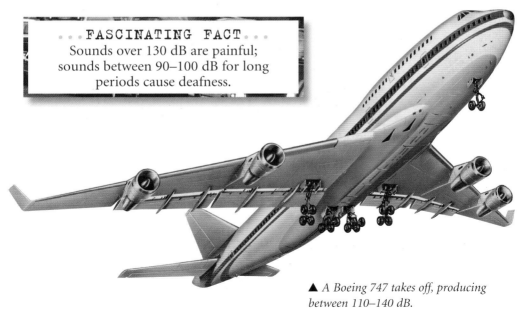

▲ *A Boeing 747 takes off, producing between 110–140 dB.*

▲ *Heavy traffic is about 90 decibels, but it can rise higher.*

● **Quiet sounds:** a rustle of leaves or a quiet whisper is 10 dB. A quiet conversation is 30–40 dB. Loud conversation is about 60 dB. A city street is about 70 dB.

● **Loud sounds:** thunder is about 100 dB. The loudest scream ever recorded was 128.4 dB. A jet taking off is 110–140 dB. The loudest sound ever made by human technology (an atom bomb) was 210 dB.

● **The amount of energy** in a sound is measured in watts per square metre (W/m^2). Zero dB is one thousand billionths of one W/m^2.

99

Musical sound

- **Like all sounds,** musical sounds are made by something vibrating. However, the vibrations of music occur at very regular intervals.

- **The pitch** of a musical note depends on the frequency of the vibrations.

- **Sound frequency** is measured in hertz (Hz) – that is, cycles or waves per second.

- **Human ears** can hear sounds as low as about 20 Hz and up to around 20,000 Hz.

- **Middle C** on a piano measures 262 Hz. A piano has a frequency range from 27.5 to 4186 Hz.

- **The highest singing voice** can reach the E above a piano top note (4350 Hz); the lowest note is 20.6 Hz.

- **A soprano's voice** has a range from 262 to 1046 Hz; an alto from 196 to 698 Hz; a tenor from 147 to 466 Hz; a baritone from 110 to 392 Hz; a bass from 82.4 to 294 Hz.

◀ *The Italian opera singer, Luciano Pavarotti, is noted for his mastery of the highest notes of a tenor's range. He is considered one of the finest singers of recent times.*

- **Very few sounds** have only one pitch. Most have a fundamental (low) pitch and higher overtones.

- **The science of vibrating strings** was first worked out by the Greek mathematician Pythagoras 2500 years ago.

▼ *In most brass and woodwind instruments, such as a tuba, different frequencies are achieved by varying the length of the air column inside.*

▲ *In stringed instruments different notes – that is, different frequencies of vibrations – are achieved by varying the length of the strings.*

. . . **FASCINATING FACT** . . .
A song can shatter glass if the pitch of a loud note coincides with the natural frequency of vibration of the glass.

101

Echoes and acoustics

- **An echo** is the reflection of a sound. You hear it a little while after the sound is made.

- **You can only hear** an echo if it comes back more than 0.1 seconds after the original sound.

- **Sound travels** 34 m in 0.1 seconds, so you only hear echoes from surfaces that are at least 17 m away.

- **Smooth hard surfaces** give the best echoes because they break up the sound waves the least.

- **Acoustics** is the study of how sounds are created, transmitted and received.

- **The acoustics** of a space is how sound is heard and how it echoes around that space, whether it is a room or a large concert hall.

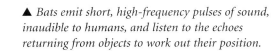

▲ *Bats emit short, high-frequency pulses of sound, inaudible to humans, and listen to the echoes returning from objects to work out their position.*

- **When concert halls** are designed, the idea is not to eliminate echoes altogether but to use them effectively.

- **A hall with too much echo** sounds harsh and unclear, as echoing sounds interfere with new sounds.

- **A hall without echoes** sounds muffled and lifeless.

- **Even in the best** concert halls, the music can be heard fading after the orchestra stops playing. This delay is called the reverberation time. Concert halls typically have a reverberation time of two seconds. A cathedral may reverberate for up to eight seconds, giving a more mellow, but less clear, sound.

▼ *Sydney Opera House in Australia is famous for its stunning design, but some orchestras have complained about its acoustics.*

Magnetism

- **Magnetism** is the invisible force between materials such as iron and nickel. Magnetism attracts or repels.

- **A magnetic field** is the area around a magnet inside which its magnetic force can be detected.

- **An electric current** creates its own magnetic field.

- **A magnet** has two poles: a north pole and a south pole.

- **Like (similar) poles** (e.g. two north poles) repel each other; unlike poles attract each other.

- **The Earth** has a magnetic field that is created by electric currents inside its iron core. The magnetic north pole is close to the geographic North Pole.

- **If left to swivel freely,** a magnet will turn so that its north pole points to the Earth's magnetic north pole.

- **The strength of a magnet** is measured in teslas. The Earth's magnetic field is 0.00005 teslas.

- **All magnetic materials** are made up of tiny groups of atoms called domains. Each one is like a mini-magnet with north and south poles. When material is magnetized, millions of domains line up.

> ...**FASCINATING FACT**...
> One of the world's strongest magnets is at the Lawrence Berkeley National Laboratory, California, USA. Its field is 250,000 times stronger than the Earth's.

▶ *Some animals seem to detect the Earth's magnetic field and use it to help them find their way when they migrate. Birds which have this built-in compass include swallows, geese and pigeons.*

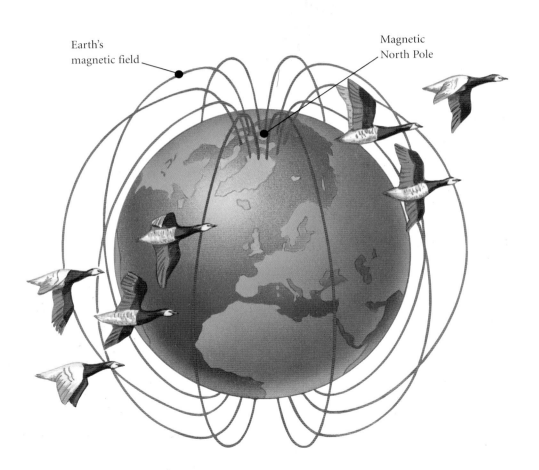

Earth's magnetic field

Magnetic North Pole

Electricity

- **Electricity** is the energy that makes everything from toasters to televisions work. It is also linked to magnetism. Together, as electromagnetism, they are one of the four fundamental forces holding the Universe together.

- **Electricity** is made by tiny bits of atoms called electrons. Electrons have an electrical charge which is a force that either pulls bits of atoms together or pushes them apart.

- **Some particles** (bit of atoms) have a negative electrical charge; others have a positive charge.

- **Particles** with the same charge push each other away. Particles with the opposite charge pull together.

▲ *Try making your own static electricity. Comb your hair quickly, if possible on a cold, dry day, and watch how it stands up.*

- **Electrons** have a negative electrical charge.

- **There are the same number** of positive and negative particles in most atoms so the charges usually balance out.

- **Electricity** is created when electrons move, building up negative charge in one place, or carrying it along.

- **Static electricity** is when the negative charge stays in one place. Current electricity is when the charge moves.

- **Electric charge** is measured with an electroscope.
- **Materials** that let electrons (and electrical charge) move through them easily, such as copper, are called conductors. Materials that stop electrons passing through, such as rubber, are called insulators.

▲ *Lightning is one of the most dramatic displays of natural electricity.*

Electric power

- **Most electricity is generated in power stations** by magnets that spin between coils of wire to induce an electric current (see electric circuits).

- **The magnets** are turned by turbines, which are themselves either turned by steam heated by burning coal, oil or gas, or by nuclear fuel, or turned by wind or water.

- **The stronger the magnet,** the faster it turns, the more coils there are, so the bigger the voltage created.

- **Simple dynamos** generate a direct current (DC) that always flows in the same direction.

- **The generators** in power stations are alternators that give an alternating current (AC) which continually swaps direction. In an alternator, as the magnets spin they pass the wires going up on one side and down on the other.

- **The system of power transmission** that takes electricity into homes was developed by Croatian-born US engineer Nikola Tesla at Niagara, USA in the 1880s.

- **Electricity from power stations** is distributed around a country in a network of cables known as the grid.

- **Power station** generators push out 25,000 volts or more. This voltage is too much to use in people's homes, but not enough to transmit over long distances.

- **To transmit** electricity over long distances, the voltage is boosted to 400,000 volts by step-up transformers. It is fed through high-voltage cables. Near its destination the electricity's voltage is reduced by step-down transformers at substations for distribution to homes, shops, offices and factories.

▼ *Electricity is brought to our homes through a network of high-tension cables. Some cables are buried underground, some are suspended high in the air from metal towers called pylons.*

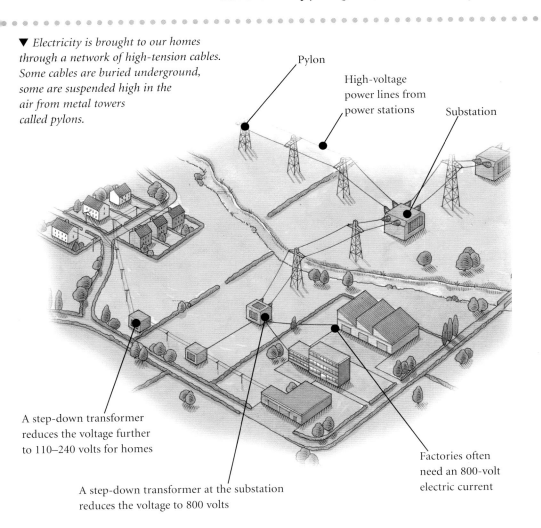

Pylon

High-voltage power lines from power stations

Substation

A step-down transformer reduces the voltage further to 110–240 volts for homes

A step-down transformer at the substation reduces the voltage to 800 volts

Factories often need an 800-volt electric current

109

Electric circuits

- **An electric charge** that does not move is called static electricity (see electricity). A charge may flow in a current providing there is an unbroken loop, or circuit.

- **A current only flows** through a good conductor such as copper, namely a material that transmits charge well.

- **A current only flows** if there is a driving force to push the charge. This force is called an electromotive force (emf).

- **The emf** is created by a battery or a generator.

- **Currents were once thought to** flow like water. In fact they move like a row of marbles knocking into each other.

- **In a good conductor** there are lots of free electrons that are unattached to atoms. These are the 'marbles'.

- **A current only flows** if there are more electrons at one point in the circuit. This difference, called the potential difference, is measured in volts.

- **The rate at which current** flows is measured in amps. It depends on the voltage and the resistance (how much the circuit obstructs the flow of current). Resistance is measured in ohms.

Spring   Batteries   Switch   Metal strip   Light bulb

▶ *A metal strip, moved by the torch's switch, connects the current from the batteries to the light bulb.*

110

● **Batteries** give out Direct Current (DC), a current that flows in one direction. Power stations send out Alternating Current (AC), which swaps direction 50–60 times per second.

▲ *Resistors, transistors, capacitors and diodes are the main components of a circuit board.*

FASCINATING FACT

The electrical resistance of dry skin is 500,000 ohms; wet skin's is just 1000 ohms.

111

Electronics

- **Electronics** are the basis of many modern technologies, from hi-fi systems to missile control systems.

- **Electronics** are systems that control things by automatically switching tiny electrical circuits on and off.

- **Transistors** are electronic switches. They are made of materials called semiconductors that change their ability to conduct electricity.

▼ *Microprocessors contain millions of transistors in a package that is no bigger than a human fingernail.*

- **Electronic systems work** by linking many transistors together so that each controls the way the others work.

- **Diodes** are transistors with two connectors. They control an electric current by switching it on or off.

- **Triodes** are transistors with three connectors that amplify the electric current (make it bigger) or reduce it.

- **A silicon chip** is thousands of transistors linked together by thin metal strips in an integrated circuit, on a single crystal of the semi-conductor, silicon.

- **The electronic areas** of a chip are those treated with traces of chemicals such as boron and phosphorus, which alter the conductivity of silicon.

- **Microprocessors** are complete Central Processing Units (see computers) on a single silicon chip.

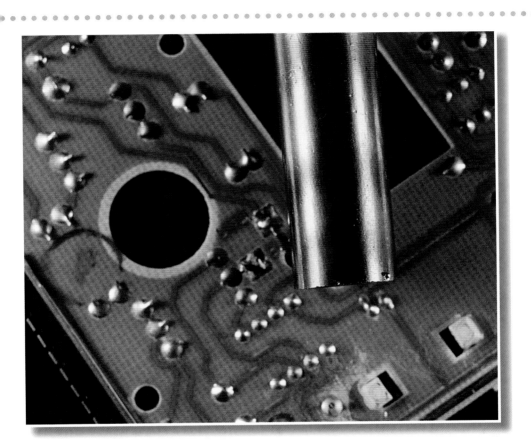

▲ *The components on silicon chips are so minute that photographing them involves using a microscope.*

113

Electromagnetism

- **Electromagnetism** is the combined effect of electricity and magnetism.

- **Every electric current** creates its own magnetic field.

- **Maxwell's screw rule** says that the magnetic field runs the same way a screw turns if you screw it in the direction of the electric current.

- **An electromagnet** is a strong magnet that is only magnetic when an electric current passes through it. It is made by wrapping a coil of wire, called a solenoid, around a core of iron.

- **Electromagnets** are used in everything from ticket machines and telephones to loudspeakers.

- **Magnetic levitation** trains use very strong electromagnets to carry the train on a cushion of magnetic repulsion.

- **When an electric wire** is moved across a magnetic field, an electric current is created, or induced, in the wire. This is the basis of every kind of electricity generation.

◀ *Wind turbines generate electricity by using the wind to turn their blades. These drive magnets around inside coils of electric wire.*

- **Fleming's right-hand rule** says that if you hold your right thumb, first and middle fingers at 90° to each other, your middle finger shows the direction of the induced current – if your thumb points in the direction the wire moves and your first finger points out the magnetic field.

- **Electromagnetism** can be switched on and off, unlike permanent magnets.

- **Around every** electric or magnetic object is an area, or electromagnetic field, where its force is effective.

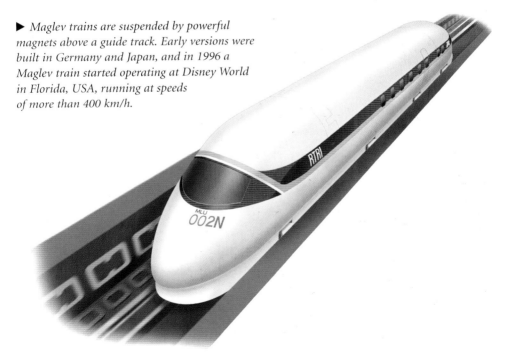

▶ *Maglev trains are suspended by powerful magnets above a guide track. Early versions were built in Germany and Japan, and in 1996 a Maglev train started operating at Disney World in Florida, USA, running at speeds of more than 400 km/h.*

Electromagnetic spectrum

- **The electromagnetic spectrum** is the complete range of radiation sent out by electrons (see light and atoms). It is given off in tiny packages of energy called photons, which can be either particles or waves (see moving light).

- **Electromagnetic waves** vary in length and frequency. The shorter the wave, the higher its frequency (and also its energy).

- **The longest waves** are over 100 kilometres long; the shortest are less than a billionth of a millimetre long.

- **All electromagnetic waves** travel at 300,000 kilometres per second, which is the speed of light.

- **Visible light** is just a small part of the spectrum.

- **Radio waves,** including microwaves and television waves, and infrared light, are made from waves that are too long for human eyes to see.

- **Long waves** are lower in energy than short waves. Long waves from space penetrate the Earth's atmosphere easily (but not solids, like short waves).

- **Ultraviolet light,** x-rays and gamma rays are made from waves that are too short for human eyes to see.

- **Short waves are very energetic.** But short waves from space are blocked out by Earth's atmosphere – which is fortunate because they are dangerous. X-rays and gamma rays penetrate some solids, and UV rays can damage living tissue, causing skin cancers.

▶ *This illustration shows the range of radiation in the electromagnetic spectrum. The waves are shown emerging from the Sun, as the Sun actually emits almost the full range of radiation. Fortunately, the atmosphere protects us from the dangerous ones.*

Gamma rays are dangerous high-energy rays with such short waves that they can penetrate solids. They are created in space and by nuclear bombs.

X-rays are longer waves than gamma rays but short enough to pass through most body tissues except bones, which show up white on medical x-rays.

The shortest ultraviolet rays in sunshine are dangerous, but longer ones give you a suntan in small doses. In large doses even long UV rays cause cancer.

Visible light varies in wavelength from violet (shortest) through all the colours of the rainbow to red (longest).

Infrared light is the radiation given out by hot objects. This is why infrared-sensitive 'thermal imaging' cameras can see hot objects such as people in the dark.

Microwaves are used to beam telephone signals to satellites – and to cook food. Radars send out fairly short microwaves (about 1 cm long).

Television broadcasts use radio waves with waves about 0.5 m long.

Radio broadcasts use radio waves from 300 to 1500 m long.

Typical wavelength in metres or millimetres. Long waves are low frequency and low energy. Short waves are high frequency and high energy.

1 billionth mm

10 millionth mm

0.00001 mm

0.0005 mm

0.2 mm

0.3 m to 1 mm

0.5 m

300–1500 m

117

Holograms

- **Holograms** are three-dimensional photographic images made with laser lights.

- **The idea of holograms** was suggested by Hungarian-born British physicist Dennis Gabor in 1947. The idea could not be tried until laser light became available.

- **The first holograms** were made by Emmett Leith and Juris Upatnieks in Michigan, USA, in 1963 and by Yuri Denisyuk in the Soviet Union.

- **To make a hologram,** the beam from a laser light is split in two. One part of the beam is reflected off the subject onto a photographic plate. The other, called the reference beam, shines directly onto the plate.

- **The interference** between light waves in the reflected beam and light waves in the reference beam creates the hologram in complex microscopic stripes on the plate.

- **Some holograms** only show up when laser light is shone through them.

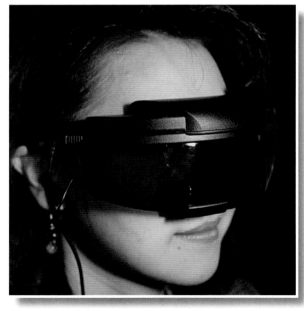

▲ *Virtual reality headsets allow the viewer to see 3-D images by showing slightly different images to each eye.*

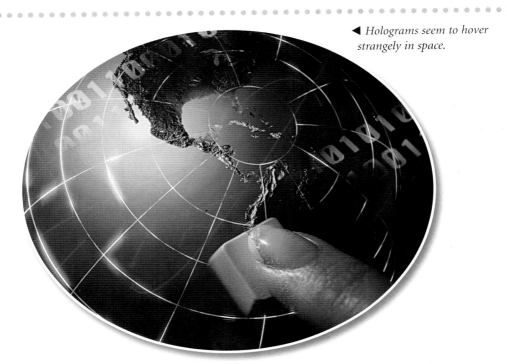

◀ *Holograms seem to hover strangely in space.*

- **Some holograms** work in ordinary light, such as those used in credit cards to stop counterfeiting.

- **Holograms** are used to detect defects in engines and aeroplanes, and forgeries in paintings by comparing two holograms made under slightly different conditions.

- **Huge amounts of digital data** can be stored in holograms in a crystal.

- **In 1993** 10,000 pages of data were stored in a lithium nobate crystal measuring just 1 cm across.

119

Microscopes

- **Microscopes** are devices for looking at things that are normally too small for the human eye to see.

- **Optical microscopes** use lenses to magnify images by up to 2000 times.

- **In an optical microscope** an objective lens bends light rays apart to enlarge what you see; an eyepiece lens makes the big image visible.

- **Electron microscopes** magnify by firing streams of electrons at the object. The electrons bounce off the object onto a fluorescent screen which makes them visible.

- **An electron microscope** can focus on something as small as one nanometre (one-billionth of a metre) and magnify it five million times.

- **Scanning Electron Microscopes** (SEMs) scan the surface of an object to magnify it by up to 100,000 times.

▶ *In the 1660s, Robert Hooke much improved the compound microscope, a powerful scientific instrument which worked by using several lenses.*

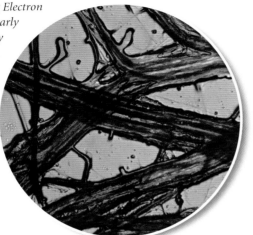

▶ *A Scanning Electron Microscope clearly reveals the tiny nerve fibres inside the human brain.*

- **Transmission Electron Microscopes** shine electrons through thin slices of an object to magnify it millions of times.

- **Scanning Tunnelling Microscopes** are so powerful that they can reveal individual atoms.

- **The idea of electron microscopes** came from French physicist Louis de Broglie in 1924.

- **Scanning Acoustic Microscopes** use sound waves to see inside tiny opaque objects.

▶ *From the 1670s, Antoni Van Leeuwenhoek used his single lens microscope to study many different subjects: fibres of fabrics, leaves, small creatures, and human blood, skin and hair.*

121

Telecommunication

- **Telecommunication** is the almost instantaneous transmission of sounds, words, pictures, data and information by electronic means.

- **Every communication system** needs three things: a transmitter, a communications link and a receiver.

- **Transmitters** can be telephones or computers with modems (see the Internet). They change the words, pictures, data or sounds into an electrical signal and send it. Similar receivers pick up the signal and change it back into the right form.

- **Communications links** carry the signal from the transmitter to the receiver in two main ways. Some give a direct link through telephone lines and other cables. Some are carried on radio waves through the air, via satellite or microwave links.

- **Telephone lines** used to be mainly electric cables which carried the signal as pulses of electricity. More and more are now fibre optics (see fibre optics) which carry the signal as coded pulses of light.

- **Communications satellites** are satellites orbiting the Earth in space. Telephone calls are beamed up on radio waves to the satellite, which beams them back down to the right part of the world.

- **Microwave links** use very short radio waves to transmit telephone and other signals from one dish to another in a straight line across Earth's surface.

- **Mobile phones** or cellular phones transmit and receive phone calls directly via radio waves. The calls are picked up and sent on from a local aerial.

- **The information superhighway** is the network of high-speed links that might be achieved by combining telephone systems, cable TV and computer networks. TV programmes, films, data, direct video links and the Internet could all enter the home in this way.all enter the home in this way.

▼ *This illustration shows some of the many ways in which telecommunications are carried. At present, TV, radio and phone links are all carried separately, but increasingly they will all be carried the same way. They will be split up only when they arrive at their destination.*

TV and radio signals are broadcast as pulses of radio waves, sent through cables or bounced off satellites.

Computer data is translated by a modem into signals that can be carried on phone lines.

Signals from individual transmitters are sent on from a telephone exchange or a service provider.

More and more communications are beamed from antenna dishes on the ground to satellites in space.

Telephones can link to the phone network by a direct cable link. Mobile phones link through to local relay towers by radio waves.

Television

- **Television relies** on the photoelectric effect – the emission of electrons by a substance when struck by photons of light. Light-sensitive photocells in cameras work like this.

- **TV cameras** have three sets of tubes with photocells (reacting to red, green and blue light) to convert the picture into electrical signals.

- **The sound signal** from microphones is added, and a 'sync pulse' is put in to keep both kinds of signal in time.

- **The combined signal** is turned into radio waves (see electromagnetic spectrum) and broadcast.

- **An aerial** picks up the signal and feeds it to your television set.

- **Most TV sets** are based on glass tubes shaped like giant lightbulbs, called cathode-ray tubes. The narrow end contains a cathode, which is a negative electrical terminal. The wide end is the TV screen.

- **The cathode** fires a non-stop stream of electrons (see electrons) at the inside of the TV screen.

◄ *TV cameras convert a scene into electrical signals that can be transmitted via radio waves.*

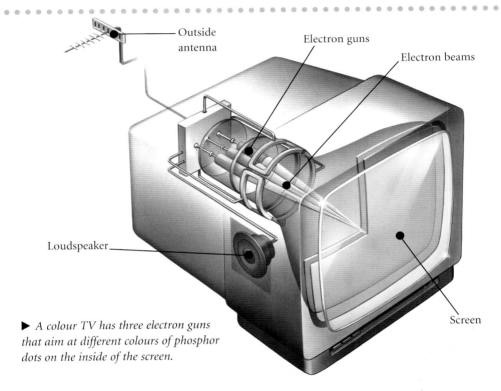

Outside antenna

Electron guns

Electron beams

Loudspeaker

Screen

▶ *A colour TV has three electron guns that aim at different colours of phosphor dots on the inside of the screen.*

- **Wherever electrons** hit the screen, the screen glows as its coating of phosphors heats up.

- **To build up the picture** the electron beam scans quickly back and forth across the screen, making it glow in certain places. This happens so quickly that it looks as if the whole screen is glowing.

- **Colour TVs** have three electron guns: one to make red phosphors glow, another for green and a third for blue. for green, and a third for blue.

125

Scanners

- **Scanners** are electronic devices that move backwards and forwards in lines in order to build up a picture.

- **Image scanners** are used to convert pictures and other material into a digital form for computers to read.

- **A photoelectric cell** in the scanner measures the amount of light reflected from each part of the picture and converts it into a digital code.

- **Various scanners** are used in medicine to build up pictures of the inside of the body. They include CT scanners, PET scanners and MRI scanners.

- **CT stands** for computerized tomography. An x-ray beam rotates around the patient and is picked up by detectors on the far side to build up a 3-D picture.

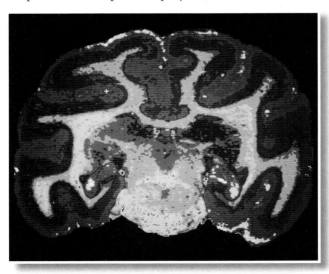

- **PET** stands for Positron Emission Tomography. The scanner picks up positrons (positively charged electrons sent out by radioactive substances injected into the blood.

- **PET scans** can show a living brain in action.

▲ *This PET scan shows a monkey's brain from above.*

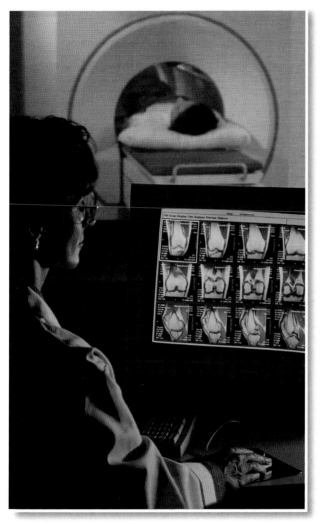

- **MRI** stands for Magnetic Resonance Imaging.

- **An MRI scan** works like CT scans but it uses magnetism, not X-rays. The patient is surrounded by such powerful magnets that all the body's protons (see atoms) line up.

- **The MRI scan begins** as a radio pulse that knocks the protons briefly out of alignment. The scanner detects radio signals sent out by the protons as they snap back into line.

◄ *A patient having an MRI scan. A computer converts signals from the scanner into images which it displays on a monitor.*

127

Computers

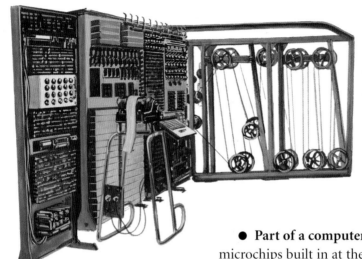

◀ *Created in the 1940s, the Colossus computer successfully cracked the German Enigma war codes.*

- **Part of a computer's** memory is microchips built in at the factory and known as ROM, or read-only memory. ROM carries the basic working instructions.

- **RAM** (random-access memory) consists of microchips that receive new data and instructions when needed.

- **Data can also** be stored as magnetic patterns on a removable floppy disk, or on the laser-guided bumps on a CD (compact disc) or DVD (digital versatile disk).

- **At the heart** of every computer is a powerful microchip called the central processing unit, or CPU.

- **The CPU** performs logical and mathematical operations on data, within the guidelines set by the computer's ROM. It carries out programmes by sending data to the right place in the RAM.

◀ *Computers are developing so rapidly that models from the 1990s already look dated.*

● **Computers** store information in bits (binary digits), either as 0 or 1.

● **The bits 0 and 1** are equivalent to the OFF and ON of electric current flow. Eight bits make a byte.

● **A kilobyte** is 1000 bytes; a megabyte (MB) is 1,000,000 bytes; a gigabyte (GB) is 1,000,000,000 bytes; a terabyte (TB) is 1,000,000,000,000 bytes.

● **A CD can hold** about 600 MB of data – approximately 375,000 pages of ordinary text.

> **. . . . FASCINATING FACT . . . .**
> The US Library of Congress's 70 million books could be stored in 25 TB of computer capacity.

129

The Internet

- **The Internet** is a vast network linking millions of computers around the world.

- **The Internet began** in the 1960s when the US Army developed a network called ARPAnet to link computers.

- **To access the Internet** computer data is translated into a form that can be sent through phone lines with a modem (short for modulator/demodulator).

- **Computers** access the Internet via a local phone to a large computer called the Internet Service Provider (ISP).

- **Each ISP** is connected to a giant computer called a main hub. There are about 100 linked main hubs worldwide.

- **Some links between** hubs are made via phone lines; some are made via satellite.

- **Links between** hubs are called fast-track connections.

▲ *The Internet links computers instantly around the world.*

- **The World Wide Web** is a way of finding your way to the data in sites on all the computers linked to the Internet. The Web makes hyperlinks (fast links) to sites with the word you select.

- **The World Wide Web** was invented in 1989 by Tim Berners-Lee of the CERN laboratories in Switzerland.

▲ *E-mail, sending electronic messages from one computer to another, is used for business and pleasure.*

...**FASCINATING FACT**...
People can now access the Internet via mobile phones.

131

Sound recording

▶ *Microphones pick up sound waves and turn them into electrical signals. These are passed on to recording, amplifying or broadcasting equipment.*

● **Sound is recorded** by using a microphone to turn the vibrations of sound into a varying electrical current.

● **Sound recording** in the past was analogue, which means that the electrical current varies continually exactly as the sound vibrations do.

● **Most sound recording** today is digital, which means that sound vibrations are broken into tiny electrical chunks.

● **To make a digital recording** a device called an analogue-to-digital converter divides the vibrations into 44,100 segments for each second of sound.

● **Each digital segment** is turned into a digital code of ON or OFF electrical pulses.

● **With analogue sound,** each time the signal is passed on to the next stage, distortion and noise are added. With digital sound no noise is added, but the original recording is not a perfect replica of the sound.

● **On a CD (compact disc)** the pattern of electrical pulses is burned by a laser as a corresponding pattern of pits on the surface of the disc.

● **During playback,** a laser beam is reflected from the tiny pits on a CD to re-create the electrical signal.

- **DVDs** work like CDs. They can store huge amounts of data on both sides, but most can only be recorded on once.

- **Minidiscs** (MDs) use magneto-optical recording to allow you to record on the disc up to one million times. A laser burns the data into a magnetic pattern on the disc.

▲ *In a recording studio, the sound is recorded either on computer or on big master tapes.*

133

Lasers

- **Laser light** is a bright artificial light. It creates an intense beam that can punch a hole in steel. A laser beam is so straight and narrow that it can hit a mirror on the Moon.

- **'Laser'** stands for light amplification by stimulated emission of radiation.

- **Laser light** is even brighter for its size than the Sun.

- **Laser light** is the only known 'coherent' source of light. This means the light waves are not only all the same wavelength (colour), but they are also perfectly in step.

- **Inside a laser** is a tube filled with gases, such as helium and neon, or a liquid or solid crystal such as ruby.

- **Lasers work** by bouncing photons (bursts of light) up and down the tube until they are all travelling together.

- **Lasing begins** when a spark excites atoms in the lasing material. The excited atoms emit photons. When the photons hit other atoms, they fire off photons too. Identical photons bounce backwards and forwards between mirrors at either end of the laser.

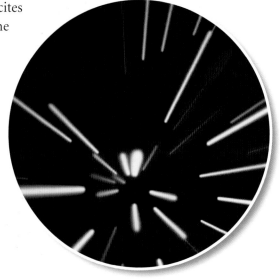

▶ *The amazingly tight, intense beam of a laser is used in a huge number of devices, from CD players to satellite guidance systems.*

134

▶ *Lasers are used for delicate plastic surgery because the laser beam can be finely focussed and because its power can be carefully controlled.*

- **Gas lasers** such as argon lasers give a lower-powered beam. It is suitable for delicate work such as eye surgery.

- **Chemical lasers** use liquid hydrogen fluoride to make intense beams for weapons.

- **Some lasers** send out a continuous beam. Pulsed lasers send out a high-powered beam at regular intervals.

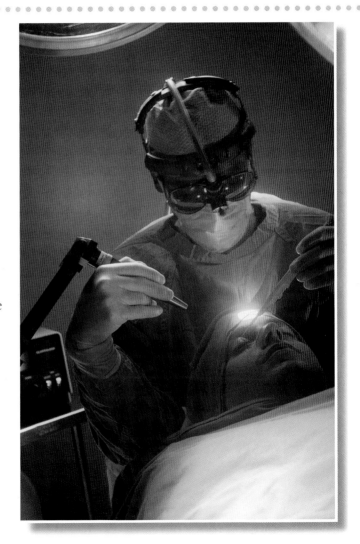

Fibre optics

- **Fibre optic cables** are bundles of thin, transparent glass threads that transmit messages by light.

- **The light is transmitted** in coded pulses.

- **A thin layer of glass,** called cladding, surrounds each fibre and stops light from escaping.

- **The cladding** reflects all the light back into the fibre so that it bends round with the fibre. This is called total internal reflection.

▲ *A bundle of optical fibres glows with transmitted light.*

- **Single-mode fibres** are very narrow and the light bounces very little from side to side. These fibres are suitable for long-distance transmissions.

- **Aiming light** into the narrow core of a single-mode fibre needs the precision of a laser beam.

- **Multi-mode fibres** are wider than single-mode fibres. They accept LED (light-emitting diodes) light, so they are cheaper but they are unsuitable for long distances.

- **The largest cables** can carry hundreds of thousands of phone calls or hundreds of television channels.

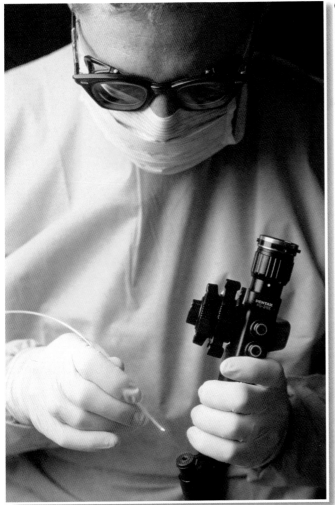

- **Underwater fibre optic** cables transmit signals under the Atlantic and Pacific Oceans.

- **Optical fibres** have many medical uses, such as in endoscopes. These are flexible tubes, with a lens on the end, that are inserted into the body to look inside it. Optical fibres are used to measure blood temperature and pressure.

◀ *A laser endoscope is used for examining the inside of a patient. An optical fibre carries a laser beam which is used for precise surgery.*

137

Nuclear power

- **Nuclear power** is based on the huge amounts of energy that bind together the nucleus of every atom in the Universe. It is an incredibly concentrated form of energy.

- **Nuclear energy** is released by splitting the nuclei of atoms in a process called nuclear fission (see nuclear energy). One day scientists hope to release energy by nuclear fusion – by fusing nuclei together as in the Sun.

- **Most nuclear reactors** use uranium-235. These are special atoms, or isotopes, of uranium with 235 protons and neutrons in their nucleus rather than the normal 238.

- **The fuel** usually consists of tiny pellets of uranium dioxide in thin tubes, separated by sheets called spacers.

- **Three kilograms of uranium fuel** provide enough energy for a city of one million people for one day.

- **The earliest reactors,** called N-reactors, were designed to make plutonium for bombs. Magnox reactors make both plutonium and electricity.

- **Pressurized water reactors** (PWRs), originally used in submarines, are now the most common kind. They are built in factories, unlike Advanced Gas Reactors (AGRs).

- **Fast-breeder reactors** actually create more fuel than they burn, but the new fuel is highly radioactive.

- **Every stage of the nuclear process** creates dangerous radioactive waste. The radioactivity may take 80,000 years to fade. All but the most radioactive liquid waste is pumped out to sea. Gaseous waste is vented into the air. Solid waste is mostly stockpiled underground. Scientists debate fiercely about what to do with radioactive waste.

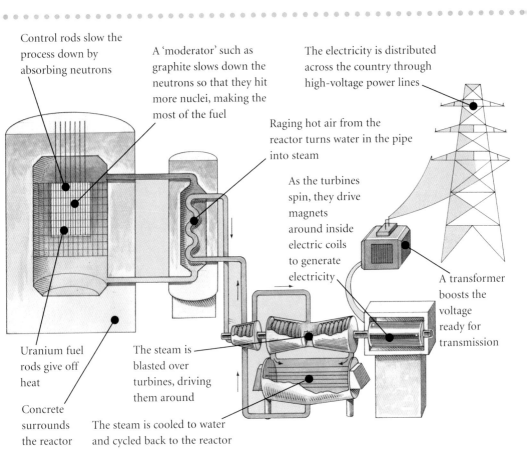

Control rods slow the process down by absorbing neutrons

A 'moderator' such as graphite slows down the neutrons so that they hit more nuclei, making the most of the fuel

The electricity is distributed across the country through high-voltage power lines

Raging hot air from the reactor turns water in the pipe into steam

As the turbines spin, they drive magnets around inside electric coils to generate electricity

A transformer boosts the voltage ready for transmission

Uranium fuel rods give off heat

The steam is blasted over turbines, driving them around

Concrete surrounds the reactor

The steam is cooled to water and cycled back to the reactor

▲ Like coal- and oil-fired power stations, nuclear power stations use steam to drive turbines to generate electricity. The difference is that nuclear power stations obtain the heat by splitting uranium atoms, not by burning coal or oil. When an atom is split, it sends out gamma rays, neutrons and immense heat. In a nuclear bomb this happens in a split second. In a nuclear power plant, control rods soak up some of the neutrons and slow the process down.

139

Nuclear energy

- **The energy** that binds the nucleus of an atom together is enormous, as Albert Einstein showed.

- **By releasing the energy** from the nuclei of millions of atoms, nuclear power stations and bombs can generate a huge amount of power.

- **Nuclear fusion** is when nuclear energy is released by fusing together small atoms such as deuterium (a kind of hydrogen).

- **Nuclear fusion** is the reaction that keeps stars glowing and gives hydrogen bombs their terrifying power.

- **Nuclear fission** releases energy by splitting the large nuclei of atoms such as uranium and plutonium.

- **To split atomic nuclei** for nuclear fission, neutrons are fired into the nuclear fuel.

- **As neutrons crash** into atoms and split their nuclei, they split off more neutrons. These neutrons bombard other nuclei, splitting off more neutrons that bombard more nuclei. This is called a chain reaction.

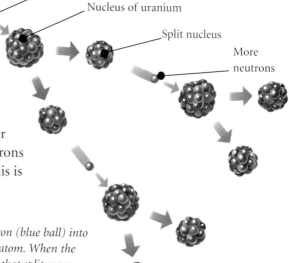

Neutron

Nucleus of uranium

Split nucleus

More neutrons

▶ *Nuclear fission involves firing a neutron (blue ball) into the nucleus of a uranium or plutonium atom. When the nucleus splits, it fires out more neutrons that split more nuclei, setting off a chain reaction.*

140

◄ *The huge mushroom-shaped cloud of a nuclear explosion. The four main effects from such an explosion are 1) a fireball leading to a blast wave of noise and air pressure 2) intense thermal radiation ie heat 3) initial nuclear radiation 4) residual radiation – given off later than a minute after the explosion.*

● **An atom bomb,** or A-bomb, is one of the two main kinds of nuclear weapon. It works by an explosive, unrestrained fission of uranium-235 or plutonium-239.

● **A hydrogen bomb (H-bomb)** or thermonuclear weapon uses a conventional explosion to fuse the nuclei of deuterium atoms in a gigantic nuclear explosion.

● **The H-bomb** tested at Novaya Zemlya in the former USSR in 1961 released 10,000 times more energy than the bombs dropped on Hiroshima, Japan, in 1945.

Thermodynamics

- **Energy cannot be destroyed** but it can be burned up. Every time energy is used, some turns into heat. This is why you feel hot after running.

- **Energy that turns into heat** may not be lost. It dissipates (spreads out thinly in all directions) and is hard to use again.

- **Every time energy is used,** some free energy (energy available to make things happen) gets lost as heat.

- **Scientists use** the word 'entropy' to describe how much energy has become unusable. The less free energy there is, the greater the entropy.

- **The word 'entropy'** was invented by the German physicist Rudolf Clausius in 1865.

- **Clausius showed** that everything really happens because energy moves from areas of high energy to areas of low energy, from hot areas to cold areas.

- **Energy goes on flowing** from high to low until there is no difference to make anything happen. This is an equilibrium state. Entropy is the maximum.

▲ *Energy cannot be reused once it has turned to heat and dissipated, just as you cannot rebuild an igloo once the snow has melted.*

▼ *Waste gases produced from this chemical plant are burnt off and released into the atmosphere as unwanted heat.*

- **Clausius summed this idea up** in 1860s with two laws of thermodynamics.

- **The first law of thermodynamics** says the total energy in the Universe was fixed forever at the beginning of time.

- **The second law of thermodynamics** says that energy is dissipated every time it is used. So the entropy of the Universe must increase.

143

Temperature

- **Temperature** is how hot or cold something is. The best-known temperature scales are Celsius and Fahrenheit.

- **The Celsius (C) scale** is part of the metric system of measurements and is used everywhere except in the USA. It is named after Swedish astronomer Anders Celsius, who developed it in 1742.

- **Celsius is also** known as centigrade because water boils at 100°C. Cent is the Latin prefix for 100. Water freezes at 0°C.

- **On the Fahrenheit (F) scale** water boils at 212°F. It freezes at 32°F.

- **To convert Celsius** to Fahrenheit, divide by 5, multiply by 9 and add 32.

- **To convert Fahrenheit** to Celsius, subtract 32, divide by 9 and multiply by 5.

- **The Kelvin (K) scale** used by scientists is like the Celsius scale, but it begins at –273.15°C. So 0°C is 273.15K.

- **Cold:** absolute zero is –273.15°C. The coldest temperature ever obtained in a laboratory is –272.99999°C. Helium turns liquid at –269°C. Oxygen turns liquid at –183°C. Gasoline freezes at –150°C. The lowest air temperature ever recorded on Earth is –89.2°C.

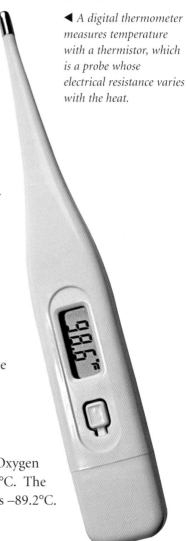

◀ *A digital thermometer measures temperature with a thermistor, which is a probe whose electrical resistance varies with the heat.*

- **Hot:** the highest shade temperature recorded on Earth is 58°C. A log fire burns at around 800°C. Molten magma is about 1200°C. Tungsten melts at 3410°C. The surface of the Sun is around 6000°C. The centre of the Earth is over 7000°C. A lightning flash reaches 30,000°C. The centre of a hydrogen bomb reaches four million°C.

- **The blood temperature** of the human body is normally 37°C. A skin temperature above 40°C is very hot, and below 31°C is very cold. Hands feel cold below 20°C and go numb below 12°C. Anything above 45°C that touches your skin hurts, although people have walked on hot coals at 800°C. The knee can tolerate 47°C for 30 seconds.

▲ *Molten iron is poured into a furnace as part of the process of producing steel. The temperature of the liquid metal is about 1500°C.*

145

Heat

- **Heat is the energy** of moving molecules. The faster molecules move, the hotter the substance is.

- **When you hold your hand** over a heater the warmth you feel is the assault of billions of fast-moving air molecules.

- **Heat** is the combined energy of all the moving molecules; temperature is how fast they are moving.

- **The coldest temperature possible** is absolute zero, or -273°C, when molecules stop moving.

▼ *Cooking helps chemical reactions to take place in food, maybe changing its flavour, its texture or consistency.*

- **When you heat a substance** its temperature rises because heat makes its molecules move faster.

- **The same amount** of heat raises the temperature of different substances by different amounts.

▶ *Fire changes the energy in fuel into heat energy. Heat makes the molecules rush about.*

- **The specific heat** of a substance is the energy needed, in joules, to heat it by 1°C.

- **Argon gas** gets hotter quicker than oxygen. The shape of oxygen molecules means they absorb some energy not by moving faster but by spinning faster.

- **Heat always spreads out** from its source. It heats up its surroundings while cooling down itself.

147

Heat movement

- **Heat moves** in three different ways: conduction, convection and radiation.

- **Conduction** involves heat spreading from hot areas to cold areas by direct contact. It works a bit like a relay race. Energetic, rapidly moving or vibrating molecules cannon into their neighbours and set them moving.

- **Good conducting materials** such as metals feel cool to the touch because they carry heat away from your fingers quickly. The best conductors of heat are the metals silver, copper and gold, in that order.

▲ *Hot-air balloons work because hot air is lighter than cold air and rises through it.*

- **Materials** that conduct heat slowly are called insulators. They help keep things warm by reducing heat loss. Wood is one of the best insulators. Water is also surprisingly effective as an insulator, which is why scuba divers and surfers often wear wetsuits.

◄ *A layer of water trapped between the diver and the wetsuit heats up to the person's body temperature keeping the diver warm.*

- **Radiation** is the spread of heat as heat rays, that is, invisible waves of infrared radiation.

- **Radiation** spreads heat without direct contact.

- **Convection** is when warm air rises through cool air, like a hot-air balloon.

- **Warm air rises** because warmth makes the air expand. As it expands the air becomes less dense and lighter than the cool air around it.

- **Convection currents** are circulation patterns set up as warm air (or a liquid) rises. Around the column of rising warmth, cool air continually sinks to replace it at the bottom. So the whole air is turning over like a non-stop fountain.

▼ *Radioactive material causes nausea, cancer or even death and so must be guarded carefully.*

. . . . FASCINATING FACT *. . . .*
Convection currents in the air bring rain; convection currents in the Earth's interior move continents.

Energy

- **Energy is the ability** to make things happen or, as scientists say, do work.

- **Energy comes in many forms,** from the chemical energy locked in sugar to the mechanical energy in a speeding train.

- **Energy does its work** either by transfer or conversion.

- **Energy transfer** is the movement of energy from one place to another, such as heat rising above a fire or a ball being thrown.

- **Energy conversion** is when energy changes from one form to another – as when wind turbines generate electric power, for instance.

- **Energy is never lost nor gained;** it simply moves or changes. The total amount of energy in the Universe has stayed the same since the beginning of time.

▼ *Power stations do not create energy. They simply convert it into a convenient form for us to use electricity.*

- **Energy and mass** are actually the same thing. They are like opposite sides of a coin and are interchangeable.

- **Potential energy** is energy stored up ready for action – as in a squeezed spring or stretched piece of elastic.

- **Kinetic energy** is energy that something has because it is moving, such as a rolling ball or a falling stone.

- **Kinetic energy** increases in proportion with the velocity of an object squared. So a car has four times more kinetic energy at 40 km/h than at 20 km/h.

▼ *Found near the Earth's surface and at various depths, coal is an important primary fossil fuel.*

▼ *Wind farms can be constructed in areas where there is a steady wind. About 47% of the kinetic energy of the wind can be harnessed.*

151

Energy conversion

- **Energy is measured** in joules (J). One joule is the energy involved in moving a force of one newton over one metre.

- **A kilojoule (kJ)** is 1000 joules.

- **A calorie** was the old measure of energy, but is now used only for food: 1 calorie is 4187 J; 1 Cal is 1000 calories.

- **For scientists,** 'work' is the transfer of energy. When you move an object, you do work. The work done is the amount of energy (in joules) gained by the object.

▲ *A hydroelectric power station is a device that converts the energy of moving water into electrical energy.*

▼ *During sleep, the body's metabolism slows right down so that less energy is needed.*

- **For scientists, 'power'** is the work rate, or the rate at which energy is changed from one form to another.

- **The power of a machine** is the amount of work it does divided by the length of time it takes to do it.

- **The power of a car's engine** is the force with which the engine turns multiplied by the speed at which it turns.

- **A transducer** is a device for turning an electrical signal into a non-electrical signal (such as sound) or vice versa. A loudspeaker is a transducer.

- **The energy in the Big Bang** was 10^{68} J. The world's coal reserves are 2×10^{23} J; a thunderstorm has 1^{14} J of energy; a large egg has 400,000 J.

- **When sleeping** you use 60 Cals an hour and 80 Cals when sitting. Running uses 600 Cals. Three hours of reading or watching TV uses 240 Cals. Seven hours' hard work uses about 1000 Cals – or about 10 eggs' worth.

Engines

- **Engines are devices** that convert fuel into movement.

- **Most engines** work by burning the fuel to make gases that expand rapidly as they get hot.

- **Engines** that burn fuel to generate power are called heat engines. The burning is called combustion.

- **An internal combustion** engine, as used in a car, a jet or a rocket, burns its fuel on the inside.

- **In engines** such as those in cars and diesel trains, the hot gases swell inside a chamber (the combustion chamber) and push against a piston or turbine.

- **An external combustion** engine burns its fuel on the outside in a separate boiler that makes hot steam to drive a piston or turbine. Steam engines on trains and boats work in this way.

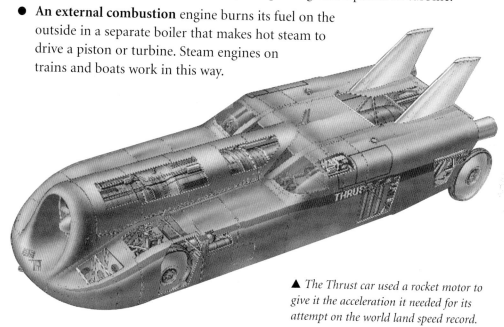

▲ *The Thrust car used a rocket motor to give it the acceleration it needed for its attempt on the world land speed record.*

- **Engines with pistons** that go back and forth inside cylinders are called reciprocating engines.

- **In jets and rockets,** hot gases swell and push against the engine as they shoot out of the back.

- **In four-stroke engines,** such as those in most cars, the pistons go up and down four times for each time they are thrust down by the hot gases.

- **In two-stroke engines,** such as those on small motorcycles, lawnmowers and chainsaws, the piston is pushed by burning gases every time it goes down.

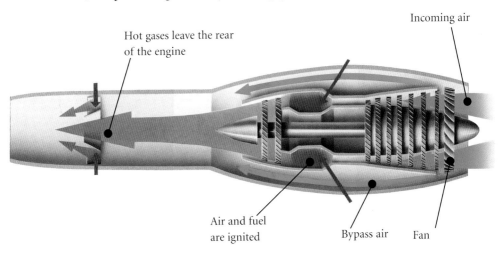

Incoming air

Hot gases leave the rear
of the engine

Air and fuel
are ignited

Bypass air   Fan

▲ *A jet engine burns fuel with air drawn in from the atmosphere in order to generate gases: it discharges these from the rear to power the craft along.*

Jet engines

- **A kind of jet engine** was built by the Ancient Greek Hero Alexander in the first century AD. It was a ball driven round by jets of steam escaping from two nozzles.

- **The first jet engines** were built at the same time in the 1930s by Pabst von Ohain in Germany and Frank Whittle in Britain.

- **Ohain's engine** was put in the Heinkel HE-178 which first flew on 27 August 1939; Whittle's was put in the Gloster E28 of 1941. The first American jet was the Bell XP-59 Aircomet of 1942.

- **Jets** work by pushing a jet of air out the back. This hits the air so fast that the reaction thrusts the plane forward like a deflating balloon.

- **Jet engines** are also called gas turbines because they burn fuel gas to spin the blades of a turbine non-stop.

- **Turbojets** are the original form of jet engine. Air is scooped in at the front and squeezed by spinning compressor blades. Fuel sprayed into the squeezed air in the middle of the engine burns, making the mixture expand dramatically. The expanding air pushes round turbines which drive the compressor, and send out a high-speed jet of hot air to propel the plane. This high-speed jet is noisy but good for fast warplanes and the supersonic Concorde.

▲ *Stealth aircraft are jet-propelled but the afterburner stream of hot gases from the jets shows up on some detection equipment. So stealth aircraft are designed to 'supercruise' – that is, fly at supersonic speeds without much afterburn.*

● **Turboprops** are turbojets that use most of their power to turn a propeller rather than force out a hot air jet.

● **Turbofans** are used by most airliners because they are quieter and cheaper to run. In these, extra turbines turn a huge fan at the front. Air driven by this fan bypasses the engine core and gives a huge extra boost at low speeds.

● **Ramjets or** 'flying stovepipes' are the simplest type of jet engine, used only on missiles. They dispense with both compressor and turbine blades and simply rely on the speed of the jet through the air to ram air in through the intake into the engine.

The engine casing is made of carbon-fibre and plastic honeycomb for lightness. Inside is an outer bypass duct for the 'cold stream' of air from the front fan. An inner duct takes the 'hot stream' through the compressor, combustion chamber and turbine to create the exhaust

Front fan to create 'cold' bypass stream

▲ *All but the very fastest warplanes are powered by turbofan jet engines, like this Russian MiG jump jet. Turbofans first came into widespread use in the 1970s and are now by far the most common kind of jet engine.*

Exhaust where a hot jet of air roars out

157

Rockets

- **Rockets** work by burning fuel. As fuel burns and swells out behind, the swelling pushes the rocket forward.

- **Solid-fuel rockets** are the oldest of all engines, used by the Chinese a thousand years ago.

- **Solid-fuel engines** are basically rods of solid, rubbery fuel with a tube down the middle.

- **Solid-fuel rockets** are usually only used for model rockets and small booster rockets. But the Space Shuttle has two solid-fuel rocket boosters (SRBs) as well as three main liquid-fuel engines.

- **Most powerful launch rockets** use liquid fuel. The Space Shuttle uses hydrogen. Other fuels include kerosene.

▶ *The mighty Atlas Rocket was used to launch America's first astronauts into space.*

158

- **Liquid fuel** only burns with oxygen, so rockets must also carry an oxidizer (a substance that gives oxygen) such as liquid oxygen (LOX) or nitrogen tetroxide.

FASCINATING FACT
The Saturn V rocket that launched the Apollo mission to the Moon is the most powerful rocket ever built.

- **Future rocket drives** include nuclear thermal engines that would use a nuclear reactor to heat the gas blasted out.

- **NASA's Deep Space-1** project is based on xenon ion engines which thrust electrically charged particles called ions, not hot gases, out of the back of the craft.

- **Solar thermal engines** of the future would collect the Sun's rays with a large mirror to heat gases.

▶ *Only powerful rockets can give the thrust to overcome gravity and launch spacecraft into space. They fall away in three stages once the spacecraft is travelling fast enough.*

Supersonic planes

- **Supersonic planes** travel faster than the speed of sound.

- **The speed of sound** is about 1220 km/h at sea level at 15°C.

- **Sound travels** slower higher up, so the speed of sound is about 1060 km/h at 12,000 m.

- **Supersonic** plane speeds are given in Mach numbers. These are the speed of the plane divided by the speed of sound at the plane's altitude.

- **A plane flying** at 1500 km/h at 12,000 m, where the speed of sound is 1060 km/h, is at Mach 1.46.

- **A plane flying** at supersonic speeds builds up shock waves in front and behind because it keeps catching up and compressing the sound waves in front of it.

- **The double shock waves** create a sharp crack called a sonic boom that is heard on the ground. Two booms can often be heard one or two seconds apart.

▲ *In 1976 Concorde became the first supersonic aircraft to carry passengers on commercial flights. It was retired from service in 2003.*

- **In 1947** Chuck Yeager of the USAF made the first supersonic flight in the Bell X-1 rocket plane. The X-15 rocket plane later reached speeds faster than Mach 6. Speeds faster than Mach 5 are called hypersonic.

- **The first jet plane** to fly supersonic was the F-100 Super Sabre fighter of 1953. The first supersonic bomber was the USAF's Convair B-58 Hustler, which was first used in 1956.

▼ *Supersonic jet fighter planes are used by the military to intercept and attack enemy aircraft.*

...FASCINATING FACT...
Spaceplanes of the near future may
reach speeds of Mach 15.

Inertia and momentum

● **Everything that is standing still** has inertia, which means that it will not move unless forced to.

● **Everything that moves** has momentum, which means that it will not slow down or speed up or change direction unless forced to.

● **There is no real difference** between inertia and momentum, because everything in the Universe is moving. Things only appear to be still because they are not moving relative to something else.

▲ *The lead shot that athletes throw when they put the shot has a large mass. It takes a lot of muscle power to overcome its inertia.*

- **An object's momentum** is its mass times its velocity.

- **Something heavy** or fast has a lot of momentum, so a large force is needed to slow it down or speed it up.

- **A ball moves** when you kick it because when a moving object strikes another, its momentum is transferred. This is the law of conservation of momentum.

- **Angular momentum** is the momentum of something spinning. It depends on its speed and the size of the circle.

- **When a spinning skater** draws his arms close to his body, the circle he is making is smaller yet his angular momentum must be the same. So he spins faster.

- **For the same reason**, a satellite orbiting close to the Earth travels faster than one orbiting farther out.

- **A spinning top stays** upright because its angular momentum is greater than the pull of gravity.

▶ *If a spinning top is given a knock it will go round at a slant. If spun with a slant at the start, it will quickly right itself until halted by friction.*

163

Motion

- **Every movement** in the Universe is governed by physical laws devised by people such as Newton and Einstein.

- **Newton's first law of motion** says an object accelerates, slows down or changes direction only when a force is applied.

- **Newton's second law of motion** says that the acceleration depends on how heavy the object is, and on how hard it is being pushed or pulled.

- **The greater the force** acting on an object, the more it will accelerate.

- **The heavier an object is** – the greater its mass – the less it will be accelerated by a particular force.

- **Newton's third law of motion** says that when a force pushes or acts one way, an equal force pushes in the opposite direction.

- **Newton's third law of motion** is summarized as follows: 'To every action, there is an equal and opposite reaction'.

◄ *To start moving, a skater uses the force of his muscles to push against the ground. As he or she pushes, the ground pushes back with equal force.*

▲ *During launch, the blast of gases shooting from the rear of the shuttle produces 31,000,000 newtons of thrust, enough to allow it to break through the force of gravity.*

- **Newton's third law** applies everywhere, but you can see it in effect in a rocket in space. In space there is nothing for the rocket to push on. The rocket is propelled by the action and reaction between the hot gases pushed out by its engine and the rocket itself.

- **You cannot always see** the reaction. When you bounce a ball on the ground, it looks as if only the ball bounces, but the Earth recoils too. The Earth's mass is so great compared to the ball's that the recoil is tiny.

- **Einstein's theory** of relativity modifies Newton's second law of motion under certain circumstances.

165

Velocity and acceleration

- **Velocity** is speed in a particular direction.

- **Uniform velocity** is when the velocity stays the same. It can be worked out simply by dividing the distance travelled (d) by the time (t): $v = d/t$.

- **Acceleration** is a change in velocity.

- **Positive acceleration** is getting faster; negative acceleration is getting slower.

- **Acceleration** is given in metres per second per second, or m/s^2. This means that a velocity gets faster by so many metres per second in each consecutive second.

▲ *A motorbike accelerates much faster than a car because of its power-to-weight ratio.*

▲ *For a brief moment as they come away from the start, sprinters accelerate faster than a Ferrari car.*

- **A rifle bullet** accelerates down the barrel at 3000 m/s². A fast car accelerates at 6 m/s².

- **When an object falls,** the Earth's gravity makes it accelerate at 9.81 m/s². This is called g.

- **Acceleration** is often described in gs.

- **In a rocket taking off** at 1g, the acceleration has little effect. But at 3 g, it is impossible to move your arms and legs; at 4.5 g you would black out in five seconds.

- **A high-speed lift** goes up at 0.2 g. An aeroplane takes off at 0.5 g. A car brakes at up to 0.7 g. In a crash, you may be able to survive a momentary deceleration of up to 100 g, but the effects are likely to be severe.

167

Machines

- **A machine** is a device that makes doing work easier by reducing the effort needed to move something.

- **There are two forces** involved in every machine: the Load that the machine has to overcome, and the effort used to move the load.

- **The amount that a machine** reduces the effort needed to move a load is called the Mechanical Advantage. This tells you how effective a machine is.

- **Basic machines include** levers, gears, pulleys, screws, wedges and wheels. More elaborate machines, such as cranes, are built up from combinations of these basic machines.

- **Machines cut** the effort needed to move a load by spreading the effort over a greater distance or time.

- **The distance** moved by the effort you apply, divided by the distance moved by the load, is called the Velocity Ratio (VR).

- **If the VR is greater** than 1, then the Effort moves farther than the Load. You need less effort to move the load, but you have to apply the effort for longer.

- **The total amount** of effort you use to move something is called Work. Work is the force you apply multiplied by the distance that the load moves.

▲ *Like many aspects of modern life, farming has become increasingly dependent on the use of machines.*

- **One of the earliest machine still used today** is a screw-like water-lifting device called a dalu, first used in Sumeria 5500 years ago.

- **One of the world's biggest machines** is the SMEC earthmover used in opencast mines in Australia. It weighs 180 tonnes and has wheels 3.5 m high.

▼ *Excavators like this can do the work of many people and are commonly seen on construction sites.*

Forces

- **A force** is a push or a pull. It can make something start to move, slow down or speed up, change direction or change shape or size. The greater a force, the more effect it has.

- **The wind is a force.** Biting, twisting, stretching, lifting and many other actions are also forces. Every time something happens, a force is involved.

- **Force is measured** in newtons (N). One newton is the force needed to speed up a mass of one kilogram by one metre per second every second.

- **When something moves** there are usually several forces involved. When you throw a ball, the force of your throw hurls it forwards, the force of gravity pulls it down and the force of air resistance slows it down.

- **The direction and speed** of movement depend on the combined effect of all the forces involved – this is called the resultant.

- **A force** has magnitude (size) and works in a particular direction.

- **A force can** be drawn on a diagram as an arrow called a vector (see vectors). The arrow's direction shows the force's direction. Its length shows the force's strength.

▶ *When a spacecraft lifts off, the force of the rocket has to overcome the forces of gravity and air resistance to power the craft upwards.*

● **Four fundamental forces** operate throughout the Universe: gravity, electric and magnetic forces (together called electromagnetic force), and strong and weak nuclear forces (see nuclear energy).

● **A force field** is the area over which a force has an effect. The field is strongest closest to the source and gets weaker farther away.

▲ *The force of the sea's waves is unpredictable. One day huge waves may crash down, on others the sea may be absolutely calm.*

....**FASCINATING FACT**....
The thrust of Saturn V's rocket engines was 33 million newtons.

171

Vectors

- **For scientists,** vectors are things that have both a particular size and a particular direction.

- **Forces** such as gravity, muscles or the wind are vector quantities.

- **Acceleration** is a vector quantity.

- **Scalar quantities** are things which have a particular size but have no particular direction.

- **Speed, density and mass** are all scalar quantities.

- **Velocity** is speed in a particular direction, so it is a vector quantity.

- **A vector** can be drawn on a diagram with an arrow that is proportional in length to its size, pointing in the right direction.

- **Several vectors** may affect something at the same time. As you sit on a chair, gravity pulls you downwards while the chair pushes you up, so you stay still. But if someone pushes the chair from behind, you may tip over. The combined effect of all the forces involved is called the resultant.

- **When several vectors** affect the same thing, they may act at different angles. You can work out their combined effect – the resultant – by drawing geometric diagrams with the vectors.

▲ *As a gymnast poses in mid-routine, she combines the forces acting on her to keep her in balance. These forces, such as her weight and forward momentum, are all vectors and could be worked out geometrically on paper.*

172

● **The parallelogram of forces** is a simple geometric diagram for working out the resultant from two forces. A vector arrow is drawn for each force from the same point. A parallel arrow is then drawn from the end of each arrow to make a parallelogram. The resultant is the simple diagonal of the parallelogram.

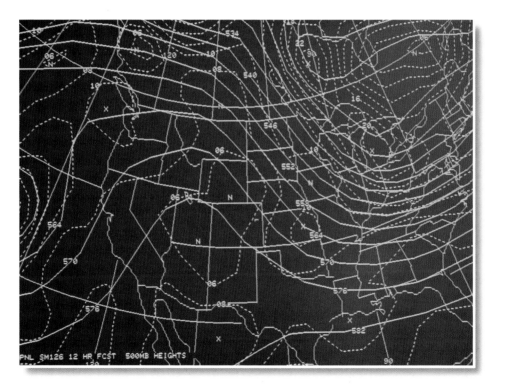

▲ *Various types of maps and charts are used to predict the weather. Vector maps are useful since they describe both speed and direction – invaluable for depicting the course of winds or storms.*

Turning forces

- **Every force** acts in a straight line. Things move round because of a 'turning effect'.

- **A turning effect** is a force applied to an object that is fixed or pivots in another place, called the fulcrum.

- **In a door** the fulcrum is the hinge.

- **The size of a turning force** is known as the moment.

- **The farther from the fulcrum** that a force is applied, the bigger the moment is.

- **A lever** makes it much easier to move a load by making use of the moment (size of turning force).

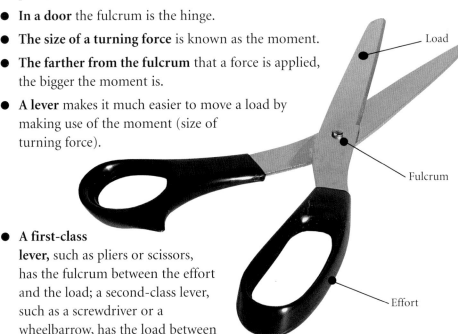

Load

Fulcrum

Effort

- **A first-class lever,** such as pliers or scissors, has the fulcrum between the effort and the load; a second-class lever, such as a screwdriver or a wheelbarrow, has the load between the effort and the fulcrum; a third-class lever, such as your lower arm or tweezers, has the effort between the load and the fulcrum.

◀ *A pair of scissors is really two knife blades joined together to form a double lever. Each blade operates as a first-class lever.*

- **Gears are sets of wheels** of different sizes that turn together. They make it easier to cycle uphill, or for a car to accelerate from a standstill, by spreading the effort over a greater distance.

- **The gear ratio** is the number of times that the wheel doing the driving turns the wheel being driven.

- **The larger the gear ratio** the more the turning force is increased, but the slower the driven wheel turns.

Fulcrum (elbow)

Effort (where the muscle joins the bone)

▶ *The human lower arm is an example of a third-class lever. The effort is between the fulcrum and the load.*

Load (in the hand)

▼ *The screwdriver is an example of a second-class lever. The load is between the effort and the fulcrum.*

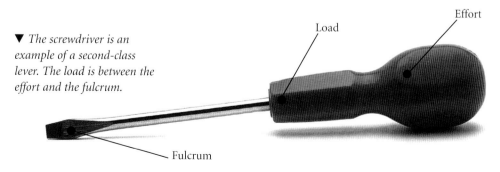

Effort

Load

Fulcrum

175

Gears

▲ *Simple cogs reverse direction of rotation.*

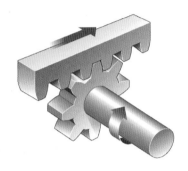

▲ *Rack and pinion changes rotation to sliding motion.*

▼ *Bevels move direction of rotation through a right angle.*

▼ *Worm gears turn fast rotation into slower, stronger rotation at right angles.*

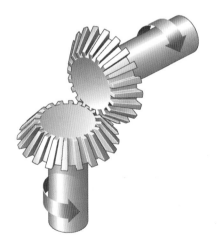

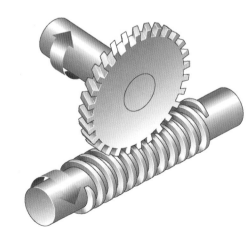

- **Gears** are pairs of toothed wheels that interlock and so transmit power from one shaft to another.

- **The first gears** were wooden, with wooden teeth. By the 6th century AD, wooden gears were used in windmills, watermills and winches.

- **Metal gears** appeared in 87 BC and were later used for clocks. Today, all gears are metal and made on a 'gear-hobbing' machine.

▶ *Gears are used in a huge range of machines, from watches to motorbikes, for transmitting movement from one shaft to another.*

- **Simple gears** are wheels with straight-cut teeth.

- **Helical gears** have slanting rather than straight teeth, and run smoother. The gears in cars are helical.

- **Bevel or mitre gears** are cone-shaped, allowing the gear shafts to interlock at right angles.

- **In worm gears** one big helical gear interlocks with a long spiral gear on a shaft at right angles.

- **Planetary gears** have a number of gear wheels known as spurs or planets that rotate around a central 'sun' gear.

- **In a planetary gear** the planet and sun gear all rotate within a ring called an annulus.

. . . FASCINATING FACT . . . .
Automatic gearboxes in cars use
planetary or epicyclic gears.

Stretching and pulling

- **Elasticity** is the ability of a solid material to return to its original shape after it has been misshapen.

- **A force** that misshapes material is called a stress.

- **All solids** are slightly elastic but some are very elastic, for example rubber, thin steel and young skin.

- **Solids** return to their original shape after the stress stops, as long as the stress is less than their 'elastic limit'.

- **Strain** is how much a solid is stretched or squeezed when under stress, namely how much longer it grows.

- **The amount** a solid stretches under a force – the ratio of stress to strain – is called the elastic modulus, or Young's modulus.

▶ *A bungee jumper stretches a piece of elasticated rope to a great extent. The rope then returns to its original length pulling the jumper back in the air.*

> ....FASCINATING FACT....
> Some types of rubber can be stretched 1000 times beyond its original length before it reaches its elastic limit.

178

- **The greater the stress**, the greater the strain. This is called Hooke's law, after Robert Hooke (1635–1703).

- **Solids** with a low elastic modulus, such as rubber, are stretchier than ones with a high modulus, such as steel.

- **Steel can be** only stretched by 1% before it reaches its elastic limit. If the steel is coiled into a spring, this 1% can allow a huge amount of stretching and squeezing.

▲ *The leverage of the bow string helps an archer to bend the elastic material of the bow so far that it has tremendous power as it snaps back into shape.*

Weight and mass

- **Mass** is the amount of matter in an object.

- **Weight** is not the same as mass. Scientists say weight is the force of gravity pulling on an object. Weight varies with the mass of the object and the strength of gravity.

- **Objects weigh more** at sea level, which is nearer the centre of the Earth, than up a mountain.

- **A person on the Moon** weighs one sixth of their weight on Earth because the Moon's gravity is one sixth of the Earth's gravity.

- **Weight varies** with gravity but mass is always the same, so scientists use mass when talking about how heavy something is.

- **The smallest** known mass is that of a photon (see light and atoms). Its mass is 5.3 times 10^{-63} (62 zeros and a 1 after the decimal point) kg.

- **The mass of the Earth** is 6 x 10^{24} (six trillion trillion) kg. The mass of the Universe may be 10^{51} (10 followed by 50 zeros) kg.

- **Density is** the amount of mass in a certain space. It is measured in grams per cubic centimetre (g/cm^3).

- **The lightest** solids are silica aerogels made for space science, with a density of 0.005 g/cm^3. The lightest gas is hydrogen, at 0.00008989 g/cm^3. The density of air is 0.00128 g/cm^3.

- **The densest** solid is osmium at 22.59 g/cm^3. Lead is 11.37 g/cm^3. A neutron star has an incredible density of about one billion trillion g/cm^3.

▲ *Brass weights are used in chemical laboratories because brass is dense and does not corrode.*

▲ *The pull of gravity at the Moon's surface is only one sixth as strong as on Earth.*

Floating and sinking

- **Things float** because they are less dense in water, which is why you can lift quite a heavy person in a swimming pool. This loss of weight is called buoyancy.

- **Buoyancy** is created by the upward push, or upthrust, of the water.

- **When an object** is immersed in water, its weight pushes it down. At the same time the water pushes it back up with a force equal to the weight of water displaced (pushed out of the way). This is called Archimedes' principle (see Archimedes).

- **An object sinks** until its weight is exactly equal to the upthrust of the water, at which point it floats.

- **Things that are less dense** than water float; those that are more dense sink.

- **Steel ships** float because although steel is denser than water, their hulls are full of air. They sink until enough water is displaced to match the weight of steel and air in the hull.

- **Oil floats** on water because it is less dense.

▲ A fishing float is made of a buoyant material such as cork or plastic in order to hold the bait suspended in the water. It bobs when a fish bites the hook.

- **Ships float** at different heights according to how heavily laden they are and how dense the water is.

- **Ships float higher** in sea water than in fresh water because salt makes the sea water more dense.

- **Ships float higher** in dense cold seas than in warm tropical ones. They float higher in the winter months.

▲ *The liner* Titanic *was said to be unsinkable. However, as soon as an iceberg breached its hull and let in water to replace the air, it sank like a stone.*

Friction

- **Friction** is the force that acts between two things rubbing together. It stops them sliding past each other.

- **The friction** that stops things starting to slide is called static friction. The friction that slows down sliding surfaces is called dynamic friction.

- **The harder** two surfaces are pressed together, the greater the force that is needed to overcome friction.

- **The coefficient of friction** (CF) is the ratio of the friction to the weight of the sliding object.

▲ *This car is streamlined to reduce drag (friction with air). The air flows over and under its 'wing', producing a downward force that presses the car to the ground, enabling it to go faster.*

▲ *Waxed skis on snow have a CF of just 0.14, allowing cross-country skiers to slide along the ground very easily.*

- **Metal sliding on metal** has a CF of 0.74; ice sliding on ice has a CF of 0.1. This means it is over seven times harder to make metal slide on metal than ice on ice.

- **Friction often makes things hot.** As the sliding object is slowed down, much of the energy of its momentum is turned into heat.

- **Fluid friction** is the friction between moving fluids or between a fluid and a solid. It is what makes thick fluids viscous (less runny).

- **Oil reduces friction** by creating a film that keeps the solid surfaces apart.

- **Brakes use dynamic friction** to slow things down.

- **Drag is friction** between air and an object. It slows a fast car, or any aircraft moving through the air.

185

Pressure

- **Pressure** is the force created by the assault of fast-moving molecules.

- **The pressure that keeps** a bicycle tyre inflated is the constant assault of huge numbers of air molecules on the inside of the tyre.

- **The water pressure that** crushes a submarine when it dives too deep is the assault of huge numbers of water molecules.

▼ The worst storms, such as this hurricane seen from space, are caused when air from high-pressure areas rushes into low-pressure areas.

- **Pressure rises** as you go deeper in the ocean. This is because of an increasing weight of water (hydrostatic pressure) pressing down from above.

- **The water pressure 10,000 m** below the surface is equivalent to seven elephants standing on a dinner plate.

- **The pressure of the air** on the outside of your body is balanced by the pressure of fluids inside. Without this internal pressure, air pressure would crush your body instantly.

- **Pressure** is measured as the force on a certain area.

- **The standard unit** of pressure is a pascal (Pa) or 1 newton per sq m (N/m^2).

- **High pressures:** the centre of the Earth may be 400 billion Pa; steel can withstand 40 million Pa; a shark bite can be 30 million Pa.

- **Low pressures:** the best laboratory vacuum is 1 trillionth Pa; the quietest sound is 200 millionths Pa. The pressure of sunlight may be 3 millionths Pa.

▲ *A submarine is protected by two hulls. The inner of these is built of thick, strong steel, and is called the pressure hull. It shields the ship from the crushing force of the water.*

Lavoisier

- **Antoine Laurent Lavoisier** (1743–1794) was a brilliant French scientist who is regarded as the founder of modern chemistry.

- **He was elected** to the French Royal Academy of Sciences at just 25 for an essay on street lighting. A year later, he worked on the first geological map of France.

- **Lavoisier earned his living** for a long while as a 'tax farmer', which meant he worked for a private company collecting taxes.

- **In 1771** he married 14-year-old Marie Paulze, who later became his illustrator and collaborator in the laboratory.

▲ *Lavoisier showed the importance of precision weighing in the laboratory.*

- **Lavoisier** was the first person to realize that air is essentially a mixture of two gases: oxygen and nitrogen.

- **Lavoisier discovered** that water is a compound of hydrogen and oxygen.

- **Lavoisier** showed that the popular phlogiston theory of burning was wrong and that burning involves oxygen instead.

▶ *Lavoisier showed that old theories about burning were wrong and that oxygen is essential in order for burning to take place.*

- **Lavoisier** gave the first working list of chemical elements in his famous book *Elementary Treatise of Chemistry* (1789), which was illustrated by his wife Marie.

- **From 1776** Lavoisier headed research at the Royal Arsenal in Paris, developing gunpowder manufacture.

- **Lavoisier ran schemes** for public education, fair taxation, old-age insurance and other welfare schemes. But his good deeds did not save him. When Lavoisier had a wall built round Paris to reduce smuggling, revolutionary leader Marat accused him of imprisoning Paris's air. His past as a tax farmer was remembered and Lavoisier was guillotined in 1794.

Splitting the atom

- **In the 1890s** scientists thought that atoms were solid like billiard balls and completely unbreakable.

- **In 1897** J. J. Thomson discovered that atoms contained even smaller particles, which he called electrons (see electrons).

- **In 1900** scientists thought atoms were like plum puddings with electrons like currants on the outside.

- **In 1909** Ernest Rutherford was firing alpha particles (see radioactivity) at a sheet of gold foil. Most went straight through, but 1 in 8000 particles bounced back!

- **Rutherford concluded** that the atom was mostly empty space (which the alpha particles passed straight through) but had a tiny, dense nucleus at its centre.

- **In 1919** Rutherford managed to split the nucleus of a nitrogen atom with alpha particles. Small atoms could be split.

- **In 1932** James Chadwick found the nucleus contained two kinds of particle: protons and neutrons.

uranium atom

▲ *By splitting uranium atoms, high levels of energy are produced. The atom's nucleus, which makes up almost all of its mass, is made up of protons and neutrons. These are held together by a very strong force. By harnessing this force, nuclear energy is made.*

- **In 1933** Italian Enrico Fermi bombarded the big atoms of uranium with neutrons. Fermi thought the new atoms that then formed had simply gained the neutrons.

- **In 1939** German scientists Hahn and Strassman repeated Fermi's experiment and found smaller atoms of barium.

- **Austrian Lise Meitner** realized that Hahn and Strassman had split the uranium atoms. This discovery opened the way to releasing nuclear energy by fission (see nuclear energy).

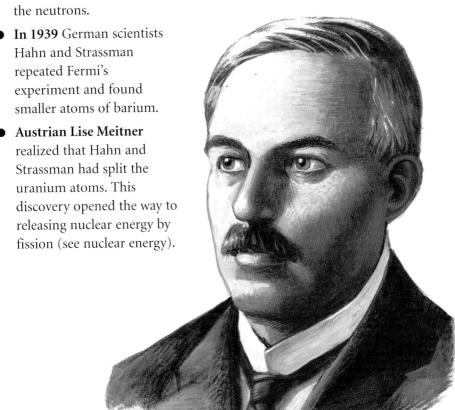

▲ *Ernest Rutherford put forward the idea that atoms are made up of particles of negative electricity orbiting around a heavy centre called the nucleus.*

191

The Curies

- **Pierre and Marie Curie** were the husband and wife scientists who discovered the nature of radioactivity. In 1903 they won a Nobel Prize for their work.

- **Marie Curie** (1867–1934) was born Marya Sklodowska in Poland. She went to Paris in 1891 to study physics.

- **Pierre Curie** (1859–1906) was a French lecturer in physics who discovered the piezoelectric effect in crystals. His discovery led to the development of devices from quartz watches to microphones.

- **The Curies** met in 1894 while Marie was a student at the Sorbonne. They married in 1895.

- **In 1896** Antoine Becquerel found that uranium salts emitted a mysterious radiation that affected photographic paper in the same way as light.

- **In 1898** the Curies found the intensity of radiation was in exact proportion to the amount of uranium – so it must be coming from the uranium atoms.

▲ *The Curies' combination of brilliant insight with exact, patient work led to their historic breakthrough in discovering radioactivity.*

- **The Curies called** atomic radiation 'radioactivity'.

- **In July 1898** the Curies discovered a new radioactive element. Marie called it polonium after her native Poland.

- **In December** the Curies found radium – an element even more radioactive than uranium.

- **In 1906** Pierre was killed by a tram. Marie died later from the effects of her exposure to radioactive materials, the dangers of which were unknown at that time.

▲ *Marie Curie had two daughters, Irène and Ève. Throughout World War 1, Marie Curie and her daughter Irène worked on the development of using x-rays for imaging.*

193

Particle physics

- **Apart from the three** basic, stable particles of atoms – electrons, protons and neutrons – scientists have found over 200 rare or short-lived particles. Some were found in cosmic rays from space; some appear when atoms are smashed to bits in devices called particle accelerators.

- **Every particle** also has a mirror-image anti-particle. Although antimatter maybe much rarer, it is every bit as real.

- **Cosmic rays** contain not only electrons, protons and neutrons, but short-lived particles such as muons and strange quarks. Muons flash into existence for 2.2 micro-seconds just before the cosmic rays reach the ground.

- **Smashing atoms** in particle accelerators creates short-lived high-energy particles such as taus and pions and three kinds of quark called charm, bottom and top.

- **Particles** are now grouped into a simple framework called the Standard Model. It divides them into elementary particles and composite particles.

- **Elementary particles** are the basic particles which cannot be broken down into anything smaller. There are three groups: quarks, leptons and bosons. Leptons include electrons, muons, taus and neutrinos. Bosons are 'messenger' particles that link the others. They include photons and gluons which 'glue' quarks together.

- **Composite particles** are hadrons made of quarks glued together by gluons. They include protons, neutrons and 'hyperons' and 'resonances'.

- **To smash atoms** scientists use particle accelerators, which are giant machines set in tunnels. The accelerators use powerful magnets to accelerate particles through a tube at huge speeds, and then smash them together.

- **Huge detectors** pick up collisions between particles.

▼ *The accelerators at Fermilab near Chicago, USA, and CERN in Switzerland, are underground tubes many kilometres long through which particles are accelerated to near the speed of light.*

.....**FASCINATING FACT**.....
When the Fermi particle accelerator is running 250,000 particle collisions occur every second.

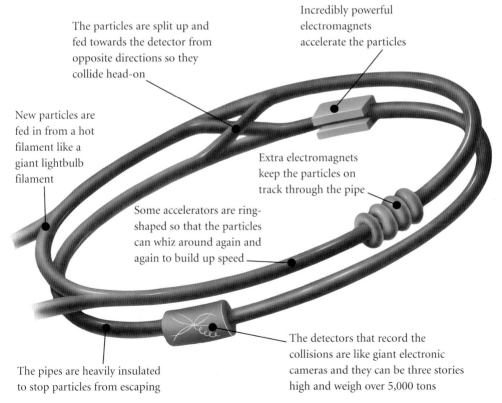

The particles are split up and fed towards the detector from opposite directions so they collide head-on

Incredibly powerful electromagnets accelerate the particles

New particles are fed in from a hot filament like a giant lightbulb filament

Extra electromagnets keep the particles on track through the pipe

Some accelerators are ring-shaped so that the particles can whiz around again and again to build up speed

The pipes are heavily insulated to stop particles from escaping

The detectors that record the collisions are like giant electronic cameras and they can be three stories high and weigh over 5,000 tons

195

Quarks

- **Quarks** are one of the three tiniest basic, or elementary, particles from which every substance is made.

- **Quarks** are too small for their size to be measured, but their mass can. The biggest quark, called a top quark, is as heavy as an atom of gold. The smallest, called an up quark, is 35,000 times lighter.

- **There are six** kinds, or flavours, of quark: up (u), down (d), bottom (b), top (t), strange (s) and charm (c).

- **Down, bottom and strange** quarks carry one-third of the negative charge of electrons; up, top and charm ones carry two-thirds of the positive charge of protons.

- **Quarks never exist** separately but in combination with one or two other quarks. Combinations of two or three quarks are called hadrons.

- **Three-quark hadrons** are called baryons and include protons and neutrons. Rare two-quark hadrons are mesons.

- **A proton** is made from two up quarks (two lots of +2/3 of a charge) and one down quark (–1/3) and has a positive charge of 1.

- **A neutron** is made from two down quarks (two lots of –1/3 of a charge) and an up quark (+2/3). The charges cancel each other out, giving a neutron no charge.

- **The theory of quarks** was first proposed by Murray Gell-Mann and Georg Zweig in 1964.

- **Quarks** are named after a famous passage in James Joyce's book *Ulysses*: 'Three quarks for Muster Mark!'

6 kinds of lepton

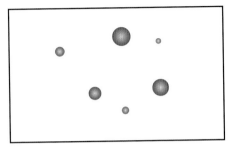

6 kinds of quark

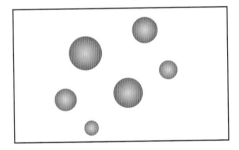

6 antiquarks

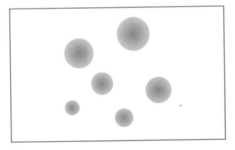

Hadrons

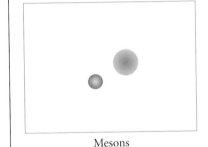

Baryons

Mesons

◀ *These are the main kinds of elementary particle. Besides quarks there are leptons, such as electrons, and antiquarks (the mirror images of quarks).*

197

Huygens

▶ *Christiaan Huygens was the leading figure of the Golden Age of Dutch science in the 17th century, making contributions in many fields.*

- **Christiaan Huygens** (1629–1695) was, after Isaac Newton, the greatest scientist of the 1600s.

- **Huygens** was born to a wealthy Dutch family in The Hague, in Holland.

- **He studied law** at the University of Leiden and the College of Orange in Breda before turning to science.

- **He worked** with his brother Constanijn to grind lenses for very powerful telescopes.

- **With his powerful telescope,** Huygens discovered in 1655 that what astronomers had thought were Saturn's 'arms' were actually rings. He made his discovery known to people in code.

- **Huygens discovered** Titan, one of Saturn's moons.

- **Huygens learned a great deal** about pendulums and built the first accurate pendulum clock.

- **Responding to Newton's theory** that light was 'corpuscles', Huygens developed the theory that light is waves (see moving light) in 1678.

- **Huygens** described light as vibrations spreading through a material called ether, which is literally everywhere and is made of tiny particles. The idea of ether was finally abandoned in the late 19th century, but not the idea of light waves.

- **Huygens' wave idea** enabled him to explain refraction (see light) simply. It also enabled him to predict correctly that light would travel more slowly in glass than in air.

▼ *Titan, Saturn's largest moon, and the only satellite in the solar system known to have clouds and a dense atmosphere, was discovered in 1655 by Christiaan Huygens.*

Quantum physics

- **By the 1890s** most scientists thought light moved in waves.

- **Max Planck** (1858–1947) realized that the range of radiation given out by a hot object is not quite what scientists would calculate it to be if radiation is waves.

- **Planck realized** that the radiation from a hot object could be explained if the radiation came in chunks, or quanta.

- **Quanta** are very, very small. When lots of quanta are emitted together they appear to be like smooth waves.

- **In 1905** Einstein showed that quanta explain the photoelectric effect.

- **In 1913** Niels Bohr showed how the arrangement of electrons in energy levels around an atom (see electrons) could be thought of in a quantum way too.

- **In the 1920s** Erwin Schrödinger and Werner Heisenberg developed Bohr's idea into quantum physics, a new branch of physics for particles on the scale of atoms.

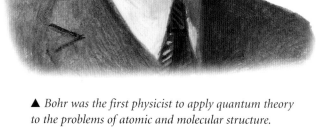

▲ *Bohr was the first physicist to apply quantum theory to the problems of atomic and molecular structure.*

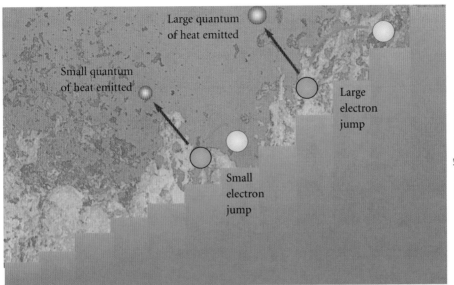

Large quantum
of heat emitted

Small quantum
of heat emitted

Large
electron
jump

Small
electron
jump

Electron energy levels

▲ *Quantum physics shows how radiation from a hot object is emitted in little chunks that are called quanta.*

● **Quantum physics** explains how electrons emit radiation (see above). It shows that an electron is both a particle and a wave, depending on how you look at it. It seems to work for all four fundamental forces (see forces) except gravity.

● **The development** of the technologies that gave us lasers and transistors came from quantum physics.

● **Quantum physics** predicts some strange things on the scale of atoms, such as particles appearing from nowhere and electrons seeming to know where each other are.

Newton

- **Sir Isaac Newton** is one of the greatest scientists of all time. His book *The Mathematical Principles of Natural Philosophy* is the most influential science book ever written.

- **Newton was born** on December 25, 1642 in Woolsthorpe in Lincoln, England. As a boy, he often made mechanical devices such as model windmills and water clocks.

- **With his theory of gravity** Newton discovered how the Universe is held together.

- **Newton** said that his theory of gravity was inspired by seeing an apple fall from a tree when he left Cambridge to escape the plague.

▲ *Newton invented a kind of telescope that is now standard for astronomers.*

- **Newton invented** an entirely new branch of mathematics called calculus. Independently, Leibniz also invented it.

- **Newton** discovered that sunlight is a mixture of all colours (see spectrum).

- **The interference** patterns from reflected surfaces (like a pool of oil) are called Newton's rings.

- **Newton** spent much of his life studying astrology and alchemy.

- **Newton never married** and at times was almost a recluse. Shortly before he died in 1727 he said: 'I seem to have been only like a boy playing on the seashore, and diverting myself in now and then finding a smoother pebble or prettier shell than ordinary, whilst the great ocean of truth lay all undiscovered before me.'

- **Newton** was a Member of Parliament, president of the Royal Society and master of the Royal Mint, where he found a way to make coins more accurately.

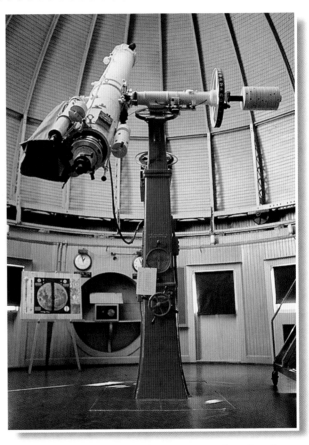

▲ *A telescope in an optical observatory stands under a large dome that has shutters. Observatories use two main kinds of telescope. Reflecting (Newtonian) telescopes use a curved mirror or set of such mirrors to focus light, and refracting telescopes use a system of lenses.*

203

Archimedes

- **Archimedes** (c.287–212BC) was one of the first great scientists. He created the sciences of mechanics and hydrostatics.

- **Archimedes** was a Greek who lived in the city of Syracuse, Sicily. His relative, Hieron II, was king of Syracuse.

- **Archimedes' screw** is a simple pump supposedly invented by Archimedes. It scoops up water with a spiral device that turns inside a tube. It is still used in the Middle East.

- **To help defend** Syracuse against Roman attackers in 215BC, Archimedes invented many war machines. They included an awesome 'claw' – a giant grappling crane that could lift whole galleys from the water and sink them.

- **Archimedes** was killed by Roman soldiers when collaborators let the Romans into Syracuse in 212BC.

- **Archimedes** analysed levers mathematically. He showed that the load you can move with a particular effort is in exact proportion to its distance from the fulcrum.

- **Archimedes discovered** that objects float because they are thrust upwards by the water.

- **Archimedes' principle** shows that the upthrust on a floating object is equal to the weight of the water that the object pushes out of the way.

- **Archimedes** realized he could work out the density, or specific gravity, of an object by comparing the object's weight to the weight of water it pushes out of a jar when completely submerged.

- **Archimedes** used specific gravity to prove a sly goldsmith had not made King Hieron's crown of pure gold.

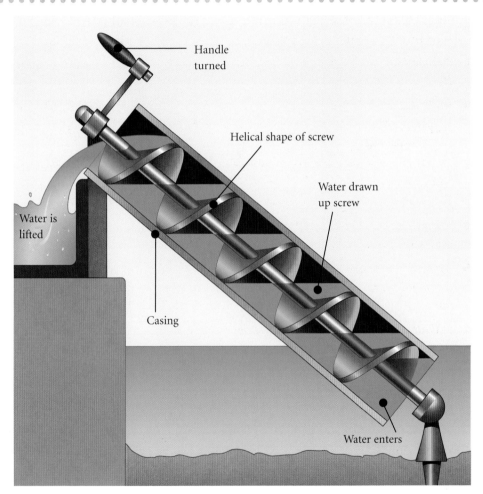

Handle
turned

Helical shape of screw

Water drawn
up screw

Water is
lifted

Casing

Water enters

▲ *Archimedes' screw draws up water by turns of a long screw held inside a tightly fitting cylinder. The casing fits snugly to stop any leakage.*

205

Faraday

- **Michael Faraday** (1791–1867) was one of the greatest scientists of the 19th century.

- **Faraday was the son** of a poor blacksmith, born in the village of Newington in Surrey, England.

- **He started work as** an apprentice bookbinder but became assistant to the great scientist Humphry Davy after taking brilliant notes at one of Davy's lectures.

- **Faraday was said** to be Davy's greatest discovery.

- **Until 1830 Faraday** was mainly a chemist. In 1825 he discovered the important chemical benzene.

▲ *Faraday drew huge crowds to his brilliant and entertaining Christmas lectures on science at the Royal Institution in London. The Royal Institution Christmas lectures continue to be a popular tradition today.*

- **In 1821** Faraday showed that the magnetism created by an electric current would make a magnet move and so made a very simple version of an electric motor.

- **In 1831** Faraday showed that when a magnet moves close to an electric wire, it creates, or induces, an electric current in the wire. This was discovered at the same time by Joseph Henry in the USA.

- **Using** his discovery of electric induction, Faraday made the first dynamo to generate electricity and so opened the way to the modern age of electricity.

- **In the 1840s** Faraday suggested the idea of lines of magnetic force and electromagnetic fields. These ideas, which were later developed by James Clerk Maxwell, underpin much of modern science.

- **Faraday** was probably the greatest scientific experimenter of all time.

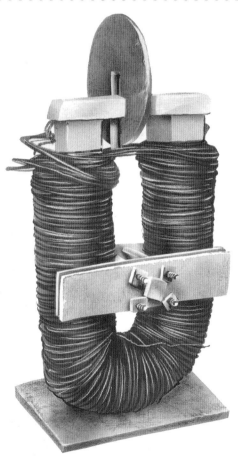

▲ *Faraday's disc generator. An electromotive force (emf) is produced in a copper disc when it is spun in the magnetic field lying between the poles of an electromagnet.*

207

Einstein

- **Albert Einstein** (1879–1955) was the most famous and influential scientist of the 20th century.

- **Einstein was half German** and half Swiss, but when Hitler came to power in 1933, Einstein made his home in the USA.

- **Einstein's fame** rests on his two theories of relativity (see Relativity).

- **His theory of special relativity** was published in 1905 while he worked in the Patent Office in Bern, Switzerland.

- **In 1905** Einstein also explained the photoelectric effect. From these ideas, photo cells were developed. These form the basis of TV cameras, burglar alarms and other devices.

- **Einstein completed his theory** of general relativity in 1915 while Germany was at war.

▲ *Einstein's equation E=mc² revealed the energy in atoms that led to nuclear bombs and nuclear power.*

- **Einstein** was not satisfied with his theory of general relativity because it did not include electromagnetism. He spent the last 25 years of his life trying to develop a 'unified field theory' to include it.

- **Einstein** was once reported to have said that only 12 people in the world could understand his theory. He later denied saying it.

- **Einstein** suggested to the US government that Germany was almost certainly developing an atomic weapon as World War 2 started. The US began developing one too.

- **Einstein was married twice.** His first wife was Mileva Maric. His second wife, Elsa, was also his first cousin.

▲ *A letter which Einstein wrote to President Roosevelt in 1939 led to the project to create the world's first atomic bomb.*

209

Time

- **No clock** keeps perfect time. For most of history clocks were set by the movement of the Sun and stars.

- **Since 1967** the world's time has been set by atomic clocks.

- **Atomic clocks** are accurate to 0.001 sec in 1000 years.

- **If a caesium atomic** clock ran for six million years it would not gain or lose a second.

- **The world's most** accurate clock is the American NIST-7 atomic clock.

- **The atomic clock** on the International Space Station is hundreds of times more accurate than clocks on Earth, because it is not affected by gravity.

- **Atomic clocks** work because caesium atoms vibrate exactly 9,192,631,770 times a second.

- **Some scientists** say that time is the fourth dimension – the other three are length, breadth and height. So time could theoretically run in any direction. Others say time only moves in one direction. Just as we cannot unburn a candle, so we cannot turn back time (see time travel).

- **Light takes** millions of years to reach us from distant galaxies, so we see them not as they are but as they were millions of years ago. Light takes a little while to reach us even from nearby things.

- **Einstein's theory of general relativity** shows that time actually runs slower nearer strong gravitational fields such as stars. This does not mean that the clock is running slower but that time itself is running slower. Time also goes slower as speed increases.

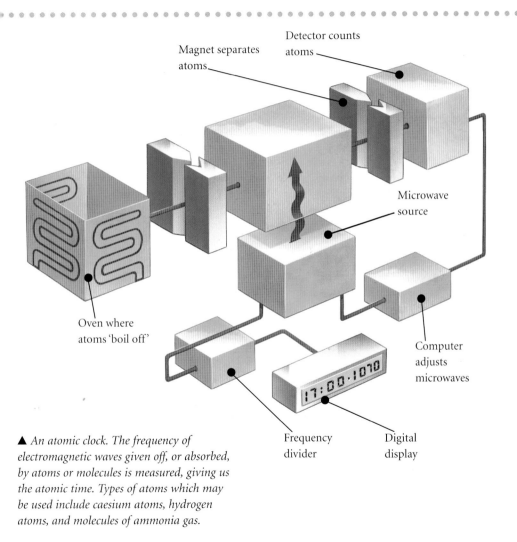

Detector counts atoms

Magnet separates atoms

Microwave source

Oven where atoms 'boil off'

Computer adjusts microwaves

Frequency divider

Digital display

▲ *An atomic clock. The frequency of electromagnetic waves given off, or absorbed, by atoms or molecules is measured, giving us the atomic time. Types of atoms which may be used include caesium atoms, hydrogen atoms, and molecules of ammonia gas.*

211

Time travel

- **Einstein showed** that time runs at different speeds in different places – and is just another dimension. Ever since, some scientists have wondered whether we could travel through time to the past or the future (see time).

- **Einstein said** you cannot move through time because you would have to travel faster than light. If you travelled as fast as light, time would stop and you would not be alive or even exist.

- **A famous argument** against time travel is about killing your grandparents. What if you travelled back in time before your parents were born and killed your grandparents? Then neither your parents nor you could have been born. So who killed your grandparents?

- **In the 1930s** American mathematician Kurt Gödel found time travel might be possible by bending space–time.

- **Scientists have come up** with all kinds of weird ideas for bending space-time, including amazing gravity machines. The most powerful benders of space-time are black holes in space.

- **Stephen Hawking** said you cannot use black holes for time travel because everything that goes into a black hole shrinks to a singularity (see Hawking). Others say you might dodge the singularity and emerge safely somewhere else in the Universe through a reverse black hole called a white hole.

- **US astronomer Carl Sagan** thought small black hole–white hole tunnels might exist without a singularity. There might be tunnels such as these linking different parts of the Universe, like a wormhole in an apple.

- **The mathematics** says that a wormhole would snap shut as soon as you stepped into it. However, it might be possible to hold it open with an anti-gravity machine based on a quantum effect called the Casimir effect.

● **Stephen Hawking** says wormholes are so unstable that they would break up before you could use them to time travel. Martin Visser says you might use them for faster than light (FTL) travel, but not for time travel.

The far end of a wormhole is the opposite of a black hole – a white hole. It pushes things out, not sucks them in.

The wormhole time machine is based on blowing a wormhole up large enough and holding it open long enough to slip through.

Although it is hard to imagine, space-time is not space with stars like this at all. It is a four-dimensional space and travelling through space-time means travelling through time and space.

If you could create a wormhole time machine, just where and when would the other end be?

▲ *If wormholes exist, they are thought to be very, very tiny – smaller than an atom. So how could they be used for time travel? Some scientists think you may be able to use an incredibly powerful electric field to enlarge them and hold them open long enough to make a tunnel through space-time.*

213

Space

- **A flat or plane surface** has just two dimensions at right angles to each other: length and width.

- **Any point** on a flat surface can be pinpointed exactly with just two figures: one showing how far along it is and the other how far across.

- **There are three** dimensions of space at right angles to each other: length, width and height.

- **A box** can be described completely with just one figure for each dimension.

- **A point in space** can be pinpointed with three figures: one shows how far along it is, one how far across it is and a third how far up or down it is.

▼ *An eclipse of the Sun in 1919 showed Einstein's suggestion that gravity can bend light is true. In bending light, gravity is also bending space–time.*

- **If something is moving,** three dimensions are not enough to locate it. You need a fourth dimension – time – to describe where the object is at a particular time.

- **In the early 1900s,** mathematician Hermann Minkowski realized that for Einstein's relativity theory you had to think of the Universe in terms of four dimensions, including time.

- **Four-dimensional** space is now called space-time.

- **Einstein's** theory of general relativity shows that space-time is actually curved.

- **After Minkowski's ideas,** mathematicians began to develop special geometry to describe four or even more dimensions.

▶ *German mathematician Hermann Minkowski used geometrical methods to solve difficult problems in number theory, in mathematical physics and the theory of relativity.*

Hawking

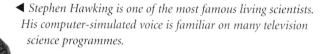

◀ *Stephen Hawking is one of the most famous living scientists. His computer-simulated voice is familiar on many television science programmes.*

- **Stephen Hawking** (b.1942) is a British physicist who is famous for his ideas on space and time.

- **Hawking was born** in Oxford, England and studied at Cambridge University, where he is now a professor.

- **Hawking suffers** from the paralysing nerve disease called amyotrophic lateral sclerosis. He cannot move any more than a few hand and face muscles, but he gets around very well in an electric wheelchair.

- **Hawking cannot speak,** but he communicates effectively with a computer-simulated voice.

- **Hawking's** book *A Brief History of Time* (1988) outlines his ideas on space, time and the history of the Universe since the Big Bang. It was one of the best-selling science books of the 20th century.

▶ *Einstein thought of, and Hawking developed, the idea of black holes. They are collapsed objects, such as stars, that have become invisible.*

216

- **Hawking's contributions** to the study of gravity are considered to be the most important since Einstein's.

- **More than anyone else,** Hawking has developed the idea of black holes – points in space where gravity becomes so extreme that it even sucks in light.

- **Hawking developed** the idea of a singularity, which is an incredibly small point in a black hole where all physical laws break down.

- **Hawking's work** provides a strong theoretical base for the idea that the Universe began with a Big Bang, starting with a singularity and exploding outwards.

- **Hawking** is trying to find a quantum theory of gravity (see quantum physics) to link in with the three other basic forces (electromagnetism and nuclear forces).

◄ *The Big Bang theory assumes the Universe started with a singularity, a point of infinite mass and energy, but almost no size.*

Relativity

- **Einstein** (see Einstein) was the creator of two theories of relativity which have revolutionized scientists' way of thinking about the Universe: the special theory of relativity (1905) and the general theory (1915).

- **Time is relative** because it depends where you measure it from (see time). Distances and speed are relative too. If you are in a car and another car whizzes past you, for instance, the slower you are travelling, the faster the other car seems to be moving.

- **Einstein showed** in his special theory of relativity that you cannot even measure your speed relative to a beam of light, which is the fastest thing in the Universe. This is because light always passes you at the same speed, no matter where you are or how fast you are going.

- **Einstein** realized that if light always travels at the same speed, there are some strange effects when you are moving very fast (see below).

- **If a rocket** passing you zoomed up to near the speed of light, you would see it shrink.

▶ In normal everyday life, the effects of relativity are so tiny that you can ignore them. However, in a spacecraft travelling very fast they may become quite significant.

◀ A spacecraft travelling almost at the speed of light seems to shrink. Of course, if you were actually on board everything would seem entirely normal. Instead, it would be the world outside that seemed to shrink, since it is travelling almost at the speed of light relative to you.

- **If a rocket** passing you zoomed up to near the speed of light, you'd see the clocks on the rocket running more slowly as time stretched out. If the rocket reached the speed of light, the clocks would stop altogether.

- **If a rocket** passing you zoomed near the speed of light, it would seem to get heavier and heavier. But it would gradually become so heavy, there wouldn't be enough energy in the Universe to speed it up any further.

- **Einstein's general relativity theory** brought in gravity. It showed that gravity works basically by bending space-time. From this theory scientists predicted black holes (see Hawking) and wormholes (see time travel).

- **In 1919** an eclipse of the Sun allowed Arthur Eddington to observe how the Sun bends light rays, proving Einstein's theory of general relativity.

▼ *In a spacecraft travelling almost at the speed of light, time runs slower. So astronauts going on a long, very fast journey into space come back a little younger than if they had stayed on the Earth.*

◄ *In a spacecraft travelling almost at the speed of light, everything becomes heavier. Many scientists believe objects will never be able to accelerate to the speed of light because the faster it goes, the heavier it gets.*

> ...FASCINATING FACT...
> When astronauts went to the Moon, their clock lost a few seconds. The clock was not faulty, but time actually ran slower in the speeding spacecraft.

Genetic engineering

- **Genetic engineering** means deliberately altering the genes of plants and animals to give them slightly different life instructions.

- **Genes** are found in every living cell on special molecules called DNA (deoxyribonucleic acid). Engineering genes means changing the DNA.

- **Scientists alter genes** by snipping them from the DNA of one organism and inserting them into the DNA of another. This is called gene splicing. The altered DNA is called recombinant DNA.

- **Genes are cut** from DNA using biological scissors called restriction enzymes. They are spliced into DNA using biological glue called DNA ligase.

- **Once a cell** has its new DNA, every time the cell reproduces the new cells will have the same altered DNA.

- **By splicing new genes** into the DNA of bacteria, scientists can turn them into factories for making valuable natural chemicals. One protein made like this is interferon, a natural body chemical which protects humans against certain viruses.

- **Scientists are now** finding ways of genetically modifying food crop, to make them resist pests or frosts, for instance. The first GM food was the 'Flavr Savr' tomato, created by the US company Calgene in 1994.

> ... FASCINATING FACT ...
> In 1999, scientists worked out the complete gene sequence for a multi-celled organism – allowing them to create a new organism artificially.

▲ *Genetic engineering may be used to make animals grow faster.*

- **Gene therapy** means altering the genes to cure diseases that are inherited from parents or caused by faulty genes.

- **Cloning** means creating an organism with exactly the same genes as another. Normally, new life grows from sex cells – cells from both parents – in which genes are mixed. Cloning takes DNA from any body cell and uses it to grow a new life. Since the new life has the same genes as the donor of the DNA, it is a perfect living replica.

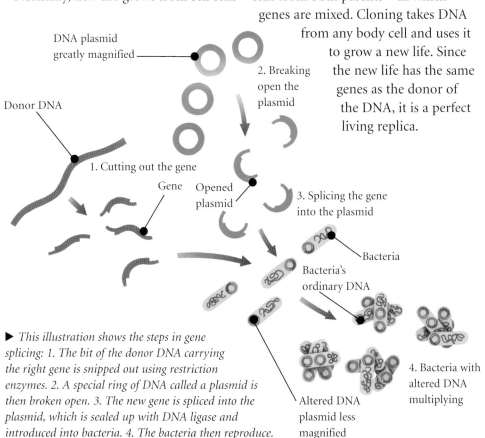

DNA plasmid greatly magnified

Donor DNA

2. Breaking open the plasmid

1. Cutting out the gene

Gene Opened plasmid

3. Splicing the gene into the plasmid

Bacteria

Bacteria's ordinary DNA

Altered DNA plasmid less magnified

4. Bacteria with altered DNA multiplying

▶ *This illustration shows the steps in gene splicing: 1. The bit of the donor DNA carrying the right gene is snipped out using restriction enzymes. 2. A special ring of DNA called a plasmid is then broken open. 3. The new gene is spliced into the plasmid, which is sealed up with DNA ligase and introduced into bacteria. 4. The bacteria then reproduce.*

The skeleton

- **Your skeleton** is a rigid framework of bones, which provides an anchor for your muscles, supports your skin and other organs, and protects vital organs.

- **An adult's skeleton has 206 bones** joined together by rubbery cartilage. Some people have extra vertebrae (the bones of the backbone, or spine).

- **A baby's skeleton has 300** or more bones, but some of these fuse (join) together as the baby grows.

- **The parts of an adult skeleton** that have fused into one bone include the skull and the pelvis (see the skull). The pelvis came from fusing the ilium bones, the ischium bones and the pubis. The ischium is the bone that you sit on.

▶ *Your skeleton is the remarkably light, but very tough framework of bones that supports your body. It is made up of more than 200 bones.*

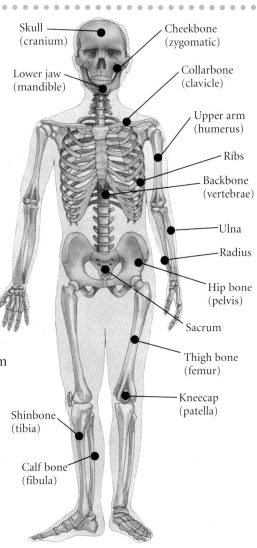

Skull (cranium)

Cheekbone (zygomatic)

Lower jaw (mandible)

Collarbone (clavicle)

Upper arm (humerus)

Ribs

Backbone (vertebrae)

Ulna

Radius

Hip bone (pelvis)

Sacrum

Thigh bone (femur)

Kneecap (patella)

Shinbone (tibia)

Calf bone (fibula)

- **The skeleton** has two main parts – the axial and the appendicular skeleton.

- **The axial skeleton** is the 80 bones of the upper body. It includes the skull, the vertebrae of the backbone, the ribs and the breastbone. The arm and shoulder bones are suspended from it.

- **The appendicular skeleton** is the other 126 bones – the arm and shoulder bones, and the leg and hip bones. It includes the femur (thigh bone), the body's longest bone.

- **The word skeleton** comes from the Ancient Greek word for 'dry'.

- **Most women and girls** have smaller and lighter skeletons than men and boys. But in women and girls, the pelvis is much wider than in men and boys. This is because the opening has to be wide enough for a baby to pass through when it is born.

... FASCINATING FACT ...
The tiniest bone in your body is only 3 mm long and is found in your ear.

▲ *There are 19 bones in the toes and foot, and 6 in the ankle, making 25 bones altogether that can be seen in this photograph.*

Bone

- **Bones are so strong** that they can cope with twice the squeezing pressure that granite can, or four times the stretching tension that concrete can.

- **Weight for weight,** bone is at least five times as strong as steel.

- **Bones are so light** they only make up 14% of your body's total weight.

- **Bones get their rigidity** from hard deposits of minerals such as calcium and phosphate.

▶ *Bones are strong but very light because, on the inside, they have many holes.*

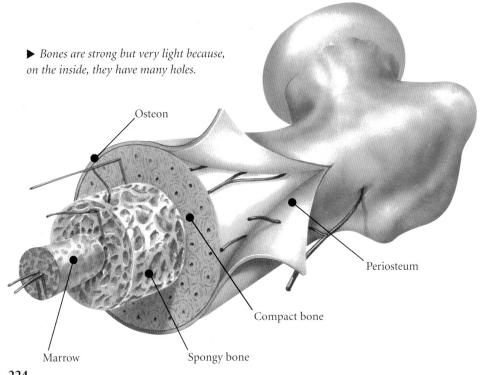

Osteon

Periosteum

Compact bone

Marrow

Spongy bone

- **Bones get their flexibility** from tough, elastic, rope-like fibres of collagen.

- **The hard outside of bones** (called compact bone) is reinforced by strong rods called osteons.

- **The inside of bones** (called spongy bone) is a light honeycomb, made of thin struts or trabeculae, perfectly angled to take stress.

- **The core of some bones,** such as the long bones in an arm or leg, is called bone marrow. It is soft and jelly-like.

- **In some parts of each bone,** there are special cells called osteoblasts which make new bone. In other parts, cells called osteoclasts break up old bone.

- **Bones grow** by getting longer near the end, at a region called the epiphyseal plate.

▲ *Milk contains a mineral called calcium, which is essential for building strong bones. Babies and children need plenty of calcium to help their bones develop properly.*

225

Marrow

- **Marrow** is the soft, jelly-like tissue in the middle of certain bones.

- **Bone marrow can be red** or yellow, depending on whether it has more blood tissue or fat tissue.

- **Red bone marrow** is the body's factory, where all blood cells apart from some white cells are made.

- **All bone marrow** is red when you are a baby, but as you grow older, more and more turns yellow.

- **In adults,** red marrow is only found in the ends of the limbs' long bones, breastbone, backbone, ribs, shoulder blades, pelvis and the skull.

- **Yellow bone marrow** is a store for fat, but it may turn to red marrow when you are ill.

- **All the different** kinds of blood cell start life in red marrow as one type of cell called a stem cell. Different blood cells then develop as the stem cells divide and re-divide.

- **Some stem cells** divide to form red blood cells and platelets.

- **Some stem cells** divide to form lymphoblasts. These divide in turn to form various different kinds of white cells, such as monocytes and lymphocytes.

- **The white cells** made in bone marrow play a key part in the body's immune system. This is why bone-marrow transplants can help people with illnesses that affect their immune system.

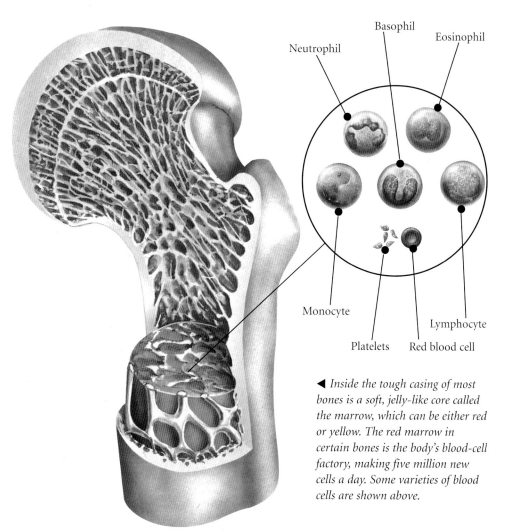

Neutrophil

Basophil

Eosinophil

Monocyte

Platelets

Lymphocyte

Red blood cell

◀ *Inside the tough casing of most bones is a soft, jelly-like core called the marrow, which can be either red or yellow. The red marrow in certain bones is the body's blood-cell factory, making five million new cells a day. Some varieties of blood cells are shown above.*

227

The skull

- **The skull** or cranium is the hard, bone case that contains and protects your brain.

- **The skull look**s as though it is a single bone. In fact, it is made up of 22 separate bones, cemented together along rigid joints called sutures.

- **The dome on top** is called the cranial vault and it is made from eight curved pieces of bone fused (joined) together.

- **As well as the sinuses** of the nose (see airways), the skull has four large cavities – the cranial cavity for the brain, the nasal cavity (the nose) and two orbits for the eyes.

- **There are holes in the skull** to allow blood vessels and nerves through, including the optic nerves to the eyes and the olfactory tracts to the nose.

▲ *Skulls vary in size and shape. A bigger skull does not necessarily mean a person is more intelligent.*

> ...**FASCINATING FACT**...
> A baby has soft spots called fontanelles in its skull
> because the bones join slowly over about 18 months.

- **The biggest hole** is in the base. It is called the foramen magnum, and the brain stem goes through it to meet the spinal cord.

- **In the 19th century**, people called phrenologists thought they could work out people's characters from little bumps on their skulls.

- **Archaeologists** can reconstruct faces from the past using computer analysis of ancient skulls.

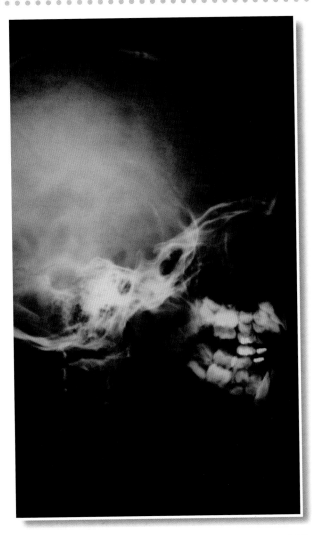

▶ *A child's skull, shown here in this X-ray photo, is quite large in relation to the rest of the child's body. As our bodies grow, our skull starts to look smaller in proportion.*

229

Backbone

- **The backbone**, otherwise known as the spine, extends from the base of the skull down to the hips.

- **The backbone is not a single bone,** but a column of drum-shaped bones called vertebrae (singular, vertebra).

  - **There are 33 vertebrae** altogether, although some of these fuse or join as the body grows.

  - **Each vertebra** is linked to the next by small facet joints, which are like tiny ball-and-socket joints.

  - **The vertebrae are separated** by discs of rubbery material called cartilage. These cushion the bones when you run and jump.

  - **The bones of the spine** are divided into five groups from top to bottom. These are the cervical (7 bones), the thoracic (12 bones), the lumbar (5 bones), the sacrum (5 bones fused together), and the coccyx (4 bones fused together).

  - **The cervical spine** is the vertebrae of the neck. The thoracic spine is the back of the chest, and each bone has a pair of ribs attached to it. The lumbar spine is the small of the back.

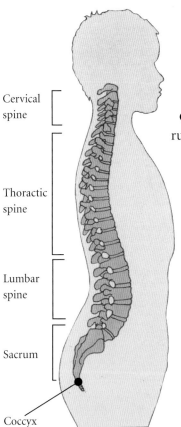

Cervical spine

Thoractic spine

Lumbar spine

Sacrum

Coccyx

◀ *The backbone is not straight – instead, its 33 vertebrae curve into an S-shape.*

- **A normal spine** curves in an S-shape, with the cervical spine curving forwards, the thoracic section curving backwards, the lumbar forwards, and the sacrum curving backwards.

FASCINATING FACT
The story character the Hunchback of Notre Dame suffered from kyphosis – excessive curving of the spine.

- **On the back** of each vertebra is a bridge called the spinal process. The bridges on each bone link together to form a tube which holds the spinal cord, the body's central bundle of nerves.

▲ *Stretching keeps the joints in your back supple and helps to release tension.*

231

Ribs

- **The ribs** are the thin, flattish bones that curve around your chest.
- **Together,** the rib bones make up the rib cage.
- **The rib cage** protects the backbone and breastbone, as well as your vital organs – heart, lungs, liver, kidneys, stomach, spleen and so on.
- **You have 12 pairs** of ribs altogether.
- **Seven pairs** are called true ribs. Each rib is attached to the breastbone in front and curves around to join on to one of the vertebrae that make up the backbone via a strip of costal cartilage.
- **There are three pairs** of false ribs. These are attached to vertebrae but are not linked to the breastbone. Instead, each rib is attached to the rib above it by cartilage.
- **There are two pairs** of floating ribs. These are attached only to the vertebrae of the backbone.
- **The gaps between** the ribs are called intercostal spaces, and they contain thin sheets of muscle which expand and relax the chest during breathing.
- **Flail chest** is when many ribs are broken (often in a car accident) and the lungs heave the chest in and out.

> ...FASCINATING FACT...
> The bones of the ribs contain red marrow and are one of the body's major blood-cell factories.

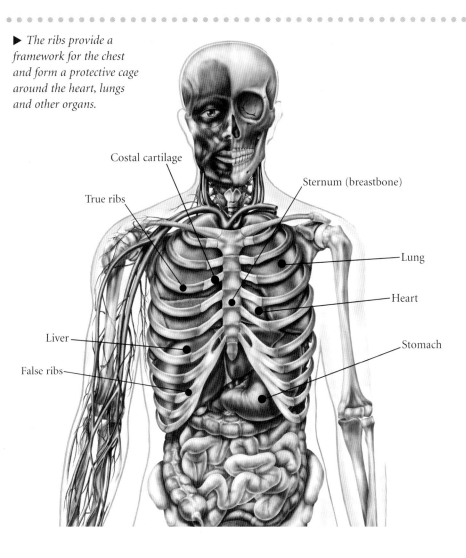

► The ribs provide a framework for the chest and form a protective cage around the heart, lungs and other organs.

Costal cartilage

True ribs

Sternum (breastbone)

Lung

Heart

Liver

Stomach

False ribs

233

Joints

▶ *Gymnasts must have supple, flexible joints in order to achieve extreme positions like this.*

- **Body joints** are places where bones meet.
- **The skull** is not one bone, but 22 separate bones bound tightly together with fibres so that they cannot move.
- **Most body joints** (apart from fixed joints like the skull's fibrous joints) let bones move, but different kinds of joint let them move in different ways.
- **Hinge joints,** such as the elbow, let the bones swing to and fro in two directions like door hinges do.

- **In ball-and-socket joints,** such as the shoulder and hip, the rounded end of one bone sits in the cup-shaped socket of the other, and can move in almost any direction.

- **Swivel joints** turn like a wheel on an axle. Your head can swivel to the left or to the right on your spine.

- **Saddle joints** such as those in the thumb have the bones interlocking like two saddles. These joints allow great mobility with considerable strength.

- **The relatively inflexible joints** between the bones (vertebrae) of the spine are cushioned by pads of cartilage.

- **Synovial joints** are flexible joints such as the hip-joint, lubricated with oily 'synovial fluid' and cushioned by cartilage.

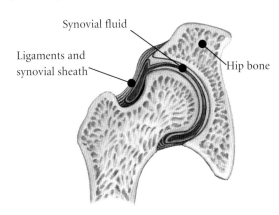

Synovial fluid

Ligaments and synovial sheath

Hip bone

▶ *The hip-joint is a ball-and-socket joint which takes a great deal of wear and tear. When the cushioning layer of cartilage breaks down, it can be replaced with an artificial joint made of special plastics.*

235

Cartilage

- **Cartilage is a rubbery** substance used in various places around the body. You can feel cartilage in your ear if you move it back and forward.

- **Cartilage is made** from cells called chondrocytes embedded in a jelly-like ground substance with fibres of collagen, all wrapped in an envelope of tough fibres.

- **There are three types:** hyaline, fibrous and elastic.

- **Hyaline cartilage** is the most widespread in your body. It is almost clear, pearly white and quite stiff.

- **Hyaline cartilage** is used in many of the joints and ribs between bones to cushion them against impacts.

▼ *A single blow to the nose can easily damage the nasal cartilage, as often happens to boxers.*

- **Fibrous cartilage** is really tough cartilage used in between the bones of the spine and in the knee.

- **Cartilage in the knee** makes two dish shapes called a menisci between the thigh and shin bones. Footballers often damage these cartilages.

- **Elastic cartilage** is very flexible and used in your airways, nose and ears.

- **Cartilage grows** quicker than bone, and the skeletons of babies in the womb are mostly cartilage, which gradually ossifies (hardens to bone).

- **Osteoarthritis** occurs when joint cartilage breaks down, making certain movements painful.

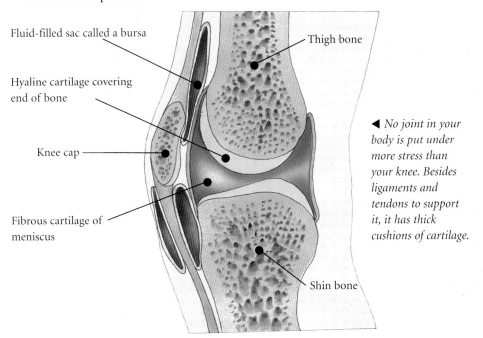

Fluid-filled sac called a bursa

Hyaline cartilage covering end of bone

Knee cap

Fibrous cartilage of meniscus

Thigh bone

Shin bone

◄ No joint in your body is put under more stress than your knee. Besides ligaments and tendons to support it, it has thick cushions of cartilage.

237

Muscles

- **Muscles are special fibres** that contract (tighten) and relax to move different parts of the body.

- **Voluntary muscles** are all the muscles you can control by will or thinking, such as your arm muscles.

- **Involuntary muscles** are the muscles you cannot control at will, but work automatically, such as the muscles that move food through your intestine.

- **Most voluntary muscles** cover the skeleton and are therefore called skeletal muscles. They are also called striated (striped) muscle because there are dark bands on the bundles of fibre that form them.

- **Most involuntary muscles** form sacs or tubes such as the intestine or the blood vessels. They are called smooth muscle because they lack the bands or stripes of voluntary muscles.

- **Most muscles are arranged in pairs,** because although muscles can shorten themselves, they cannot make themselves longer. So the flexor muscle that bends a joint is paired with an extensor muscle to straighten it again.

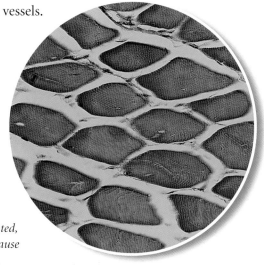

▶ *This microscopic cross-section shows striated, or striped, skeletal muscle. It is so-called because its fibres are made of light and dark stripes.*

238

- **The heart muscle** is a unique combination of skeletal and smooth muscle. It has its own built-in contraction rhythm of 70 beats per minute, and special muscle cells that work like nerve cells for transmitting the signals for waves of muscle contraction to sweep through the heart.

- **Your body's longest muscle** is the sartorius on the inner thigh.

- **Your body's widest muscle** is the external oblique which runs around the side of the upper body.

- **Your body's biggest muscle** is the gluteus maximus in your buttocks (bottom).

▶ *You have more than 640 skeletal muscles and they make up over 40% of your body's entire weight, covering your skeleton like a bulky blanket. This illustration shows only the main surface muscles of the back, but your body has at least two, and sometimes three, layers of muscle beneath its surface muscles. Most muscles are firmly anchored at both ends and attached to the bones either side of a joint, either directly or by tough fibres called tendons.*

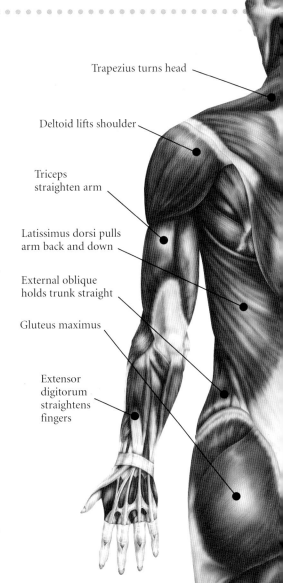

Trapezius turns head

Deltoid lifts shoulder

Triceps straighten arm

Latissimus dorsi pulls arm back and down

External oblique holds trunk straight

Gluteus maximus

Extensor digitorum straightens fingers

Muscle movement

▲ *Athletes sometimes suffer from muscle fatigue, when their muscles are overworked. This is caused by a build-up of lactic acid, a waste product made when muscles contract.*

- **Most muscles are long and thin** and they work by pulling themselves shorter – sometimes contracting by up to half their length.

- **Skeletal muscles,** the muscles that make you move, are made of special cells which have not just one nucleus like other cells do, but many nuclei in a long fibre, called a myofibre.

- **Muscles are made** from hundreds or thousands of these fibres bound together like fibres in string.

- **Muscle fibres** are made from tiny strands called myofibrils, each marked with dark bands, giving the muscle its name of stripey or 'striated' muscle.

- **The stripes** in muscle are alternate bands of filaments of two substances: actin and myosin.

- **The actin and myosin** interlock, like teeth on a zip.

- **When a nerve signal** comes from the brain, chemical 'hooks' on the myosin twist and yank the actin filaments along, shortening the muscle.

- **The chemical hooks** on myosin are made from a stem called a cross-bridge and a head made of a chemical called adenosine triphosphate or ATP.

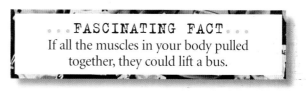

⋯FASCINATING FACT⋯
If all the muscles in your body pulled together, they could lift a bus.

- **ATP is sensitive to calcium,** and the nerve signal transmitted from the brain that tells the muscle to contract does its work by releasing a flood of calcium to trigger the ATP.

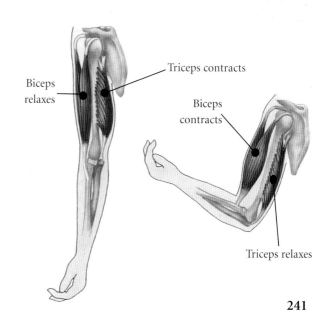

Triceps contracts

Biceps relaxes

Biceps contracts

▶ *Muscles, such as the biceps and triceps in your upper arm, work in pairs, pulling in opposite directions to one another.*

Triceps relaxes

241

The arm

- **The arm is made** from three long bones, linked by a hinge joint at the elbow.

- **The two bones** of the lower arm are the radius and the ulna.

- **The radius** supports the thumb side of the wrist.

- **The ulnar** supports the outside of the wrist.

- **The wrist** is one of the best places to test the pulse, since major arteries come nearer the surface here than at almost any other place in the body.

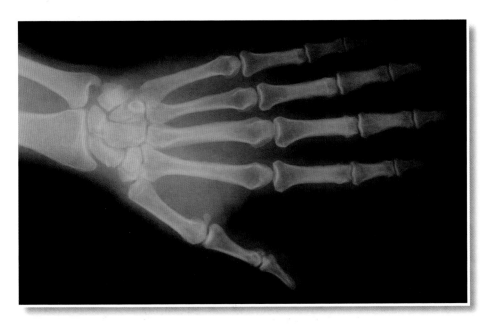

▲ *The intricate network of bones in your hands enables you to perform delicate and complex movements like writing or playing a musical instrument.*

- **The two major muscles** of the upper arm are the biceps (which bends the elbow) and the triceps (which straightens it).

- **The hand is made** from 26 bones, including the carpals (wrist bones), the metacarpals (hand bones) and the phalanges (finger bones).

- **There are no strong muscles** in the hand. When you grip firmly, most of the power comes from muscles in the lower arm, linked to the bones of the hand by long tendons.

- **The shoulder** is one of the most flexible but least stable joints of the skeleton, since it is set in a very shallow socket. But it is supported by six major muscle groups, including the powerful deltoid (shoulder) muscle.

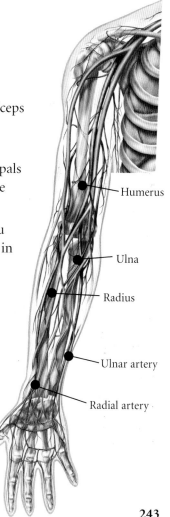

Humerus

Ulna

Radius

Ulnar artery

Radial artery

▶ *Look at the inside of your wrist on a warm day and you may be able to see the radial artery beneath the skin.*

243

Tendons
and ligaments

- **Tendon**s are cords that tie a muscle to a bone or tie a muscle to another muscle.

- **Most tendons** are round, rope-like bundles of fibre. A few, such as the ones in the abdomen wall, are flat sheets called aponeuroses.

- **Tendon fibres are made** from a rubbery substance called collagen.

- **Your fingers are moved** mainly by muscles in the forearm, which are connected to the fingers by long tendons.

▲ *Tendons provide a link between muscle and bone. They prevent muscles tearing when they are put under strain.*

- **The Achilles tendon** pulls up your heel at the back.

- **Ligaments** are cords attached to bones on either side of a joint. They strengthen the joint.

- **Ligaments** also support various organs, including the liver, bladder and uterus (womb).

- **Women's breasts** are held in shape by bundles of ligaments.

- **Ligaments are made up** of bundles of tough collagen and a stretchy substance called elastin.

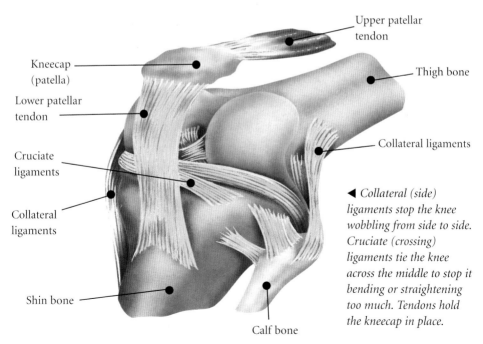

Upper patellar tendon

Kneecap (patella)

Thigh bone

Lower patellar tendon

Cruciate ligaments

Collateral ligaments

Collateral ligaments

Shin bone

Calf bone

◀ *Collateral (side) ligaments stop the knee wobbling from side to side. Cruciate (crossing) ligaments tie the knee across the middle to stop it bending or straightening too much. Tendons hold the kneecap in place.*

245

Teeth

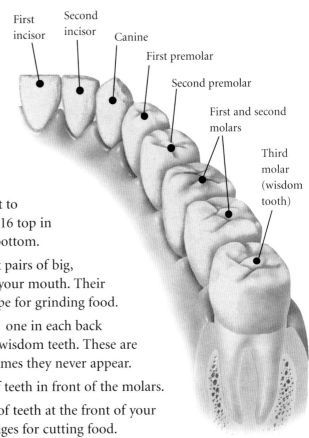

▶ *This shows one side of an adult's lower jaw. Not every adult grows the full set of eight teeth on each side of the jaw.*

First incisor

Second incisor

Canine

First premolar

Second premolar

First and second molars

Third molar (wisdom tooth)

- **Milk teeth** are the 20 teeth that start to appear when a baby is about six months old.

- **When you are six,** you start to grow your 32 adult teeth – 16 top in the top row and 16 in the bottom.

- **Molars** are the (usually) six pairs of big, strong teeth at the back of your mouth. Their flattish tops are a good shape for grinding food.

- **The four rearmost molars,** one in each back corner of each jaw, are the wisdom teeth. These are the last to grow and sometimes they never appear.

- **Premolars** are four pairs of teeth in front of the molars.

- **Incisors** are the four pairs of teeth at the front of your mouth. They have sharp edges for cutting food.

- **Canines** are the two pairs of big, pointed teeth behind the incisors. Their shape is good for tearing food.

246

- **The enamel** on teeth is the body's hardest substance.
- **Dentine** inside teeth is softer but still hard as bone.
- **Teeth** sit in sockets in the jawbones.

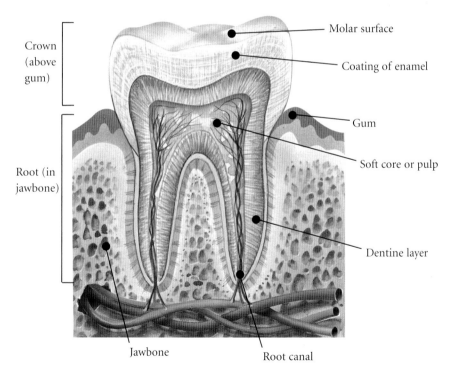

Crown (above gum)

Molar surface

Coating of enamel

Gum

Soft core or pulp

Root (in jawbone)

Dentine layer

Jawbone

Root canal

▲ *Teeth have long roots that slot into sockets in the jawbones, but they sit in a fleshy ridge called the gums. In the centre of each tooth is a living pulp of blood and nerves. Around this is a layer of dentine, then on top of that a tough shield of enamel.*

Body systems

▲ *Fresh air and exercise are vital for keeping our body systems working to their best potential.*

- **Your body systems** are interlinked – each has its own task, but they are all dependent on one another.

- **The skeleton** supports the body, protects the major organs, and provides an anchor for the muscles.

- **The nervous system** is the brain and the nerves – the body's control and communications network.

- **The digestive system** breaks down food into chemicals that the body can use to its advantage.

248

- **The immune system** is the body's defence against germs. It includes white blood cells, antibodies and the lymphatic system.

- **The urinary system** controls the body's water balance, removing extra water as urine and getting rid of impurities in the blood.

- **The respiratory system** takes air into the lungs to supply oxygen, and lets out waste carbon dioxide.

- **The reproductive system** is the smallest of all the systems. It is basically the sexual organs that enable people to have children. It is the only system that is different in men and women.

- **The other body systems** are the hormonal system (controls growth and internal co-ordination by chemical hormones), integumentary system (skin, hair and nails), and the sensory system (eyes, ears, nose, tongue, skin, balance).

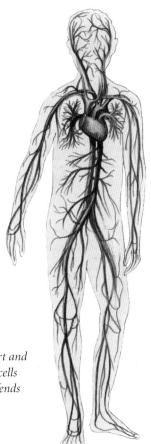

▶ *The cardiovascular system is the heart and the blood circulation. It keeps the body cells supplied with food and oxygen, and defends them against germs.*

... FASCINATING FACT ...
The reproductive system is the only system that can be removed without threatening life.

249

Breathing

- **You breathe** because every single cell in your body needs a continuous supply of oxygen to burn glucose, the high-energy substance from digested food that cells get from blood.

- **Scientists** call breathing 'respiration'. Cellular respiration is the way that cells use oxygen to burn glucose.

- **The oxygen in air** is taken into your lungs, and then carried in your blood to your body cells.

- **Waste carbon dioxide** from your cells is returned by your blood to your lungs, to be breathed out.

- **On average** you breathe in about 15 times a minute. If you run hard, the rate soars to around 80 times a minute.

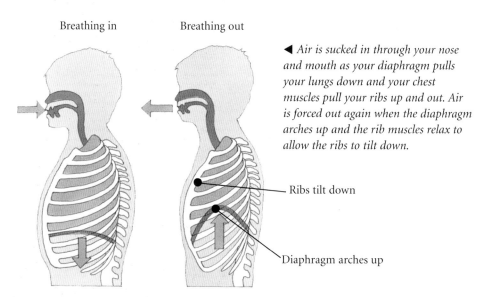

Breathing in   Breathing out

◀ *Air is sucked in through your nose and mouth as your diaphragm pulls your lungs down and your chest muscles pull your ribs up and out. Air is forced out again when the diaphragm arches up and the rib muscles relax to allow the ribs to tilt down.*

Ribs tilt down

Diaphragm arches up

- **Newborn babies** breathe about 40 times a minute.

- **If you live to the age of 80,** you will have taken well over 600 million breaths.

- **A normal breath** takes in about 0.4 litres of air. A deep breath can take in ten times as much.

- **Your diaphragm** is a dome-shaped sheet of muscle between your chest and stomach, which works with your chest muscles to make you breathe in and out.

- **Scientists** call breathing in 'inhalation', and breathing out 'exhalation'.

▶ *Wind musicians, such as this trumpeter, use their diaphragm and chest to control the air flowing in and out of their lungs. This allows them to produce a better quality sound.*

Airways

- **The upper airways** include the nose and the sinuses, the mouth and the pharynx (throat).

- **The lower airways** include the larynx (see vocal cords), the trachea (windpipe) and the airways of the lungs.

- **The sinuses** are air chambers within the bones of the skull that form the forehead and face.

▶ *After air is taken in through the nose or mouth, it travels down the throat, down the windpipe held open by cartilage rings, and into the lungs.*

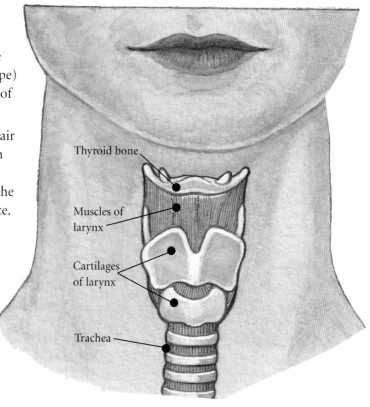

Thyroid bone

Muscles of larynx

Cartilages of larynx

Trachea

- **The soft palate** is a flap of tissue at the back of the mouth, which is pressed upwards when you swallow to stop food getting into your nose.

- **Your throat** is the tube that runs down through your neck from the back of your nose and mouth.

- **Your throat branches** in two at the bottom. One branch, the oesophagus, takes food to the stomach. The other, the larynx, takes air to the lungs.

- **The epiglottis** is the flap that tilts down to the larynx to stop food entering it when you swallow.

- **The tonsils and the adenoids** are bunches of lymph nodes (see lymphatic system) that swell to help fight ear, nose and throat infections, especially in young children.

- **The adenoids** are at the back of the nose, and the tonsils are at the back of the upper throat.

- **If tonsils or adenoids** swell too much, they are sometimes taken out.

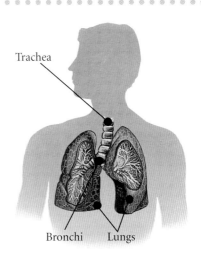

Trachea

Bronchi   Lungs

▲ *The lower airways include the larynx, the trachea (windpipe), and the bronchi which branch into the lungs.*

The vocal cords

- **Speaking and singing** depend on the larynx (voice-box) in your neck (see airways).

- **The larynx** has bands of stretchy fibrous tissue called the vocal cords, which vibrate (shake) as you breathe air out over them.

- **When you are silent**, the vocal cords are relaxed and apart, and air passes freely.

- **When you speak or sing,** the vocal cords tighten across the airway and vibrate to make sounds.

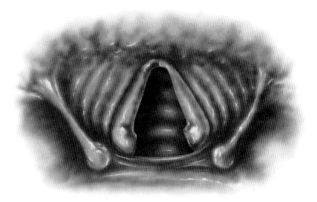

When the cords are apart no sound is made, as air can move freely past them

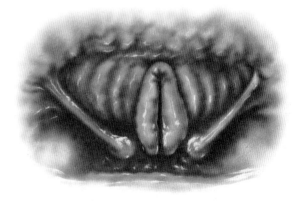

▶ *The vocal cords are soft flaps in the larynx, situated at the base of the throat. Our voices make sounds by vibrating these cords, as shown in the diagram.*

When the cords are pulled together by tiny muscles, air is forced through a small gap and the cords vibrate to create a sound

254

- **The tighter** the vocal cords are stretched, the less air can pass through them, so the higher pitched the sounds you make.

- **The basic sound** produced by the vocal cords is a simple 'aah'. But by changing the shape of your mouth, lips and especially your tongue, you can change this simple sound into letters and words.

Pharynx (throat)

Epiglottis (a fold of cartilage) blocks the airway as you swallow food

Vocal cords

Trachea (windpipe) to the lungs

Oesophagus to the stomach

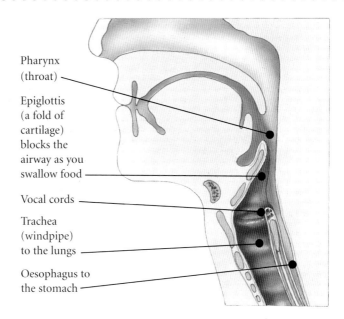

- **Babies' vocal cords** are just 6 mm long.

▲ *This shows a cross-section of your mouth, nose and throat, with the vocal cords at the top of the trachea.*

- **Women's vocal cords** are about 20 mm long.

- **Men's vocal cords** are about 30 mm long. Because men's cords are longer than women's, they vibrate more slowly and give men deeper voices.

- **Boys' vocal cords** are the same length as girls' until they are teenagers – when they grow longer, making a boy's voice 'break' and get deeper.

255

The lungs

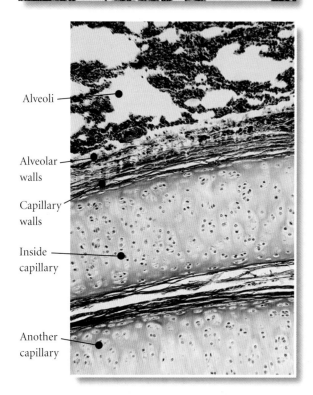

Alveoli

Alveolar
walls

Capillary
walls

Inside
capillary

Another
capillary

▲ *Taken through a powerful microscope, this*
photo of a slice of lung tissue shows a blood vessel
and the very thin walls of an alveolus next to it.

- **Your lungs** are a pair of soft, spongy bags inside your chest.

- **When you breathe** in, air rushes in through your nose or mouth, down your windpipe and into the millions of branching airways in your lungs.

- **The two biggest airways** are called bronchi (singular bronchus), and they both branch into smaller airways called bronchioles.

- **The surface of your airways** is protected by a slimy film of mucus, which gets thicker to protect the lungs when you have a cold.

- **At the end of each bronchiole** are bunches of minute air sacs called alveoli (singular alveolus).

- **Alveoli** are wrapped around with tiny blood vessels, and alveoli walls are just one cell thick – thin enough to let oxygen and carbon dioxide seep through them.

- **There are around 300 million alveoli** in your lungs.

- **The large surface area** of all these alveoli makes it possible for huge quantities of oxygen to seep through into the blood. Equally huge quantities of carbon dioxide can seep back into the airways for removal when you breathe out.

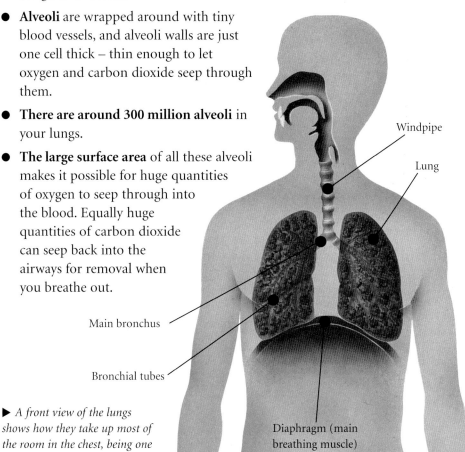

Windpipe

Lung

Main bronchus

Bronchial tubes

Diaphragm (main breathing muscle)

▶ *A front view of the lungs shows how they take up most of the room in the chest, being one of our most vital organs.*

257

Circulation

- **Your circulation** is the system of tubes called blood vessels which carries blood out from your heart to all your body cells and back again.

- **Blood circulation** was discovered in 1628 by the English physician William Harvey (1578–1657), who built on the ideas of Matteo Colombo.

- **Each of the body's** 600 billion cells gets fresh blood continuously, although the blood flow is pulsating.

- **On the way out** from the heart, blood is pumped through vessels called arteries and arterioles.

- **On the way back** to the heart, blood flows through venules and veins.

- **Blood flows** from the arterioles to the venules through the tiniest tubes called capillaries.

- **The blood circulation** has two parts – the pulmonary and the systemic.

- **The pulmonary circulation** is the short section that carries blood which is low in oxygen from the right side of the heart to the lungs for 'refuelling'. It then returns oxygen-rich blood to the left side of the heart.

- **The systemic circulation** carries oxygen-rich blood from the left side of the heart all around the body, and returns blood which is low in oxygen to the right side of the heart.

- **Inside the blood,** oxygen is carried by the haemoglobin in red blood cells (see blood cells).

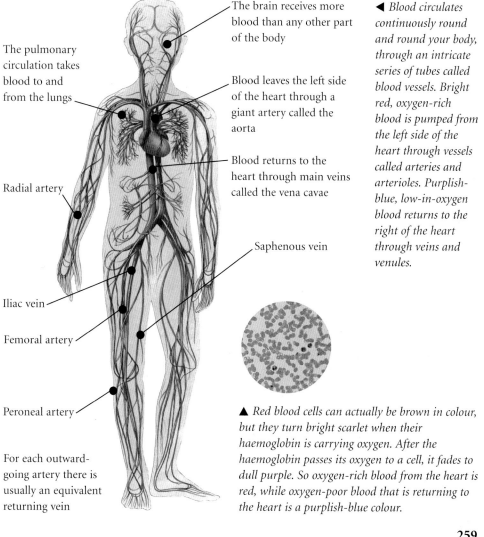

The pulmonary circulation takes blood to and from the lungs

Radial artery

Iliac vein

Femoral artery

Peroneal artery

For each outward-going artery there is usually an equivalent returning vein

The brain receives more blood than any other part of the body

Blood leaves the left side of the heart through a giant artery called the aorta

Blood returns to the heart through main veins called the vena cavae

Saphenous vein

◄ *Blood circulates continuously round and round your body, through an intricate series of tubes called blood vessels. Bright red, oxygen-rich blood is pumped from the left side of the heart through vessels called arteries and arterioles. Purplish-blue, low-in-oxygen blood returns to the right of the heart through veins and venules.*

▲ *Red blood cells can actually be brown in colour, but they turn bright scarlet when their haemoglobin is carrying oxygen. After the haemoglobin passes its oxygen to a cell, it fades to dull purple. So oxygen-rich blood from the heart is red, while oxygen-poor blood that is returning to the heart is a purplish-blue colour.*

259

Arteries

▶ *This illustration shows how the main kinds of blood vessel in the body are connected. The artery (red) branches into tiny capillaries, which join up to supply the vein (blue).*

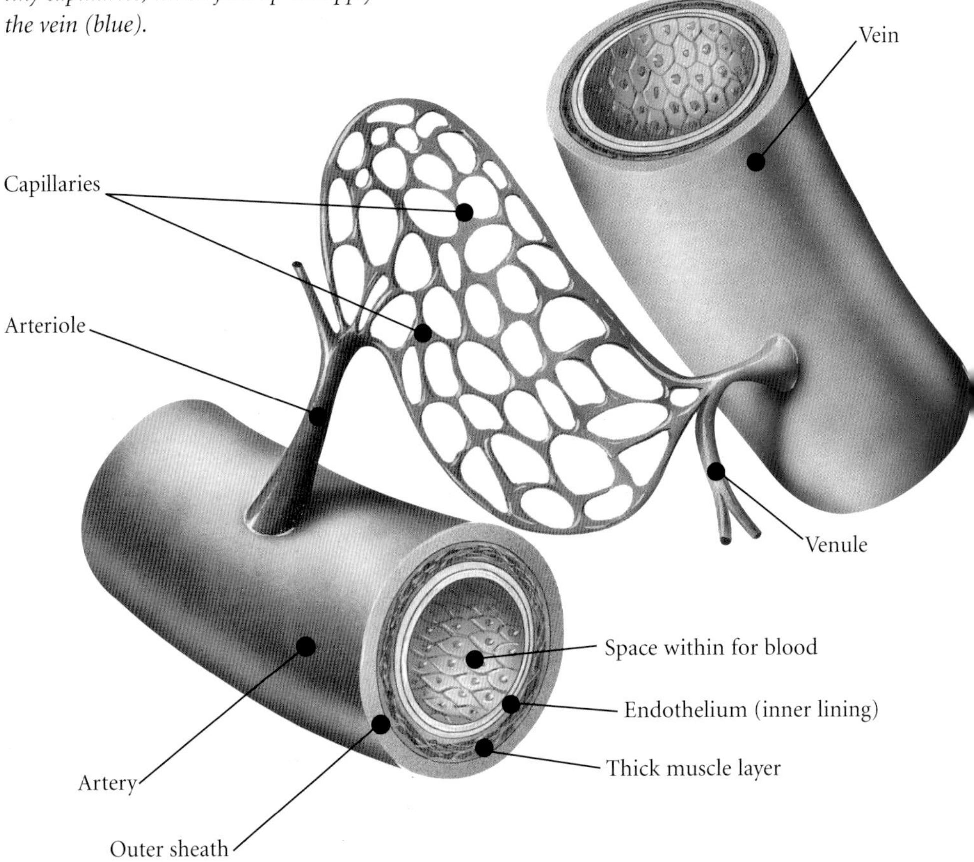

Vein

Capillaries

Arteriole

Venule

Space within for blood

Endothelium (inner lining)

Thick muscle layer

Artery

Outer sheath

- **An artery** is a tube-like blood vessel that carries blood away from the heart.

- **Systemic arteries deliver oxygenated blood** around the body. Pulmonary arteries deliver deoxygenated blood to the lungs.

- **An arteriole** is a smaller branch off an artery. Arterioles branch into microscopic capillaries.

- **Blood flows through** arteries at 30 cm per second in the main artery, down to 2 cm or less per second in the arterioles.

- **Arteries run alongside** most of the veins that return blood to the heart.

- **The walls of arteries** are muscular and can expand or relax to control the blood flow.

- **Arteries have** thicker, stronger walls than veins, and the pressure of the blood in them is a lot higher.

- **Over-thickening of the artery walls** may be one of the causes of hypertension (high blood pressure).

- **In old age** the artery walls can become very stiff. This hardening of the arteries, called arteriosclerosis, can cut blood flow to the brain.

. . . . FASCINATING FACT . . . .
Blood in an artery moves in a fast, pulsing
way, while blood in a vein oozes slowly.

Capillaries

- **Capillaries** are the smallest blood vessels, visible only under a microscope. They link the arterioles to the venules (see circulation).

- **Capillaries** were discovered by Marcello Malphigi in 1661.

- **There are 10 billion capillaries** in your body.

- **The largest capillary** is just 0.2 mm wide – thinner than a hair.

- **Each capillary** is about 0.5 mm to 1 mm long.

- **Capillary walls** are just one cell thick, so it is easy for chemicals to pass through them.

▲ *The work done by an athlete's muscles generates a lot of heat – which the body tries to lose by opening up capillaries in the skin, turning the skin bright red.*

. . . **FASCINATING FACT** . . .
The average capillary is 0.001 mm in diameter – just wide enough for red blood cells to pass through one at a time.

- **It is through the capillary walls** that your blood passes oxygen, food and waste to and from each one of your body cells.

- **There are many more capillaries** in active tissues such as muscles, liver and kidneys than there are in tendons and ligaments.

- **Capillaries** carry less or more blood according to need. They carry more to let more blood reach the surface when you are warm. They carry less to keep blood away from the surface and save heat when you are cold.

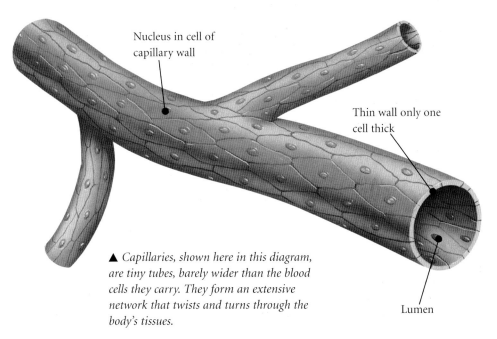

Nucleus in cell of
capillary wall

Thin wall only one
cell thick

Lumen

▲ *Capillaries, shown here in this diagram, are tiny tubes, barely wider than the blood cells they carry. They form an extensive network that twists and turns through the body's tissues.*

Veins

- **Veins** are pipes in the body for carrying blood back to the heart.

- **Unlike arteries,** most veins carry 'used' blood back to the heart – the body cells have taken the oxygen they need from the blood, so it is low in oxygen.

- **When blood** is low in oxygen, it is a dark, purplish blue colour – unlike the bright red of the oxygenated blood carried by the arteries.

- **The only veins** that carry oxygenated blood are the four pulmonary veins, which carry blood from the lungs the short distance to the heart.

- **The two largest veins** in the body are the vena cavae that flow into the heart from above and below.

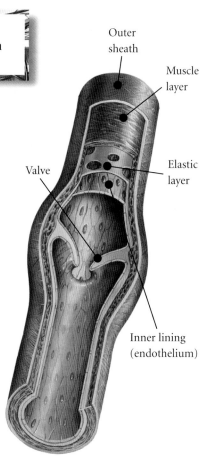

Outer sheath

Muscle layer

Elastic layer

Valve

Inner lining (endothelium)

▶ *This shows a greatly enlarged cutaway of a small vein. The valve prevents the blood from flowing backwards away from the heart.*

- **Inside most veins** are flaps that act as valves to make sure that the blood only flows in one direction.

- **The blood in veins** is pumped by the heart, but the blood pressure is much lower than in arteries and vein walls do not need to be as strong.

- **Unlike arteries,** veins collapse when empty.

- **Blood is helped through** the veins by pressure that is placed on the vein walls by the surrounding muscles.

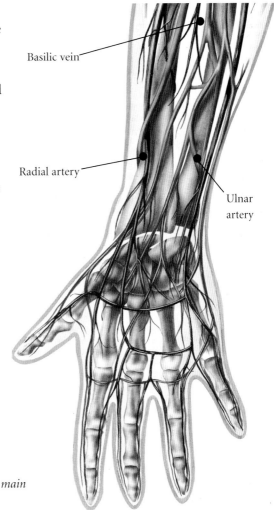

Basilic vein

Radial artery

Ulnar artery

▶ *This illustration of the lower arm shows the main veins (in blue) and the main arteries (in red).*

265

The heart

- **Your heart** is the size of your fist. It is inside the middle of your chest, slightly to the left.

- **The heart is a powerful pump** made almost entirely of muscle.

- **The heart contracts** (tightens) and relaxes automatically about 70 times a minute to pump blood out through your arteries.

- **The heart has two sides** separated by a muscle wall called the septum.

- **The right side** is smaller and weaker, and it pumps blood only to the lungs.

- **The stronger left side** pumps blood around the body.

- **Each side of the heart** has two chambers. There is an atrium (plural atria) at the top where blood accumulates (builds up) from the veins, and a ventricle below which contracts to pump blood out into the arteries.

- **Each side of the heart** (left and right) ejects about 70 ml of blood every beat.

- **There are two valves** in each side of the heart to make sure that blood flows only one way – a large one between the atrium and the ventricle, and a small one at the exit from the ventricle into the artery.

- **The coronary arteries** supply the heart. If they become clogged, the heart muscle may be short of blood and stop working. This is what happens in a heart attack.

> **...FASCINATING FACT...**
> During an average lifetime, the heart pumps
> 200 million litres of blood – enough to fill
> New York's Central Park to a depth of 15 m.

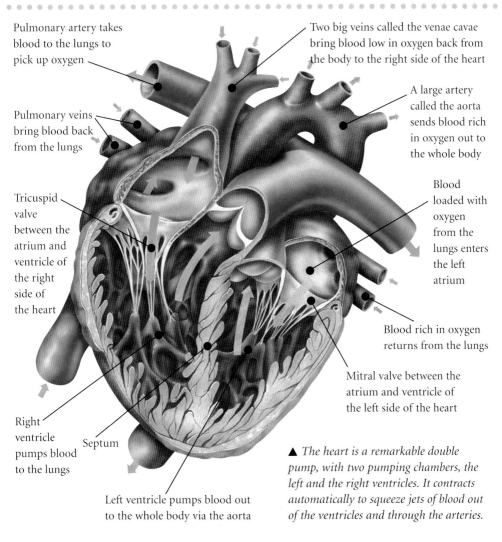

Pulmonary artery takes blood to the lungs to pick up oxygen

Two big veins called the venae cavae bring blood low in oxygen back from the body to the right side of the heart

A large artery called the aorta sends blood rich in oxygen out to the whole body

Pulmonary veins bring blood back from the lungs

Tricuspid valve between the atrium and ventricle of the right side of the heart

Blood loaded with oxygen from the lungs enters the left atrium

Blood rich in oxygen returns from the lungs

Mitral valve between the atrium and ventricle of the left side of the heart

Right ventricle pumps blood to the lungs

Septum

▲ *The heart is a remarkable double pump, with two pumping chambers, the left and the right ventricles. It contracts automatically to squeeze jets of blood out of the ventricles and through the arteries.*

Left ventricle pumps blood out to the whole body via the aorta

267

Heartbeat

- **The heartbeat** is the regular squeezing of the heart muscle to pump blood around the body.

- **Four heart valves** make sure blood only moves one way.

- **The heartbeat** is a sequence called the cardiac cycle and it has two phases – systole and diastole.

- **Systole** is when the heart muscle contracts (tightens). Diastole is the resting phase between contractions.

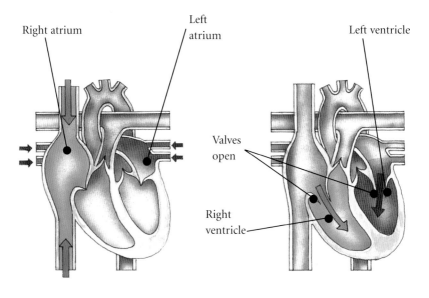

Right atrium

Left atrium

Left ventricle

Valves open

Right ventricle

▲ *Blood floods into the relaxed atria.*

▲ *The wave of contraction squeezes blood into the ventricles.*

- **Systole begins** when a wave of muscle contraction sweeps across the heart and squeezes blood from each of the atria into the two ventricles.

- **When the contraction** reaches the ventricles, they squeeze blood out into the arteries.

- **In diastole,** the heart muscle relaxes and the atria fill with blood again.

- **Heart muscle** on its own would contract automatically.

- **Nerve signals** make the heart beat faster or slower.

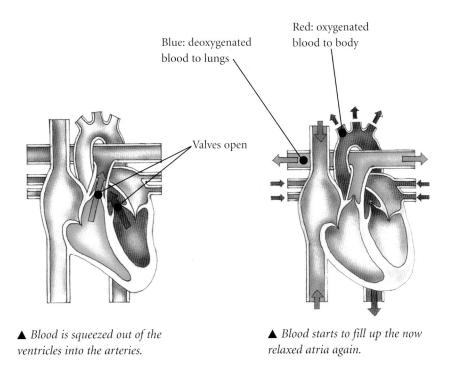

Blue: deoxygenated blood to lungs

Red: oxygenated blood to body

Valves open

▲ *Blood is squeezed out of the ventricles into the arteries.*

▲ *Blood starts to fill up the now relaxed atria again.*

Pulse

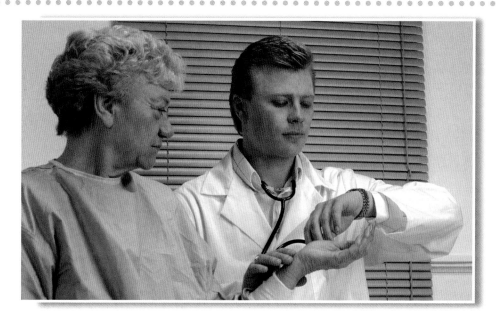

▲ *A doctor tests his patient's pulse rate by timing how many beats there are per minute.*

- **Your pulse** is the powerful high-pressure surge or wave that runs through your blood and vessels as the heart contracts strongly with each beat.

- **You can feel your pulse** by pressing two fingertips on the inside of your wrist where the radial artery nears the surface (see the arm).

- **Other pulse points** include the carotid artery in the neck and the brachial artery inside the elbow.

- **Checking the pulse** is a good way of finding out how healthy someone is, which is why doctors do it.

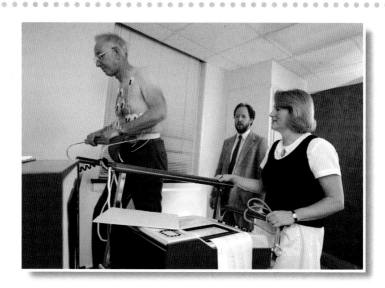

▶ *An ECG machine can show how healthy someone's heart is, by monitoring how much their heart rate goes up and down during exercise.*

● **Normal pulse rates** vary between 50 and 100 beats a minute. The average for a man is about 71, for a woman it is 80, and for children it is about 85.

● **Tachycardia** is the medical word for an abnormally fast heartbeat.

● **Someone who has tachycardia** when sitting down may have drunk too much coffee or tea, or taken drugs, or be suffering from anxiety or a fever, or have heart disease.

● **Bradycardia** is an abnormally slow heartbeat rate.

● **Arrhythmia** is any abnormality in a person's heartbeat rate.

● **Anyone with a heart problem** may be connected to a machine called an electrocardiogram (ECG) to monitor (watch) their heartbeat.

Blood

- **Blood** is the reddish liquid that circulates around your body. It carries oxygen and food to body cells, and takes carbon dioxide and other waste away. It fights infection, keeps you warm, and distributes chemicals that control body processes.

- **Blood is made up of** red cells, white cells and platelets, all carried in a liquid called plasma.

- **Plasma** is 90% water, plus hundreds of other substances, including nutrients, hormones and special proteins for fighting infection.

- **Blood plasma** turns milky immediately after a meal high in fats.

- **Blood platelets** are tiny pieces of cell that make blood clots start to form in order to stop bleeding.

◀ A centrifuge is used to separate the different components of blood. The spinning action of the machine separates the heavier blood cells from the lighter plasma.

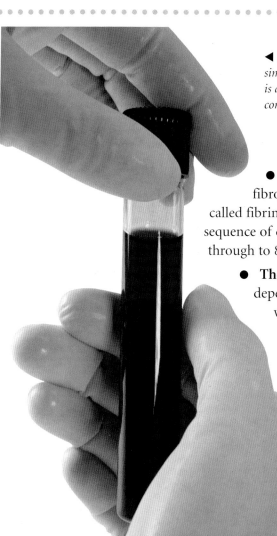

◀ Blood may look like a simple sticky red liquid, but it is actually a watery liquid containing millions of cells.

● **Blood clots also** involve a lacy, fibrous network made from a protein called fibrin. Fibrin is set in action by a sequence of chemicals called factors (factors 1 through to 8).

● **The amount of blood** in your body depends on your size. An adult who weighs 80 kg has about 5 litres of blood. A child who is half as heavy has half as much blood.

● **A drop of blood** the size of the dot on this i contains around 5 million red cells.

● **If a blood donor** gives 0.5 litres of blood, the body replaces the plasma in a few hours, but it takes a few weeks to replace the red cells.

273

Blood cells

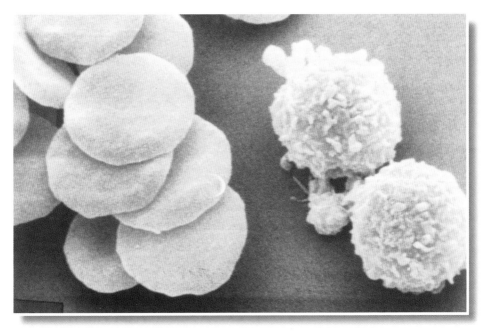

▲ *This is a highly magnified photograph of red blood cells (left) and white blood cells (right).*

- **Your blood has two main kinds of cell** – red cells and white cells – plus pieces of cell called platelets (see blood).

- **Red cells** are button-shaped and they contain mainly a red protein called haemoglobin.

- **Haemoglobin** is what allows red blood cells to ferry oxygen around your body.

- **Red cells** also contain enzymes which the body uses to make certain chemical processes happen (see enzymes).

274

- **White blood cells** are big cells called leucocytes and most types are involved in fighting infections.

- **Most white cells** contain tiny little grains and are called granulocytes.

- **Most granulocytes** are giant white cells called neutrophils. They are the blood's cleaners, and their task is to eat up invaders.

- **Eosinophils and basophils** are granulocytes that are involved in fighting disease. Some release antibodies that help fight infection (see antibodies).

- **Lymphocytes** are also types of white cells (see lymphocytes and antibodies).

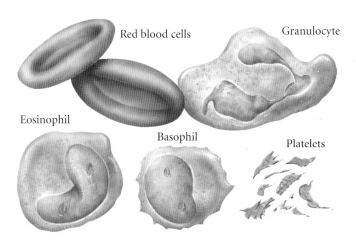

Red blood cells

Granulocyte

Eosinophil

Basophil

Platelets

▲ *These are some important kinds of cell in the blood – red cells, three kinds of white cells, and platelets.*

. . . **FASCINATING FACT** . . .
Each red blood cell contains more than 200 million molecules of haemoglobin.

Blood groups

- **Most people's blood** belongs to one of four different groups or types – A, O, B and AB.

- **Blood type O** is the most common, followed by blood group A.

- **Blood is also** either Rhesus positive (Rh+) or Rhesus negative (Rh-).

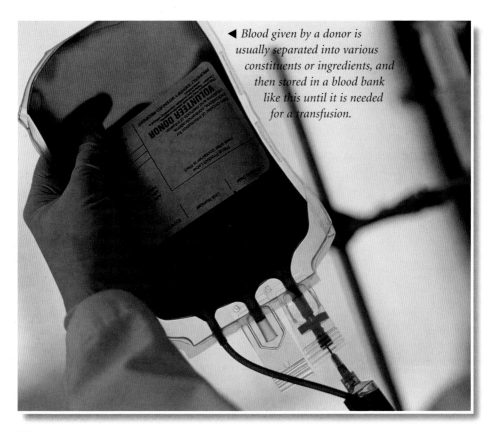

◀ *Blood given by a donor is usually separated into various constituents or ingredients, and then stored in a blood bank like this until it is needed for a transfusion.*

A pregnant mother who is Rh- may develop damaging
antibodies against the baby in her own womb if it is Rh+.

- **Around 85% of people** are Rh+. The remaining 15% are Rh-.

- **If your blood is Rh**+ and your group is A, your blood group is said to be A
  positive. If your blood is Rh- and your group is O, you are O negative, and so on.

- **The Rhesus factors** got their name because they were first identified in
  Rhesus monkeys.

- **A transfusion** is when you
  are given blood from
  another person's body. Your
  blood is 'matched' with
  other blood considered safe
  for transfusion.

- **Blood transfusions** are given
  when someone has lost a lot
  of blood due to an injury or
  operation. They are also given
  to replace diseased blood.

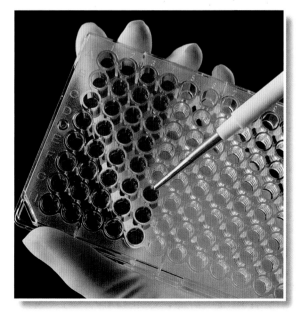

▶ *Donated blood is tested to*
determine its blood group. The blood
must belong to a suitable group,
otherwise patients undergoing a blood
transfusion could become very ill.

The lymphatic system

- **The lymphatic system** is your body's sewer, the network of pipes that drains waste from the cells.

- **The 'pipes' of the lymphatic system** are called lymphatics or lymph vessels.

- **The lymphatics** are filled by a watery liquid called lymph fluid which, along with bacteria and waste chemicals, drains from body tissues such as muscles.

- **The lymphatic system** has no pump, such as the heart, to make it circulate. Instead, lymphatic fluid is circulated as a side effect of the heartbeat and muscle movement.

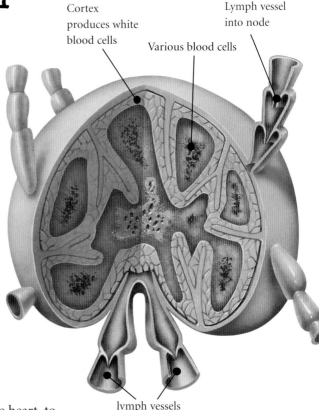

Cortex produces white blood cells

Various blood cells

Lymph vessel into node

lymph vessels from node

▲ *This shows a cross-section of a lymph node. White blood cells are produced and stored here, and are released through the lymph vessels into the bloodstream.*

- **At places** in the lymphatic system there are tiny lumps called nodes. These are filters which trap germs that have got into the lymph fluid.

- **In the nodes**, armies of white blood cells called lymphocytes neutralize or destroy germs.

- **When you have** a cold or any other infection, the lymph nodes in your neck or groin, or under your arm, may swell, as lymphocytes fight germs. This is sometimes called 'swollen glands'.

- **Lymph fluid** drains back into the blood via the body's main vein, the superior vena cava (see heart).

- **The lymphatic system** is not only the lymphatics and lymph nodes, but includes the spleen, the thymus, the tonsils and the adenoids (see the immune system).

- **On average**, at any time about 1 to 2 litres of lymph fluid circulate in the lymphatics and body tissues.

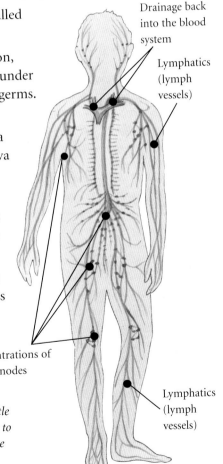

Drainage back into the blood system

Lymphatics (lymph vessels)

Concentrations of lymph nodes

Lymphatics (lymph vessels)

▶ *The lymphatic system is a branching network of little tubes that reaches throughout the body. It drains back to the centre of the body, running into the branches of the superior vena cava, the body's main vein to the heart.*

279

Digestion

- **Digestion** is the process by which your body breaks down the food you eat into substances that it can absorb (take in) and use.

- **Your digestive tract** is basically a long, winding tube called the alimentary canal (gut). It starts at your mouth and ends at your anus.

- **If you could lay** your gut out straight, it would be nearly six times as long as you are tall.

- **The food you eat** is softened in your mouth by chewing and by chemicals in your saliva (spit).

- **When you swallow,** food travels down your oesophagus (gullet) into your stomach. Your stomach is a muscular-walled bag which mashes the food into a pulp, helped by chemicals called gastric juices.

- **When empty,** your stomach holds barely 0.5 litres, but after a big meal it can stretch to more than 4 litres.

- **The half-digested food** that leaves your stomach is called chyme. It passes into your small intestine.

- **Your small intestine** is a 6-m-long tube where chyme is broken down into molecules small enough to be absorbed through the intestine wall into the blood.

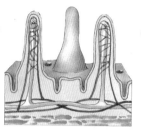

▲ *The small intestine is lined with tiny, finger-like folds called villi. On the surface of each villus are even tinier, finger-like folds called microvilli. These folds give a huge area for absorbing food.*

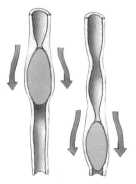

▲ *Swallowed food is pushed through the long, winding digestive tract by waves of contraction (tightening) that pass along its muscular walls. These waves are called peristalsis.*

> ... **FASCINATING FACT** ...
> On average, food takes 24 hours to pass right through your alimentary canal and out the other end.

- **Food that cannot be** digested in your small intestine passes on into your large intestine. It is then pushed out through your anus as faeces when you go to the toilet (see excretion).

- **Digestive enzymes** play a vital part in breaking food down so it can be absorbed by the body.

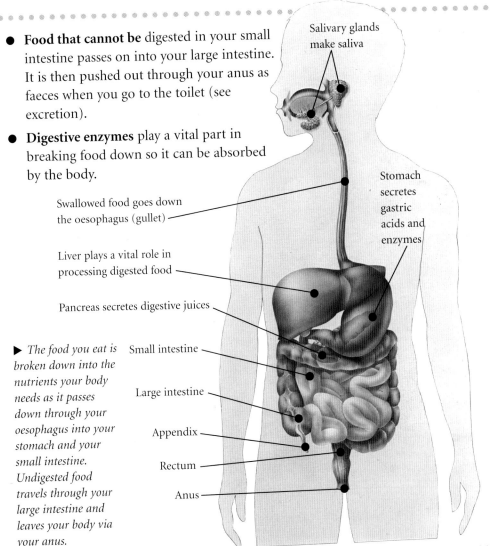

Salivary glands make saliva

Stomach secretes gastric acids and enzymes

Swallowed food goes down the oesophagus (gullet)

Liver plays a vital role in processing digested food

Pancreas secretes digestive juices

Small intestine

Large intestine

Appendix

Rectum

Anus

▶ *The food you eat is broken down into the nutrients your body needs as it passes down through your oesophagus into your stomach and your small intestine. Undigested food travels through your large intestine and leaves your body via your anus.*

281

The liver

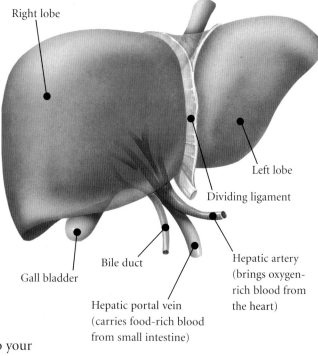

▶ *The liver is a large organ situated to the right of the stomach.*

Right lobe

Left lobe

Dividing ligament

Hepatic artery (brings oxygen-rich blood from the heart)

Bile duct

Gall bladder

Hepatic portal vein (carries food-rich blood from small intestine)

- **The liver** is your body's chemical processing centre.

- **The liver is your body's biggest internal organ,** and the word hepatic means 'to do with the liver'.

- **The liver's prime task** is handling all the nutrients and substances digested from the food you eat and sending them out to your body cells when they are needed.

- **The liver turns** carbohydrates into glucose, the main energy-giving chemical for body cells.

- **The liver keeps** the levels of glucose in the blood steady. It does this by releasing more when levels drop, and by storing it as glycogen, a type of starch, when levels rise.

- **The liver packs off** excess food energy to be stored as fat around the body.

▲ *The liver filters harmful substances such as alcohol and food additives to keep the body safe.*

- **The liver breaks down** proteins and stores vitamins and minerals.

- **The liver produces bile,** the yellowish or greenish bitter liquid that helps dissolve fat as food is digested in the intestines.

- **The liver clears the blood** of old red cells and harmful substances such as alcohol, and makes new plasma (see blood).

- **The liver's chemical processing units**, called lobules, take in unprocessed blood on the outside and dispatch it through a collecting vein.

The pancreas

- **The pancreas** is a large, carrot-shaped gland which lies just below your stomach.

- **The larger end** of the pancreas is on the right, tucking into the gut (see digestion). The tail end is on the left, touching your spleen.

- **The pancreas** is made from a substance called exocrine tissue, embedded with hundreds of nests of hormone glands called the islets of Langerhans.

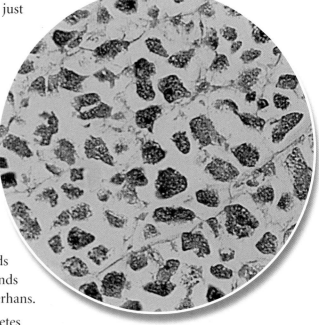

- **The exocrine tissue** secretes (releases) pancreatic enzymes such as amylase into the intestine to help digest food (see enzymes).

▲ *This is a microscopic view of the pancreas, with the islets of Langerhans (shown in purple) embedded in the exocrine tissue.*

- **Amylase** breaks down carbohydrates into simple sugars such as maltose, lactose and sucrose.

- **The pancreatic enzymes** run into the intestine via a pipe called the pancreatic duct, which joins on to the bile duct. This duct also carries bile (see liver).

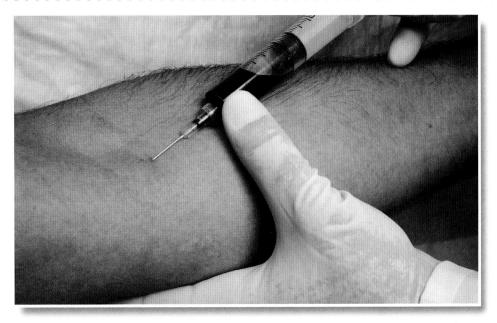

▲ *Diabetics, who suffer from the condition diabetes, produce little or no insulin in their pancreas. They control their blood glucose by injecting insulin, without which they might not survive.*

- **The pancreatic enzymes** only start working when they meet other kinds of enzyme in the intestine.

- **The pancreas** also secretes the body's own antacid, sodium bicarbonate, to settle an upset stomach.

- **The islets of Langerhans** secrete two important hormones , which are insulin and glucagon.

- **Insulin and glucagon** regulate blood sugar levels (see glucose).

285

Glucose

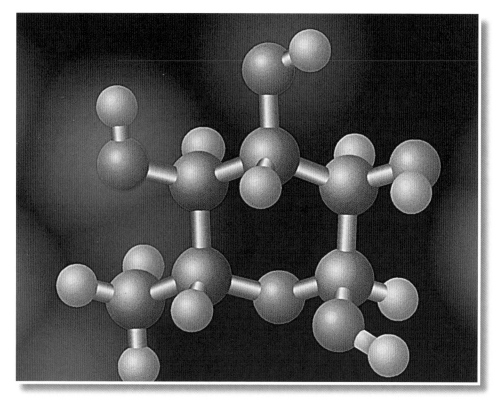

▲ *Glucose is built from 6 carbon, 12 hydrogen and 6 oxygen atoms.*

- **Glucose** is the body's energy chemical, used as the fuel in all cell activity.
- **Glucose is a kind of sugar** made by plants as they take energy from sunlight. It is commonly found in many fruits and fruit juices, along with fructose (see carbohydrates).

- **The body gets its glucose** from carbohydrates in food, broken down in stages in the intestine.

- **From the intestine,** glucose travels in the blood to the liver, where excess is stored as starchy glycogen.

- **For the body to work effectively,** levels of glucose in the blood (called blood sugar) must always be correct.

- **Blood sugar levels** are controlled by two hormones, glucagon and insulin, sent out by the pancreas.

- **When blood sugar is low,** the pancreas sends out glucagon and this makes the liver change more glycogen to glucose.

- **When blood sugar is high,** the pancreas sends out insulin and this makes the liver store more glucose as glycogen.

- **Inside cells,** glucose may be burned for energy, stored as glycogen, or used to make triglyceride fats (see fats).

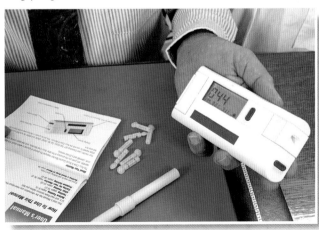

▶ *A blood glucose monitor checks that a person's blood sugar is at a healthy level.*

Carbohydrates

- **Carbohydrates** in food are your body's main source of energy. They are plentiful in sweet things and in starchy food such as bread, cakes and potatoes (see diet).

- **Carbohydrates** are burned by the body in order to keep it warm and to provide energy for growth and muscle movement, as well as to maintain basic body processes.

- **Carbohydrates** are among the most common of organic (life) substance – plants, for instance, make carbohydrates by taking energy from sunlight.

- **Carbohydrates** include chemical substances called sugars. Sucrose (the sugar in sugar lumps and caster sugar) is just one of these sugars.

- **Simple carbohydrates** such as glucose, fructose (the sweetness in fruit) and sucrose are sweet and soluble (they will dissolve in water).

- **Complex carbohydrates** (or polysaccharides) such as starch are made when molecules of simple carbohydrates join together.

▼ *Bread is especially rich in complex carbohydrates such as starch, as well as simpler ones such as glucose and sucrose.*

▲ *Carbohydrates give us the instant energy we need to help us lead a full and active life.*

● **A third type of carbohydrate** is cellulose (see diet).

● **The carbohydrates** you eat are turned into glucose for your body to use at once, or stored in the liver as the complex sugar glycogen (body starch).

● **The average adult** needs 2000 to 4000 Calories a day.

● **A Calorie** is the heat needed to warm 1 litre of water by 1°C.

289

Fats

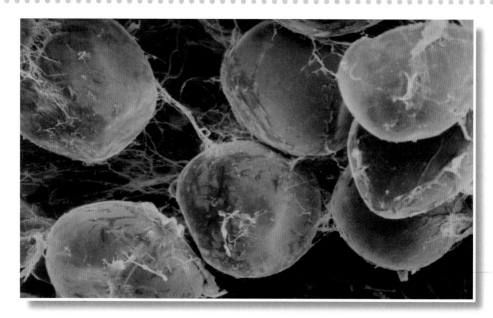

▲ *Fat cells are numerous under the skin, providing your body with a store of energy and a layer of insulation to keep you warm.*

- **Fats** are an important source of energy. Together with carbohydrates and proteins, they make up your body's three main components of foods.

- **While carbohydrates** are generally used for energy immediately, your body often stores fat to use for energy in times of shortage.

- **Weight for weight,** fats contain twice as much energy as carbohydrates.

- **Fats** are important organic (life) substances, found in almost every living thing. They are made from substances called fatty acids and glycerol.

- **Food fats** are greasy, vegetable or animal fats that will not dissolve in water.

- **Most vegetable fats** such as corn oil and olive oil are liquid, although some nut fats are solid.

- **Most animal fats,** as in meat, milk and cheese, are solid. Milk is mainly water with some solid animal fats. Most solid fats melt when warmed.

- **Fats called triglycerides** are stored around the body as adipose tissue (body fat). These act as energy stores and also insulate the body against the cold.

- **Fats called phospholipids** are used to build body cells.

- **In your stomach,** bile from your liver and enzymes from your pancreas break fats down into fatty acids and glycerol. These are absorbed into your body's lymphatic system or enter the blood.

◄ *Fats are either saturated or unsaturated. Cheese is a saturated fat. Saturated fats are linked to high levels of the substance cholesterol in the blood and may increase certain health risks, such as heart attack.*

Water

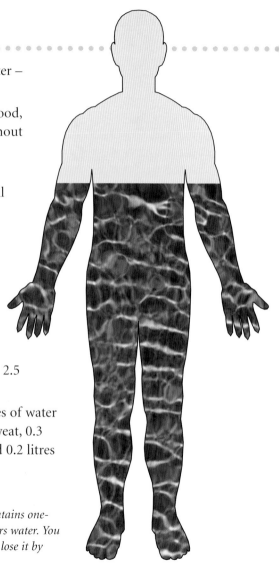

- **Your body** is mainly made of water – more than 60%.

- **You can survive weeks** without food, but no more than a few days without water.

- **You gain water** by drinking and eating, and as a by-product of cell activity.

- **You lose water** by sweating and breathing, and in your urine and faeces (see excretion).

- **The average person** takes in 2.2 litres of water a day – 1.4 litres in drink and 0.8 litres in food. Body cells add 0.3 litres, bringing the total water intake to 2.5 litres.

- **The average person** loses 1.5 litres of water every day in urine, 0.5 litres in sweat, 0.3 litres as vapour in the breath, and 0.2 litres in faeces.

▶ *Your body is mostly water. Even bone contains one-fifth water, while your brain is three-quarters water. You take it in through drinking and eating, and lose it by urinating, sweating and even breathing.*

- **The water balance** in the body is controlled mainly by the kidneys and adrenal glands.

- **The amount of water** the kidneys let out as urine depends on the amount of salt there is in the blood (see body salts).

- **If you drink a lot,** the saltiness of the blood is diluted (watered down). To restore the balance, the kidneys let out a lot of water as urine.

- **If you drink little** or sweat a lot, the blood becomes more salty, so the kidneys restore the balance by holding on to more water.

▶ *If you sweat a lot during heavy exercise, you need to make up for all the water you have lost by drinking. Your kidneys make sure that if you drink too much, you lose water as urine.*

Diet

- **Your diet** is what you eat. A good diet includes the correct amount of proteins, carbohydrates, fats, vitamins, minerals, fibre and water.

- **Most of the food** that you eat is fuel for the body, provided mostly by carbohydrates and fats.

- **Carbohydrates** are foods made from kinds of sugar, such as glucose and starch. They are found in foods such as bread, rice, potatoes and sweet things.

- **Fats** are greasy foods that will not dissolve in water. Some, such as the fats in meat and cheese, are solid. Some, such as cooking oil, are liquid.

- **Fats are not** usually burned up straight away, but are stored around your body until they are needed.

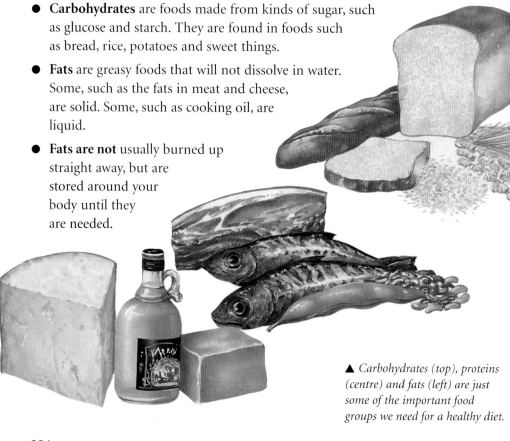

▲ *Carbohydrates (top), proteins (centre) and fats (left) are just some of the important food groups we need for a healthy diet.*

● **Proteins** are needed to build and repair cells. They are made from special chemicals called amino acids.

● **There are 20** different amino acids. Your body can make 11 of them. The other nine are called essential acids and they come from food.

● **Meat and fish** are very high in protein.

● **A correctly balanced vegetarian diet** of eggs, milk and cheese can provide all the essential amino acids.

▲ *Fresh fruit and vegetables provide us with an assortment of vital vitamins and minerals.*

● **Fibre or roughage** is supplied by cellulose from plant cell walls. Your body cannot digest fibre, but needs it to keep the bowel muscles exercised.

▶ *These foods contain fibre, which helps keep the digestive system healthy.*

Vitamins

- **Vitamins** are special substances the body needs to help maintain chemical processes inside cells.

- **Plants can make** their own vitamins, but humans must take most of their vitamins from food.

- **A lack of any vitamin** in the diet can cause certain illnesses.

- **Before the 18th century,** sailors on long voyages used to suffer the disease scurvy, caused by a lack in their diet of vitamin C from fresh fruit.

- **There are at least 15 known** vitamins .

◀ *Vegetables like these are rich in vitamins B and C, which is why we must eat plenty of them.*

▲ *This is a microscope photograph of a crystal of vitamin C, also known as ascorbic acid. This vitamin helps the body fight infections such as colds.*

- **The first vitamins** discovered were given letter names like B. Later discoveries were given chemical names, such as E vitamins, which are known as tocopherols.

- **Some vitamins** such as A, D, E and K dissolve in fat and are found in animal fats and vegetable oils. They may be stored in the body for months.

- **Some vitamins** such as C and the Bs dissolve in water and are found in green leaves, fruits and cereal grains. They are used daily.

- **Vitamins D and K** are the only ones made in the body. Vitamin D is essential for bone growth in children.

Body salts

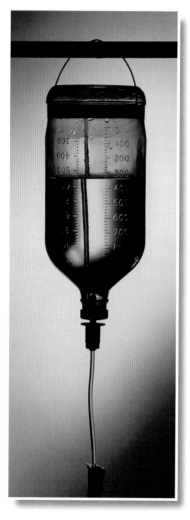

- **Body salts** are not simply the salt (sodium chloride) some people sprinkle on food – they are an important group of chemicals which play a vital role in your body.

- **Examples of components** in body salts include potassium, sodium, manganese, chloride, carbonate and phosphate.

- **Body salts are important** in maintaining the balance of water in the body, and on the inside and the outside of body cells.

- **The body's thirst centre** is the hypothalamus (see the brain). It monitors salt levels in the blood and sends signals telling the kidneys to keep water or to let it go.

- **You gain salt** in the food you eat.

- **You can lose salt** if you sweat heavily. This can make muscles cramp, which is why people take salt tablets in the desert or drink a weak salt solution.

- **Too much salt** in food may result in high blood pressure in certain people.

◄ *A saline drip is a salt solution injected via a tube into a patient who has lost blood.*

.. .FASCINATING FACT.. .
The kidneys control the amount of salts
and water you have inside your body.

▲ *People who live in hot countries must eat plenty of salt on their food to make up for the loss of salt in their blood caused by continuous sweating.*

- **When dissolved in water,** the chemical elements that salt is made from split into ions – atoms or groups of atoms with either a positive or a negative electrical charge.

- **The balance** of water and salt inside and outside of body cells often depends on a balance of potassium ions entering the cell and sodium ions leaving it.

299

Osmosis and diffusion

- **To survive,** every living cell must constantly take in the chemicals it needs and let out the ones it does not need through its thin membrane (casing). Cells do this in several ways, including osmosis, diffusion and active transport.

- **Osmosis** is when water moves to even the balance between a weak solution and a stronger one.

- **Diffusion** is when the substances that are dissolved in water or mixed in air move to even the balance.

- **Osmosis happens** when the molecules of a dissolved substance are too big to slip through the cell membrane – only the water is able to move.

- **Osmosis is vital** to many body processes, including the workings of the kidney and the nerves.

- **Urine gets its water** from the kidneys by osmosis.

▲ *Water swallowed into the stomach passes through its lining into the blood, mainly by the process of osmosis.*

- **In diffusion,** a substance such as oxygen moves in and out of cells, while the air or water it is mixed in mainly stays put.

- **Diffusion is vital** to body processes such as cellular respiration (see breathing), when cells take in oxygen and push out waste carbon dioxide.

- **Active transport** is the way a cell uses protein-based 'pumps' or 'gates' in its membrane to draw in and hold substances that might otherwise diffuse out.

- **Active transport** uses energy and is how cells draw in most of their food such as glucose.

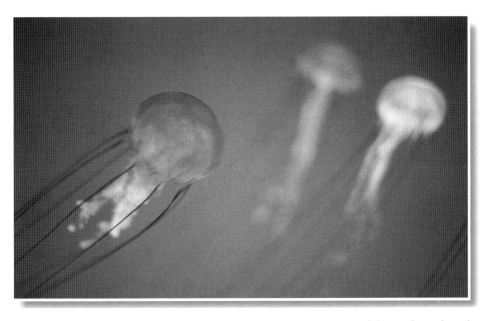

▲ *Like these jellyfish, every living cell must maintain the correct balance of chemicals inside and outside of them.*

Enzymes

- **Enzymes are** molecules that are mostly protein, and which alter the speed of chemical reactions in living things.

- **There are thousands of enzymes** inside your body – it would not be able to function without them.

- **Some enzymes** need an extra substance, called a coenzyme, to work. Many coenzymes are vitamins.

- **Most enzymes** have names ending in 'ase', such as lygase, protease and lipase.

▲ *After you eat a meal, a complex series of enzymes gets to work, breaking the food down into the simple molecules that can be absorbed into your blood.*

- **Pacemaker enzymes** play a vital role in controlling your metabolism – the rate at which your body uses energy.

- **One of the most important** enzyme groups is that of the messenger RNAs, which are used as communicators by the nuclei of body cells (see cells).

- **Many enzymes** are essential for the digestion of food, including lipase, protease, amylase, and the peptidases. Many of these enzymes are made in the pancreas.

◀ *From the moment you take your first bite of food, enzymes in your saliva begin to break carbohydrates down into glucose, preparing the food for digestion.*

- **Lipase is released** mainly from the pancreas into the alimentary canal (gut) to help break down fat.

- **Amylase breaks down starches** such as those in bread and fruit into simple sugars (see carbohydrates). There is amylase in saliva and in the stomach.

- **In the gut**, the sugars maltose, sucrose and lactose are broken down by maltase, sucrase and lactase.

Excretion

- **Digestive excretion** is the way your body gets rid
  of food that it cannot digest.

- **Undigested food** is prepared for excretion in your
  large intestine or bowel.

- **The main part** of the large intestine is the colon,
  which is almost as long as you are tall.

- **The colon** converts the semi-liquid 'chyme' (see
  digestion) of undigested food into solid waste, by
  absorbing water.

- **The colon** soaks up 1.5 litres of water every day.

- **The colon walls** also absorb sodium and chlorine
  and get rid of bicarbonate and potassium.

▲ *To work well, your bowel
needs plenty of roughage – the
indigestible cellulose plant
fibres found in food such as
beans and wholemeal bread.
Roughage keeps the muscles of
the bowel properly exercised.*

- **Billions of bacteria** live inside the colon and help turn the chyme into faeces.
  These bacteria are harmless as long as they do not spread to the rest of the
  body.

- **Bacteria in the colon** make vitamins K and B –
  as well as smelly gases such as methane and
  hydrogen sulphide.

- **The muscles of the colon** break the waste food
  down into segments ready for excretion.

▶ *This is an X-ray of the
colon. Patients drink a liquid
called barium to enable their
doctor to see the colon more
clearly and check it is in
working order.*

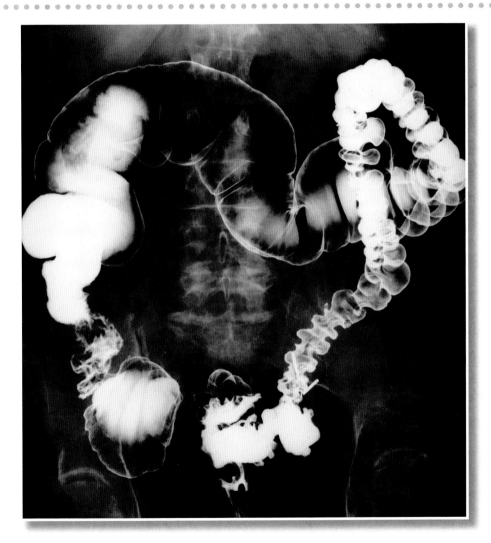

The kidneys

- **The kidneys** are a pair of bean-shaped organs inside the small of the back.

- **The kidneys** are the body's water control and blood-cleaning plants.

- **The kidneys** are high-speed filters that draw off water and important substances from the blood. They let unwanted water and waste substances go (see urine).

- **The kidneys filter** about 1.3 litres of blood a minute.

- **All the body's blood** flows through the kidneys every ten minutes, so blood is filtered 150 times a day.

- **The kidneys manage** to recycle or save every re-useable substance from the blood. They take 85 litres of water and other blood substances from every 1000 litres of blood, but only let out 0.6 litres as urine.

- **The kidneys** save nearly all the amino acids and glucose (see diet) from the blood and 70% of the salt.

- **Blood entering each kidney** is filtered through a million or more filtration units called nephrons.

- **Each nephron** is an incredibly intricate network of little pipes called convoluted tubules, wrapped around countless tiny capillaries. Useful blood substances are filtered into the tubules, then re-absorbed back into the blood in the capillaries.

- **Blood enters each nephron** through a little cup called the Bowman's capsule via a bundle of capillaries.

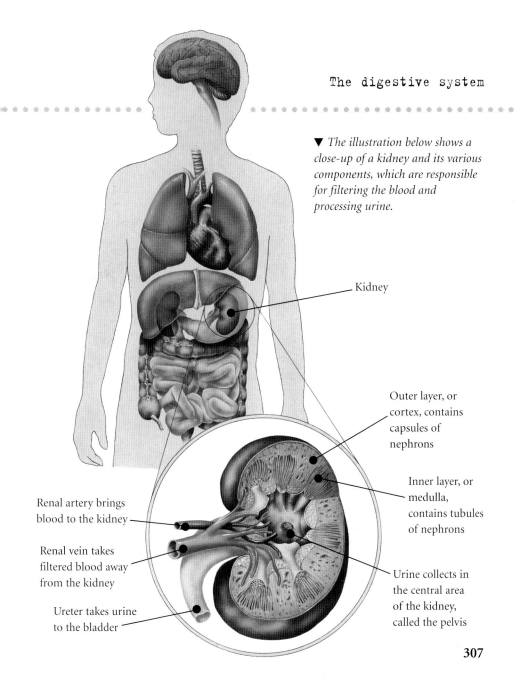

▼ *The illustration below shows a close-up of a kidney and its various components, which are responsible for filtering the blood and processing urine.*

Kidney

Outer layer, or cortex, contains capsules of nephrons

Inner layer, or medulla, contains tubules of nephrons

Renal artery brings blood to the kidney

Renal vein takes filtered blood away from the kidney

Ureter takes urine to the bladder

Urine collects in the central area of the kidney, called the pelvis

307

Urine

- **Urine** is one of your body's ways of getting rid of waste (see water).

- **Your kidneys** produce urine, filtering it from your blood.

- **Urine runs from** each kidney down a long tube called the ureter, to a bag called the bladder.

- **Your bladder fills** up with urine over several hours. When it is full, you feel the need to urinate.

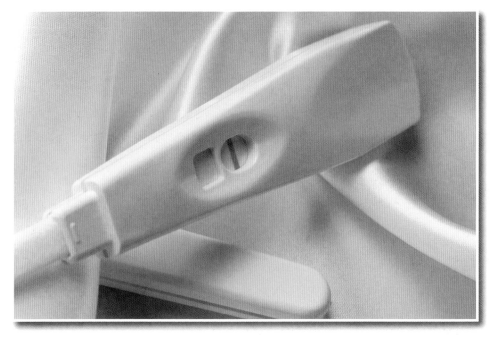

▲ *Urine can be used to test for pregnancy. A woman may use a home pregnancy test kit (above) to check her urine for a particular hormone, which, if present, will mean she is pregnant.*

- **Urine is mostly made up of water,** but there are several substances dissolved in it. These include urea, various salts, creatinine, ammonia and blood wastes.

- **Urea** is a substance that is left after the breakdown of amino acids (see diet).

- **Urine gets its smell** from substances such as ammonia.

- **Urine gets its colour** from a yellowish blood waste called urochrome. Urochrome is left after proteins are broken down.

- **If you sweat a lot** – perhaps during a fever – your kidneys will let less water go and your urine will be stronger in colour.

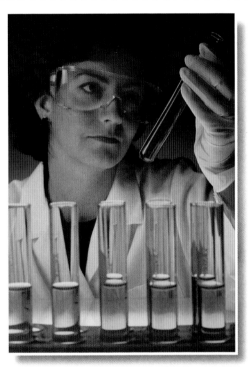

▲ *Doctors can get clues to illnesses by testing the substances in urine. Diabetes, for instance, is shown up by the presence of glucose in urine.*

...FASCINATING FACT...
During your life you will urinate 45,000 litres
– enough to fill a small swimming pool!

Reflexes

▲ *Many sportsmen rely on lightning reflexes – actions too fast for the brain to even think about.*

- **Reflexes** are muscle movements that are automatic (they happen without you thinking about them).

- **Inborn reflexes** are reflexes you were born with, such as urinating or shivering when you are cold.

- **The knee-jerk** is an inborn reflex that makes your leg jerk up when the tendon below your knee is tapped.

- **Primitive reflexes** are reflexes that babies have for a few months after they have been born.

- **One primitive reflex** is when you put something in a baby's hand and it automatically grips it.

- **Conditioned reflexes** are those you learn through habit, as certain pathways in the nervous system are used again and again.

- **Conditioned reflexes** help you do anything from holding a cup to playing football without thinking.

- **Reflex reactions** make you pull your hand from hot things before you have had time to think about it.

- **Reflex reactions** work by short-circuiting the brain. The alarm signal from your hand sets off motor signals in the spinal cord to move the hand.

- **A reflex arc** is the nerve circuit from sense to muscle via the spinal cord.

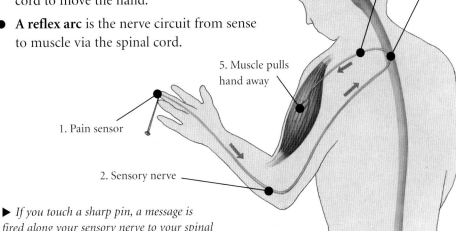

6. Brain is informed a split second later

4. Motor nerve

3. Reflex connection in spinal cord

5. Muscle pulls hand away

1. Pain sensor

2. Sensory nerve

▶ *If you touch a sharp pin, a message is fired along your sensory nerve to your spinal cord. A motor nerve then moves your hand away immediately. This response is a reflex action.*

311

Temperature

- **The inside of your body** stays at a constant temperature of 37°C (98°F), rising a few degrees only when you are ill.

- **Your body creates heat** by burning food in its cells, especially the 'energy sugar' glucose.

- **Even when you are resting,** your body generates so much heat that you are comfortable only when the air is slightly cooler than you are.

- **When you are working hard,** your muscles can generate as much heat as a 2 kW heater (a typical room heater).

- **Your body loses heat** when you breathe in cool air and breathe out warm air. Your body also loses heat by giving it off from your skin.

- **The body's temperature control** is the tiny hypothalamus in the lower front of the brain.

- **Temperature sensors** in the skin, in the body's core, and in the blood by the hypothalamus tell the hypothalamus how hot or cold your body is.

◄ *The body's temperature can be easily monitored using an electronic thermometer. This digital reading shows a normal body temperature of 98.6 degrees Farenheit.*

▶ *A very hot day can sometimes make us feel uncomforatble. Splashing ourselves with cool water is often welcome relief!*

- **If it is too hot,** the hypothalamus sends signals to your skin telling it to sweat more. Signals also tell blood vessels in the skin to widen – this increases the blood flow, increasing the heat loss from your blood.

- **If it is too cold,** the hypothalamus sends signals to the skin to cut back skin blood flow, as well as signals to tell the muscles to generate heat by shivering.

- **If it is too cold,** the hypothalamus may also stimulate the thyroid gland to send out hormones to make your cells burn energy faster and so make more heat.

313

The eye

- **Your eyes** are tough balls that are filled with a jelly-like substance called vitreous humour.

- **The cornea** is a thin, glassy dish across the front of your eye. It allows light rays through the eye's window, the pupil, and into the lens.

- **The iris** is the coloured, muscular ring around the pupil. The iris narrows in bright light and widens when light is dim.

- **The lens** is just behind the pupil. It focuses the picture of the world on to the back of the eye.

- **The back of the eye** is lined with millions of light-sensitive cells. This lining is called the retina, and it registers the picture and sends signals to the brain via the optic nerve.

- **There are two kinds** of light-sensitive cell in the retina – rods and cones. Rods are very sensitive and work in even dim light, but they cannot detect colours. Cones respond to colour.

- **Some kinds of cone** are very sensitive to red light, some to green and some to blue. One theory says that the colours we see depend on how strongly they affect each of these three kinds of cone (see colour vision).

- **Each of your two eyes** gives you a slightly different view of the world. The brain combines these views to give an impression of depth and 3-D solidity.

- **Although each eye** gives a slightly different view of the world, we see things largely as just one eye sees it. This dominant eye is usually the right eye.

> ...**FASCINATING FACT**...
> The picture received by your retina looks large and real –
> yet it is upside down and just a few millimetres across.

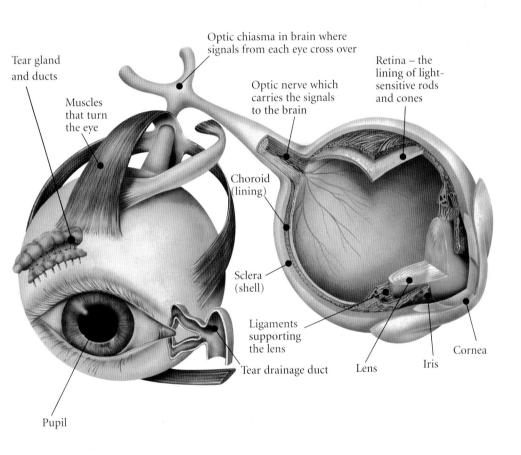

Optic chiasma in brain where
signals from each eye cross over

Tear gland
and ducts

Muscles
that turn
the eye

Optic nerve which
carries the signals
to the brain

Retina – the
lining of light-
sensitive rods
and cones

Choroid
(lining)

Sclera
(shell)

Ligaments
supporting
the lens

Tear drainage duct

Lens

Iris

Cornea

Pupil

▲ *This illustration shows your two eyeballs, with a cutaway to reveal
the cornea and lens (which projects light rays through the eye's
window) and the light-sensitive retina (which registers them).*

315

Colour vision

▲ *Seeing all the colours of the world around you depends on the colour-sensitive cone cells inside your eyes.*

- **Seeing in colour** depends on eye cells called cones.

- **Cones do not** work well in low light, which is why things seem grey at dusk.

- **Some cones** are more sensitive to red light, some are more sensitive to green and some to blue.

- **The old trichromatic theory** said that you see different colours by comparing the strength of the signals from each of the three kinds of cone – red, green and blue.

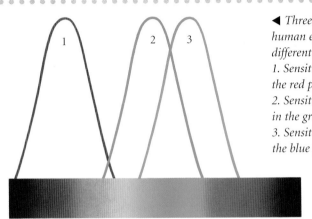

◀ *Three different types of cone in the human eye are each sensitive to a different part of the spectrum:*
1. Sensitivity of the red cone peaks in the red part of the spectrum.
2. Sensitivity of the green cone peaks in the green part of the spectrum.
3. Sensitivity of the blue cone peaks in the blue part of the spectrum.

White light spectrum

- **The trichromatic theory** does not explain how we see colours such as gold, silver and brown.

- **The opponent-process theory** said that you see colours in opposing pairs – blue and yellow, red and green.

- **In opponent-process theory,** lots of blue light is thought to reduce your awareness of yellow, and vice versa. Lots of green reduces your awareness of red, and vice versa.

- **Now scientists** combine these theories and think that colour signals from the three kinds of cone are further processed in the brain in terms of the opposing pairs.

- **Ultraviolet light** is light waves too short for you to see, although some birds and insects can see it.

. . . . **FASCINATING FACT** . . . .
You have over 5 million colour-detecting cones in the retina of each eye.

The ear

- **Pinnae** (singular, pinna) are the ear flaps you can see on the side of your head, and they are simply collecting funnels for sounds.

- **A little way inside your head,** sounds hit a thin, tight wall of skin, called the eardrum, making it vibrate.

- **When the eardrum vibrates,** it shakes three little bones called ossicles. These are the smallest bones in the body.

- **The three ossicle bones** are the malleus (hammer), the incus (anvil) and the stapes (stirrup).

- **When the ossicles vibrate,** they rattle a tiny membrane called the oval window, intensifying the vibration.

- **The oval window** is 30 times smaller in area than the eardrum.

- **Beyond the oval window** is the cochlea – a winding collection of three, liquid-filled tubes, which looks a bit like a snail shell.

- **In the middle tube** of the cochlea there is a flap which covers row upon row of tiny hairs. This is called the organ of Corti.

- **When sounds make** the eardrum vibrate, the ossicles tap on the oval window, making pressure waves shoot through the liquid in the cochlea and wash over the flap of the organ of Corti, waving it up and down.

- **When the organ of Corti waves,** it tugs on the tiny hairs under the flap. These send signals to the brain via the auditory nerve, and you hear a sound.

▼ *Most of your ear is hidden inside your head. It is an amazingly complex and delicate structure for picking up the tiny variations in air pressure created by a sound.*

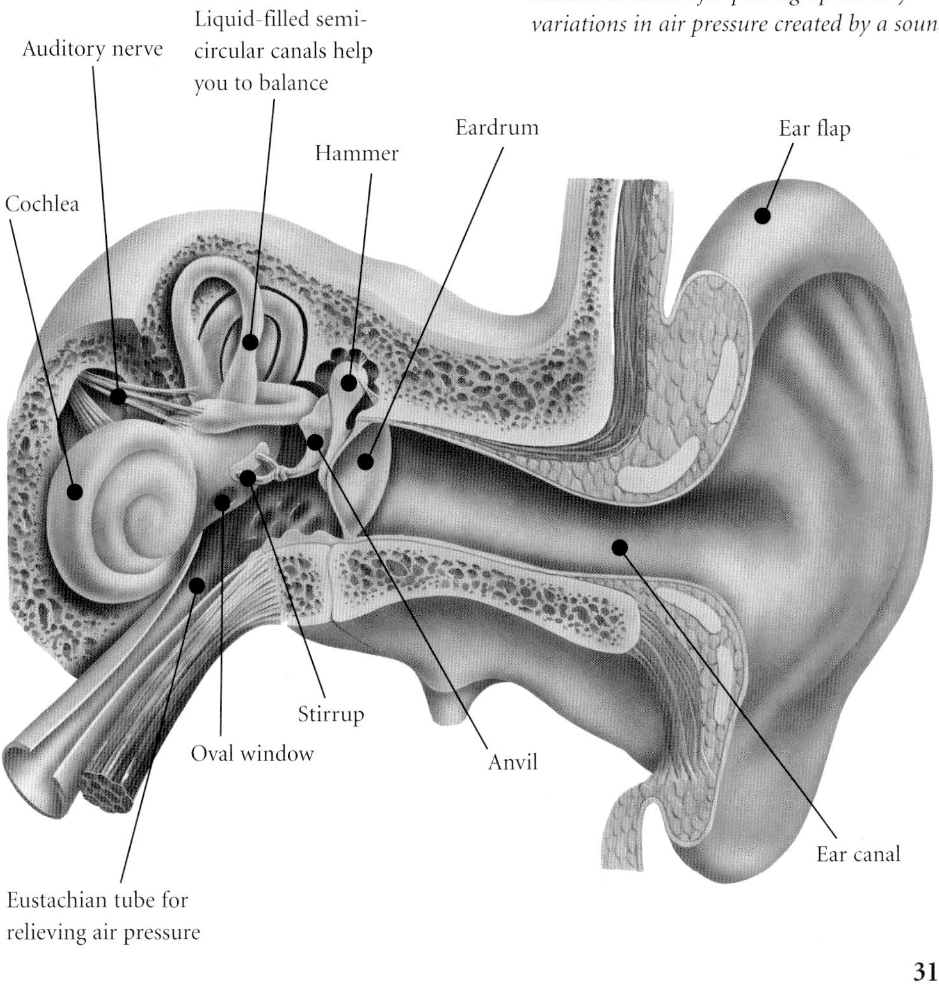

Auditory nerve

Liquid-filled semi-circular canals help you to balance

Hammer

Eardrum

Ear flap

Cochlea

Stirrup

Anvil

Oval window

Eustachian tube for relieving air pressure

Ear canal

319

Balance

- **To stay upright,** your body must send a continual stream of data about its position to your brain – and your brain must continually tell your body how to move to keep its balance.

- **Balance** is controlled in many parts of the brain, including the brain's cerebellum.

- **Your brain** finds out about your body position from many sources, including your eyes, proprioceptors around the body, and the semicircular canals and other chambers in the inner ear.

▶ *To stop you losing your balance, it helps to fix your eyes on a single focal point, so that your brain does not become confused or distracted.*

▲ *A rollercoaster ride can make you feel dizzy because the liquid inside your inner ear keeps spinning after you have stopped.*

- **Proprioceptors** are sense receptors in your skin, muscles and joints (see co-ordination).

- **The semicircular canals** are three, tiny, fluid-filled loops in your inner ear (see the ear).

- **Two chambers** (holes) called the utricle and saccule are linked to the semicircular canals.

- **When you move your head,** the fluid in the canals and cavities lags a little, pulling on hair detectors which tell your brain what is going on.

- **The canals** tell you whether you are nodding or shaking your head, and which way you are moving.

- **The utricle and saccule** tell you if you tilt your head or if its movement

321

Smell

- **Smells are scent molecules** which are taken into your nose by breathed-in air. A particular smell may be noticeable even when just a single scent molecule is mixed in with millions of air molecules.

- **The human nose** can tell the difference between more than 10,000 different chemicals.

- **Dogs can pick up** smells that are 10,000 times fainter than the ones humans are able to detect.

- **Inside the nose,** scent molecules are picked up by a patch of scent-sensitive cells called the olfactory epithelium.

▲ *Scents are closely linked to emotions in the brain, and perfume can be a powerful way of triggering feelings.*

- **Olfactory** means 'to do with the sense of smell'.

- **The olfactory epithelium** contains over 25 million receptor cells.

- **Each of the receptor cells** in the olfactory epithelium has up to 20 or so scent-detecting hairs called cilia.

- **When they are triggered** by scent molecules, the cilia send signals to a cluster of nerves called the olfactory bulb, which then sends messages to the part of the brain that recognizes smell.

- **The part of the brain** that deals with smell is closely linked to the parts that deal with memories and emotions. This may be why smells can evoke vivid memories.

- **By the age of 20,** you will have lost 20% of your sense of smell. By 60, you will have lost 60% of it.

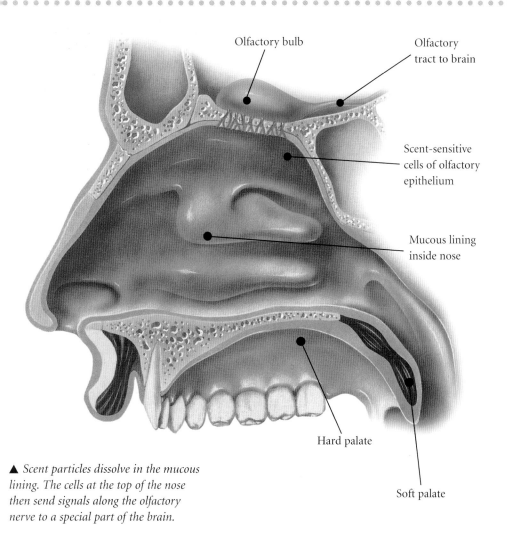

Olfactory bulb

Olfactory tract to brain

Scent-sensitive cells of olfactory epithelium

Mucous lining inside nose

Hard palate

Soft palate

▲ *Scent particles dissolve in the mucous lining. The cells at the top of the nose then send signals along the olfactory nerve to a special part of the brain.*

Taste

▲ *As well as tasting the flavour of ice cream, the tongue can also tell that it is cold and smooth.*

- **The sense of taste** is the crudest of our five senses, giving us less information about the world than any other sense.

- **Taste** is triggered by certain chemicals in food, which dissolve in the saliva in the mouth, and then send information to a particular part of the brain via sensory nerve cells on the tongue.

▶ *Certain parts of the tongue are more sensitive to one flavour than to others, as shown in this diagram.*

- **Taste buds** are receptor cells found around tiny bumps called papillae on the surface of your tongue.

- **Taste buds** are sensitive to four basic flavours: sweet, sour, bitter and salty.

- **The back of the tongue** contains big round papaillae shaped like an upside-down V. This is where bitter flavours are sensed.

- **The front of the tongue** is where fungiform (mushroom-like) papillae and filiform (hairlike) papillae carry taste buds that detect sweet, sour and salty flavours.

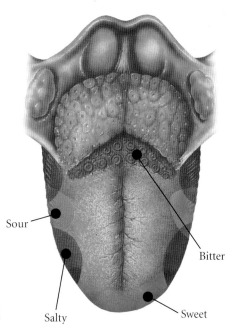

Sour

Bitter

Salty

Sweet

- **As well as taste,** the tongue can also feel the texture and temperature of food.

- **Your sense of taste** works closely together with your sense of smell to make the flavour of food more interesting.

- **Strong tastes,** such as spicy food, rely less on the sense of smell than on pain-sensitive nerve endings in the tongue.

- **People can learn** to distinguish more flavours and tastes than normal, as is the case with tea- or wine-tasters.

325

Touch

- **Touch,** or physical contact, is one of five sensations that are spread all over your body in your skin. The others are pressure, pain, heat and cold.

- **There are sense receptors** everywhere in your skin, but places like your face have more than your back.

- **There are 200,000** hot and cold receptors in your skin, plus 500,000 touch and pressure receptors, and nearly 3 million pain receptors.

- **Free nerve-endings** are rather like the bare end of a wire. They respond to all five kinds of skin sensation and are almost everywhere in your skin.

- **There are specialized receptors** in certain places, each named after their discoverer.

▲ *The fingertips are where your sense of touch is most sensitive.*

. . . **FASCINATING FACT** . . .
Your brain knows just how hard you are touched from how fast nerve signals arrive.

▲ *As we grow up, we gradually learn to identify more and more things instantly through the sense of touch.*

- **Pacini's corpuscles** and Meissner's endings react instantly to sudden pressure.
- **Krause's bulbs,** Merkel's discs and Ruffini's endings respond to steady pressure.
- **Krause's bulbs** are also sensitive to cold.
- **Ruffini's endings** also react to changes in temperature.

327

Co-ordination

▲ *Dancing of any kind tests the body's balance and co-ordination to its limits.*

- **Co-ordination** means balanced or skilful movement.

- **To make you move,** your brain has to send signals out along nerves telling all the muscles involved exactly what to do.

- **Co-ordination of the muscles** is handled by the cerebellum at the back of your brain (see the brain).

- **The cerebellum** is given instructions by the brain's motor cortex (see the cortex).

- **The cerebellum sends** its commands via the basal ganglia in the middle of the brain.

- **Proprioceptors** are nerve cells that are sensitive to movement, pressure or stretching. Proprioceptor means 'one's own sensors'.

- **Proprioceptors are all over your body** – in muscles, tendons and joints – and they all send signals to your brain telling it the position or posture of every part of your body.

- **The hair cells** in the balance organs of your ear are also proprioceptors (see balance).

▲ *Ball skills demand incredible muscle co-ordination, relying on high-speed signals sent from the brain.*

····FASCINATING FACT····
Proprioceptors allow you to touch forefingers behind your back.

Skin

▲ *Skin colour varies from person to person because of melanin, a pigment which protects skin from the sun's harmful rays. The more melanin you have in your skin, the darker it is.*

- **Skin is your protective coat,** shielding your body from the weather and from infection, and helping to keep it at just the right temperature.

- **Skin is your largest sense receptor**, responding to touch, pressure, heat and cold (see touch).

- **Skin makes** vitamin D for your body from sunlight.

- **The epidermis** (the thin outer layer) is just dead cells.

... **FASCINATING FACT** ...
Even though its thickness averages just 2 mm, your skin gets an eighth of all your blood supply.

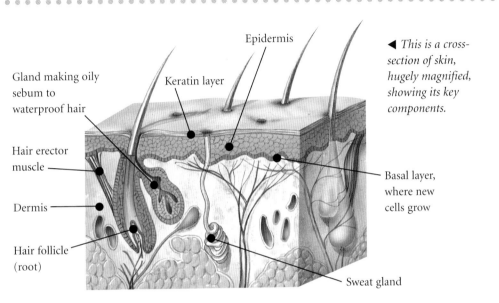

◄ This is a cross-section of skin, hugely magnified, showing its key components.

Epidermis

Keratin layer

Gland making oily sebum to waterproof hair

Hair erector muscle

Dermis

Hair follicle (root)

Basal layer, where new cells grow

Sweat gland

- **The epidermis is made mainly** of a tough protein called keratin – the remains of skin cells that die off.

- **Below the epidermis** is a thick layer of living cells called the dermis, which contains the sweat glands.

- **Hair roots** have tiny muscles that pull the hair upright when you are cold, giving you goose bumps.

- **Skin is 6 mm thick** on the soles of your feet, and just 0.5 mm thick on your eyelids.

- **The epidermis** contains cells that make the dark pigment melanin – this gives dark-skinned people their colour and fair-skinned people a tan.

Hair

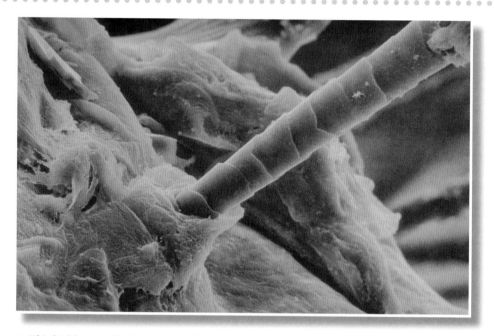

▲ *This highly magnified photograph shows a human hair growing from inside the skin.*

- **Humans are one of** very few land mammals to have almost bare skin. But even humans have soft, downy hair all over, with thicker hair in places.

- **Lanugo** is the very fine hair babies are covered in when they are inside the womb, from the fourth month of pregnancy onwards.

- **Vellus hair** is fine, downy hair that grows all over your body until you reach puberty.

- **Terminal hair** is the coarser hair on your head, as well as the hair that grows on men's chins and around an adult's genitals.

- **The colour of your hair** depends on how much there are of pigments called melanin and carotene in the hairs.

- **Hair is red or auburn** if it contains carotene.

- **Black, brown and blonde hair** get its colour from black melanin.

- **Each hair** is rooted in a pit called the hair follicle. The hair is held in place by its club-shaped tip, the bulb.

- **Hair grows** as cells fill with a material called keratin and die, and pile up inside the follicle.

- **The average person** has 120,000 head hairs and each grows about 3 millimetres per week.

▲ *The colour of your hair depends upon melanin made in melanocytes at the root.*

...FASCINATING FACT...
Hair in poor condition is said to be lifeless. In fact, all hair is lifeless since it is made of keratin, the material left by dead cells.

The nervous system

- **The nervous system** is your body's control and communication system, made up of nerves and the brain. Nerves are your body's hot-lines, carrying instant messages from the brain to every organ and muscle – and sending back an endless stream of data to the brain about what is going on both inside and outside your body.

- **The central nervous system** (CNS) is the brain and spinal cord (see central nervous system).

- **The peripheral nervous system** (PNS) is made up of the nerves that branch out from the CNS to the rest of the body.

▲ *A spider has a nervous system with about 100,000 nerve cells, while a human being has around 60 billion.*

- **The main branches of the PNS** are the 12 cranial nerves located in the head, and the 31 pairs of spinal nerves that branch off the spinal cord.

- **The nerves of the PNS** are made up of long bundles of nerve fibres, which in turn are made from the long axons (tails) of nerve cells, bound together like the wires in a telephone cable.

334

Brain

Cranial nerves

Spinal cord

Brachial 'plexus'
(nerve junction)

Ulnar
nerve

Lateral
pectoral
nerve

Lumbar
nerves

Sacral
nerves

Radial nerve

Sciatic nerve

Peroneal nerve

Femoral
nerve

Lateral
plantar
nerve

- **In many places**, sensory nerves (which carry sense signals from the body to the brain) run alongside motor nerves (which carry the brain's commands telling muscles to move).

- **Some PNS nerves** are as wide as your thumb. The longest is the sciatic, which runs from the base of the spine to the knee.

- **The autonomic nervous system** (ANS) is the body's third nervous system. It controls all internal body processes such as breathing automatically, without you even being aware of it.

- **The ANS** is split into two complementary (balancing) parts – the sympathetic and the parasympathetic. The sympathetic system speeds up body processes when they need to be more active, such as when the body is exercising or under stress. The parasympathetic slows them down.

◄ *The nervous system is an incredibly intricate network of nerves linking your brain to every part of the body. The nerves of the peripheral nervous system branch out to every limb and body part from the central nervous system (the brain and spinal cord).*

335

Nerve cells

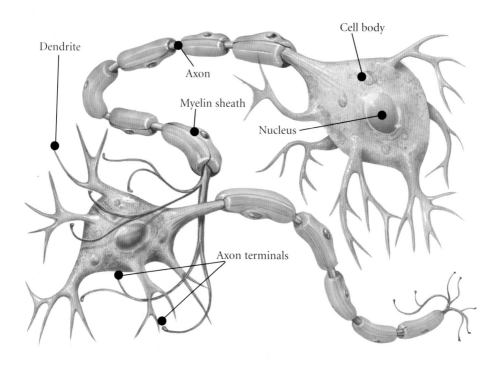

Dendrite

Axon

Myelin sheath

Cell body

Nucleus

Axon terminals

▲ *Nerve cells, or neurons, are the 'wires' of the body's nervous system. They carry messages within, to and from the central nervous system along fine branches called dendrites and long tails called axons.*

- **Nerves** are made of very specialized cells called neurons.

- **Neurons** are shaped like a spider, with a nucleus at the centre, lots of branching threads called dendrites, and a winding tail called an axon which can be up to 1 m long.

- **Axon terminals** on the axons of one neuron link to the dendrites or body cell of another neuron.

- **Neurons link up** like beads on a string to make your nervous system.

- **Most cells are** short-lived and are constantly being replaced by new ones. Neurons, however, are very long-lived – some are never actually replaced after you are born.

- **Nerve signals** travel as electrical pulses, each pulse lasting about 0.001 seconds.

- **When nerves are resting** there are extra sodium ions with a positive electrical charge on the outside of the nerve cell, and extra negative ions inside.

- **When a nerve fires,** gates open in the cell wall all along the nerve, and positive ions rush in to join the negative ions. This makes an electrical pulse.

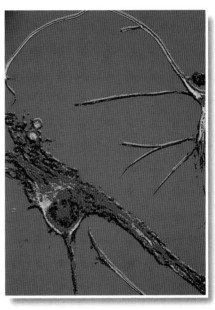

▲ *Microscopically tiny nerve cells like this were first seen when stained with silver nitrate by the Italian scientist Camillo Golgi in the 1870s.*

- **Long-distance nerves** are insulated (covered) by a sheath of a fatty substance, myelin, to keep the signal strong.

- **Myelinated (myelin-sheathed) nerves** shoot signals through very fast – at more than 100 metres per second.

- **Ordinary nerves** send signals at about 1 to 2 metres per second.

Synapses

◀ Our changes of mood can be caused by imbalances of the neurotransmitter, serotonin, in our nervous system.

- **Synapses** are the tiny gaps between nerve cells.

- **When a nerve signal** goes from one nerve cell to another, it must be transmitted (sent) across the synapse by special chemicals called neurotransmitters.

- **Droplets of neurotransmitter** are released into the synapse whenever a nerve signal arrives.

- **As the droplets of neurotransmitter** lock on to the receiving nerve's receptors, they fire the signal onwards.

338

- **Each receptor site** on a nerve-ending only reacts to certain neurotransmitters. Others have no effect.

- **Sometimes** several signals must arrive before enough neurotransmitter is released to fire the receiving nerve.

- **More than 40 neurotransmitter chemicals** have been identified.

- **Dopamine** is a neurotransmitter that works in the parts of the brain that control movement and learning. Parkinson's disease may develop when the nerves that produce dopamine break down.

- **Serotonin** is a neurotransmitter that is linked to sleeping and waking up, and also to your mood.

- **Acetylcholine** is a neurotransmitter that may be involved in memory, and also in the nerves that control muscle movement.

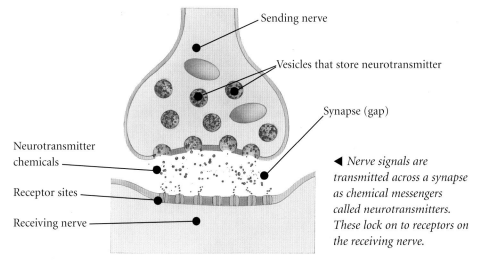

Sending nerve

Vesicles that store neurotransmitter

Synapse (gap)

Neurotransmitter chemicals

Receptor sites

Receiving nerve

◀ *Nerve signals are transmitted across a synapse as chemical messengers called neurotransmitters. These lock on to receptors on the receiving nerve.*

Sensory nerves

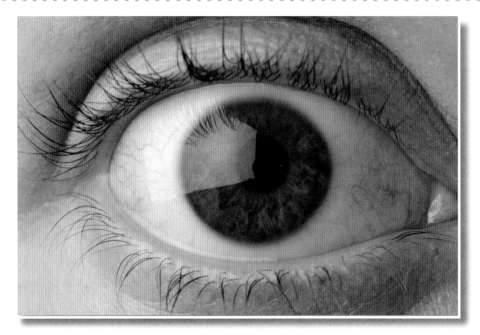

▲ *Sight is the sense most people rely on above all the others.*

- **Sensory nerves** are the nerves that carry information to your brain from sense receptors all over your body.

- **Each sense receptor** in the body is linked to the brain by a sensory nerve.

- **Most sensory nerves** feed their signals to the somatosensory cortex, which is the strip situated around the top of the brain where sensations are registered (see the cortex).

- **Massive bundles** of sensory nerve cells form the nerves that link major senses such as the eyes, ears and nose to the brain.

▶ *Some of our most pleasant feelings, such as being hugged or stroked, are sent to the brain by sensory nerves.*

- **The eyes are linked to the brain** by the optic nerves.

- **The ears are linked to the brain** by the auditory nerves.

- **The nose is linked to the brain** by the olfactory tracts.

- **In the skin**, many sense receptors are simply 'free' – meaning they are exposed sensory nerve-endings.

- **The sciatic nerve** to each leg is the longest nerve in the body. Its name is from the Latin for 'pain in the thigh'.

- **We can tell** how strong a sensation is by how fast the sensory nerve fires signals to the brain. But no matter how strong the sensation is, the nerve does not go on firing at the same rate and soon slows down.

341

Motor nerves

- **Motor nerves** are connected to your muscles and tell your muscles to move.

- **Each major muscle** has many motor nerve-endings that instruct it to contract (tighten).

- **Motor nerves cross over** from one side of your body to the other at the top of your spinal cord. This means that signals from the right side of your brain go to the left side of your body, and vice versa.

- **Each motor nerve** is paired to a proprioceptor on the muscle and its tendons (see co-ordination). This sends signals to the brain to say whether the muscle is tensed or relaxed.

- **If the strain** on a tendon increases, the proprioceptor sends a signal to the brain. The brain adjusts the motor signals to the muscle so it contracts more or less.

- **Motor nerve signals** originate in a part of the brain called the motor cortex (see the cortex).

- **All the motor nerves** (apart from those in the head) branch out from the spinal cord.

- **The gut** has no motor nerve-endings but plenty of sense endings, so you can feel it but cannot move it consciously.

- **The throat** has motor nerve-endings but few sense endings, so you can move it but not feel it.

- **Motor neuron disease** attacks motor nerves within the central nervous system.

◀ *Motor nerves fire signals to the muscles to make them move to hit the ball.*

Central nervous system

- **The central nervous system** (CNS) is made up of the brain and the spinal cord (the nerves of the spine).

- **The CNS** contains billions of densely packed interneurons – nerve cells with very short connecting axons (see nerve cells).

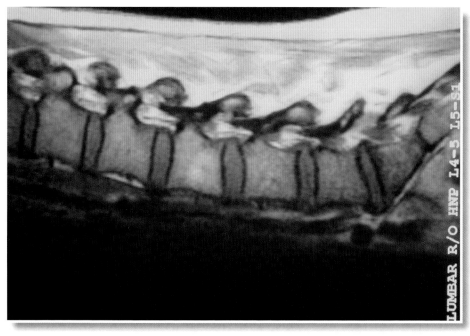

▲ *The spinal cord, shown here in this CAT scan, together with the brain and nerves, form the body's central information system, making sure all its different parts work together efficiently.*

Brain

Spinal cord

Thoracic nerves

Cervical nerves

Lumbar nerves

Sacral nerves

▲ *Spinal nerves branch off the spinal cord in pairs, with one nerve on either side. They are arranged in four groups, and there is one pair between each of the neighbouring 32 vertebrae.*

- **The CNS is cushioned** from damage by a surrounding bath of liquid called cerebrospinal fluid.

- **There are 86 main nerves** branching off the CNS.

- **There are 12 pairs of cranial nerves,** and 31 pairs of spinal nerves.

- **Cranial nerves** are the 12 pairs of nerves that branch off the CNS out of the brain.

- **Spinal nerves** are the 31 pairs of nerves that branch off the spinal cord.

- **The spinal nerves** are made up of 8 cervical nerve pairs, 12 thoracic pairs, 5 lumbar pairs, 5 sacral pairs and one coccyx pair.

- **Many spinal nerves** join up just outside the spine in five spaghetti junctions called plexuses.

The spinal cord

- **The spinal cord** is the bundle of nerves running down the middle of the backbone.

- **The spinal cord** is the route for all nerve signals travelling between the brain and the body.

- **The spinal cord** can actually work independently of the brain, sending out responses to the muscles directly.

- **The outside** of the spinal cord is made of the long tails or axons of nerve cells and is called white matter; the inside is made of the main nerve bodies and is called grey matter.

- **Your spinal cord** is about 43 cm long and 1 cm thick. It stops growing when you are about five years old.

White matter

Grey matter

Nerve root

Spinal nerve

Vertebra (single backbone)

Disc between two vertebrae

▶ *The spinal cord is encased in a tunnel in the backbone at the back of each vertebra. Nerves branch off to the body in pairs either side.*

- **Damage to the spinal cord** can cause paralysis.

- **Injuries below the neck** can cause paraplegia – paralysis below the waist.

- **Injuries to the neck** can cause quadriplegia – paralysis below the neck.

- **Descending pathways** are groups of nerves that carry nerve signals down the spinal cord – typically signals from the brain for muscles to move.

- **Ascending pathways** are groups of nerves that carry nerve signals up the spinal cord – typically signals from the skin and internal body sensors going to the brain.

◀ *When the spinal cord gets damaged, nerves cannot carry messages from the brain to the muscles to tell the body to move. This is called paraplegia, or paralysis below the waist, and means the person will be unable to walk.*

347

The brain

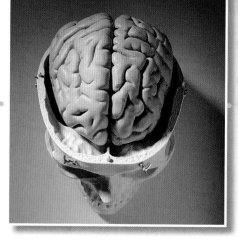

- **The human brain** is made up of over 100 billion nerve cells called neurons.

- **Each neuron** is connected to as many as 25,000 other neurons – so the brain has trillions and trillions of different pathways for nerve signals.

- **Girls' brains** weigh 2.5% of their body weight, on average, while boys' brains weigh 2%.

▲ *Taking the top off the skull shows the brain to be a pinky-grey mass which looks rather like a giant walnut.*

- **About 0.85 litres** of blood shoots through your brain every minute. The brain may be as little as 2% of your body weight, but it demands 12 – 15% of your blood supply.

- **An elephant's brain** weighs four times as much as the human brain. Some apes, monkeys and dolphins are quite near our brain–body ratio.

- **The cerebral cortex** is the outside of the brain. If laid out flat, it would cover a bed.

- **The left hemisphere (half)** of the upper part of the brain is more dominant in speech, writing and general language, the right half in pictures and ideas.

- **Conscious thoughts and actions** happen in the cerebral cortex.

- **A human brain** has a cerebral cortex four times as big as a chimpanzee, about 20 times as big as a monkey's, and about 300 times as big as a rat's.

- **Unconscious, automatic activities** like breathing, hunger and sleep are controlled by structures such as the brain stem and the hypothalamus.

> ... **FASCINATING FACT** ...
> Scientists can now grow human brain
> cells in a laboratory dish.

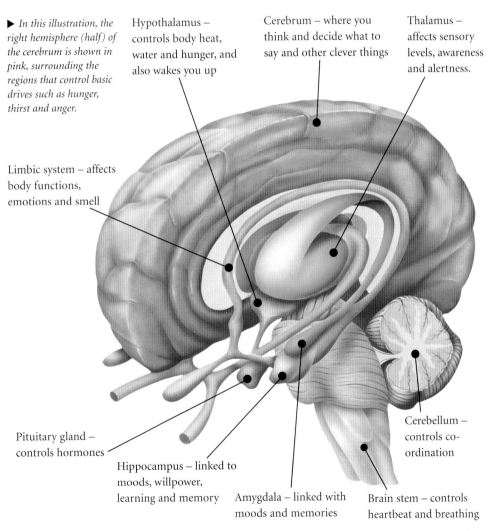

▶ *In this illustration, the right hemisphere (half) of the cerebrum is shown in pink, surrounding the regions that control basic drives such as hunger, thirst and anger.*

Hypothalamus – controls body heat, water and hunger, and also wakes you up

Cerebrum – where you think and decide what to say and other clever things

Thalamus – affects sensory levels, awareness and alertness.

Limbic system – affects body functions, emotions and smell

Pituitary gland – controls hormones

Hippocampus – linked to moods, willpower, learning and memory

Amygdala – linked with moods and memories

Cerebellum – controls co-ordination

Brain stem – controls heartbeat and breathing

349

The cortex

- **A cortex** is the outer layer of any organ, such as the brain or the kidney.

- **The brain's cortex** is also known as the cerebral cortex. It is a layer of interconnected nerve cells around the outside of the brain, called 'grey matter'.

- **The cerebral cortex** is where many signals from the senses are registered in the brain.

- **The visual cortex** is around the lower back of the brain. It is the place where all the things you see are registered in the brain.

- **The somatosensory cortex** is a band running over the top of the brain like a headband. This where a touch on any part of the body is registered.

- **The motor cortex** is a band just in front of the sensory cortex. It sends out signals to body muscles to move.

- **The more nerve ending**s there are in a particular part of the body, the more of the sensory cortex it occupies.

- **The lips and face** take up a huge proportion of the sensory cortex.

- **The hands** take up almost as much of the sensory cortex as the face.

▶ *The cortex is only 5 mm thick, but flattened out would cover an area almost as big as an office desk, and contains at least 50 billion nerve cells.*

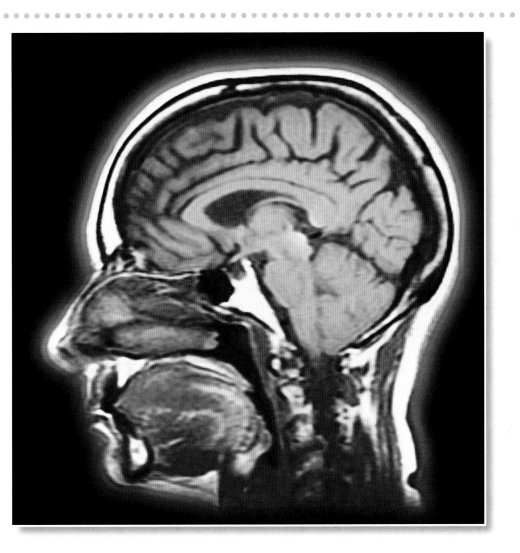

Sleeping

- **When you are asleep,** many of your body functions go on as normal – even your brain goes on receiving sense signals. But your body may save energy and do routine repairs.

- **Lack of sleep** can be dangerous. A newborn baby needs 18 to 20 hours sleep a day. An adult needs around 7 to 8.

- **Sleep is controlled** in the brain stem (see the brain). Dreaming is stimulated by signals fired from a part of the brain stem called the pons.

▲ *The traditional tale of Rip Van Winkle tells of how he fell into a deep sleep for 20 years. When he finally woke up, he couldn't understand why the world was so different.*

- **When you are awake,** there is little pattern to the electricity created by the firing of the brain's nerve cells. But as you sleep, more regular waves appear.

- **While you are asleep,** alpha waves sweep across the brain every 0.1 seconds. Theta waves are slower.

◀ *We all shut our eyes to sleep. Other marked changes to the body include the pattern of the brain's activity, relaxation of skeletal muscles, reduced urine production and slower heartbeat, breathing and digestive activity.*

- **For the first 90 minutes** of sleep, your sleep gets deeper and the brain waves become stronger.

- **After about 90 minutes** of sleep, your brain suddenly starts to buzz with activity, yet you are hard to wake up.

- **After 90 minutes** of sleep, your eyes begin to flicker from side to side under their lids. This is called Rapid Eye Movement (REM) sleep.

- **REM sleep** is thought to show that you are dreaming.

- **While you sleep**, ordinary deeper sleep alternates with spells of REM lasting up to half an hour.

353

Mood

- **Mood is** your state of mind – whether you are happy or sad, angry or afraid, overjoyed or depressed.

- **Moods and emotions** seem to be strongly linked to the structures in the centre of the brain, where unconscious activities are controlled (see the brain).

- **Moods** have three elements – how you feel, what happens to your body, and what moods make you do.

- **Some scientists** think the way you feel causes changes in the body – you are happy so you smile, for example.

- **Other scientists** think changes in the body alter the way you feel – smiling makes you happy.

▶ *The reasons why we react the way we do in certain situations, such as feeling happy, is still unclear to scientists. But emotions like these are what make us unique as human beings.*

- **Yet other scientists** think moods start automatically – before you even know it – when something triggers off a reaction in the thalamus in the centre of the brain.

- **The thalamus** then sends mood signals to the brain's cortex and you become aware of the mood.

- **The thalamus** also sets off automatic changes in the body through the nerves and hormones.

- **Certain memories or experiences** are so strongly linked in your mind that they can often trigger a mood automatically.

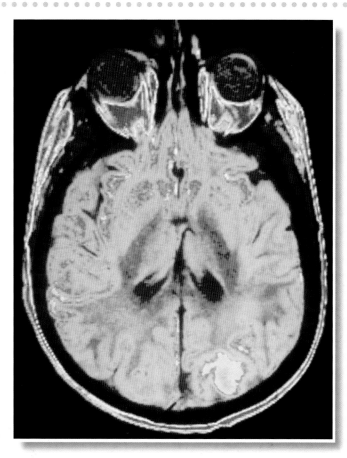

▲ *Scientists are only just beginning to discover how moods and emotions are linked to particular parts of the brain.*

Thinking

- **Some scientists** claim that we humans are the only living things that are selfconscious, meaning that we alone are actually aware that we are thinking.

- **No one knows** how consciousness works – it is one of science's last great mysteries.

- **Most of your thoughts** seem to take place in the cerebrum (at the top of your brain), and different kinds of thought are linked to different areas, called association areas.

- **Each half of the cerebrum** has four rounded ends called lobes – two at the front, called frontal and temporal lobes, and two at the back, called occipital and parietal lobes.

- **The frontal lobe** is linked to your personality and it is where you have your bright ideas.

- **The temporal lobe** enables you to hear and understand what people are saying to you.

- **The occipital lobe** is where you work out what your eyes see.

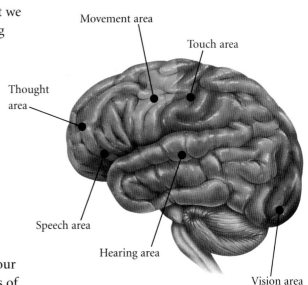

Movement area

Touch area

Thought area

Speech area

Hearing area

Vision area

▲ *The 'thought' area at the front of the brain helps us to think, solve problems and be creative.*

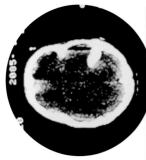

▲ ▶ *Modern scanning techniques have taught us a great deal about the human brain and brain processes by allowing us to see brains in action.*

- **The left half of the brain** (left hemisphere) controls the right side of the body. The right half (right hemisphere) controls the left side.

- **One half of the brain** is always dominant (in charge). Usually, the left brain is dominant, which is why 90% of people are right-handed.

- **The parietal lobe** is where you register touch, heat and cold, and pain.

Memory

▲ *Special moments like birthday parties leave long-lasting memories.*

- **When you remember** something, your brain probably stores it by creating new nerve connections.

- **You have** three types of memory – sensory, short-term and long-term.

- **Sensory memory** is when you go on feeling a sensation for a moment after it stops.

- **Short-term memory** is when the brain stores things for a few seconds, like a phone number you remember long enough to press the buttons.

- **Long-term memory** is memory that can last for months or maybe even your whole life.

- **Your brain** seems to have two ways of remembering things for the long term. Scientists call these two different ways declarative and non-declarative memories.

- **Non-declarative memories** are skills you teach yourself by practising, such as playing badminton or the flute. Repetition establishes nerve pathways.

- **Declarative memories** are either episodic or semantic. Each may be sent by the hippocampus region of the brain to the correct place in the cortex, the brain's wrinkly outer layer where you do most of your thinking.

▲ *Learning to play the violin involves non-declarative memory – in which nerve pathways become reinforced by repeated use. This is why practising is so important.*

- **Episodic memories** are memories of striking events in your life, such as breaking your leg or your first day at a new school. You not only recall facts, but sensations too.

- **Semantic memories** are facts such as dates. Scientists think these are stored in the left temporal lobe, at the front left-hand side of your brain.

359

The thyroid gland

- **The thyroid** is a small gland about the size of two joined cherries. It is situated at the front of your neck, just below the larynx (see airways and vocal cords).

- **The thyroid** secretes (releases) three important hormones – tri-iodothyronine (T3), thyroxine (T4) and calcitonin.

- **The thyroid hormones** affect how energetic you are by controlling your metabolic rate.

- **Your metabolic rate** is the rate at which your body cells use glucose.

▶ *The thyroid is part of your energy control system, telling your body cells to work faster or slower in order to keep you warm or to make your muscles work harder.*

- **T3 and T4** hormones control metabolic rate by circulating into the blood and stimulating cells to convert more glucose.

- **If the thyroid** sends out too little T3 and T4, you get cold and tired, your skin gets dry and you put on weight.

- **If the thyroid** sends out too much T3 and T4, you become nervous, sweaty and overactive, and you will also lose weight.

- **The amount of T3 and T4** sent out by the thyroid depends on how much thyroid-stimulating hormone is sent to it from the pituitary gland (see the brain).

- **If the levels of T3 and T4** in the blood drop, the pituitary gland sends out extra thyroid-stimulating hormone to tell the thyroid to produce more.

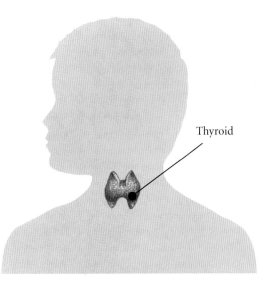

Thyroid

▲ *The thyroid gland is usually described as the size and shape of a bow tie, and is even situated in the same place.*

361

Chromosomes

- **Chromosomes** are the microscopically tiny, twisted threads inside every cell that carry your body's life instructions in chemical form.

- **There are 46 chromosomes** in each of your body cells, divided into 23 pairs.

- **One of each chromosome pair** came from your mother and the other from your father.

- **In a girl's 23 chromosome pairs,** each half exactly matches the other (the set from the mother is equivalent to the set from the father).

- **Boys** have 22 matching chromosome pairs, but the 23rd pair is made up of two odd chromosomes.

- **The 23rd chromosome pair** decides what sex you are, and the sex chromosomes are called X and Y.

▶ *A girl turns out to be a girl because she gets an X chromosome from her father. A boy gets a Y chromosome from his father.*

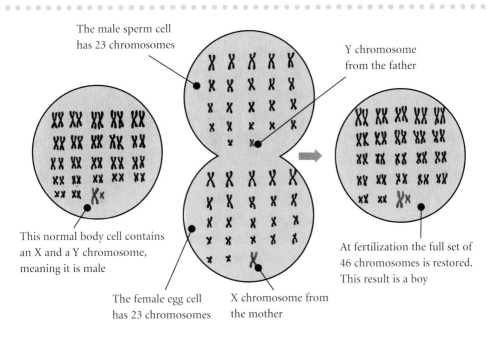

The male sperm cell has 23 chromosomes

Y chromosome from the father

This normal body cell contains an X and a Y chromosome, meaning it is male

At fertilization the full set of 46 chromosomes is restored. This result is a boy

The female egg cell has 23 chromosomes

X chromosome from the mother

▲ *Two sets of chromosomes, one each from the mother and the father, combine at fertilization.*

- **Girls have two X chromosomes,** but boys have an X and a Y chromosome.

- **In every matching pair,** both chromosomes give your body life instructions for the same thing.

- **The chemical instructions** on each chromosome come in thousands of different units called genes.

- **Genes for the same feature** appear in the same locus (place) on each matching pair of chromosomes in every human body cell. Scientists one day hope to find out how the entire pattern, called the genome, works.

Genes

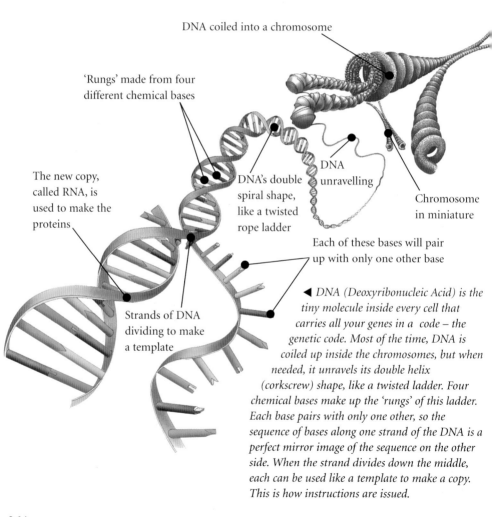

DNA coiled into a chromosome

'Rungs' made from four different chemical bases

The new copy, called RNA, is used to make the proteins

DNA's double spiral shape, like a twisted rope ladder

DNA unravelling

Chromosome in miniature

Each of these bases will pair up with only one other base

Strands of DNA dividing to make a template

◄ *DNA (Deoxyribonucleic Acid) is the tiny molecule inside every cell that carries all your genes in a code – the genetic code. Most of the time, DNA is coiled up inside the chromosomes, but when needed, it unravels its double helix (corkscrew) shape, like a twisted ladder. Four chemical bases make up the 'rungs' of this ladder. Each base pairs with only one other, so the sequence of bases along one strand of the DNA is a perfect mirror image of the sequence on the other side. When the strand divides down the middle, each can be used like a template to make a copy. This is how instructions are issued.*

- **Genes** are the body's chemical instructions for your entire life – for growing up, surviving, having children and, perhaps, even for dying.

- **Individual genes** are instructions to make particular proteins – the body's building-block molecules.

- **Small sets of genes** control features such as the colour of your hair or your eyes, or create a particular body process such as digesting fat from food.

- **Each of your body cells** (except egg and sperm cells) carries identical sets of genes. This is because all your cells were made by other cells splitting in two, starting with the original egg cell in your mother.

- **Your genes are a mixture** – half come from your mother and half from your father (see chromosomes). But none of your brothers or sisters will get the same mix, unless you are identical twins.

- **Genes make us unique** – making us tall or short, fair or dark, brilliant dancers or speakers, healthy or likely to get particular illnesses, and so on.

- **Genes are sections** of DNA – a microscopically tiny molecule inside each cell.

- **DNA** is shaped in a double helix with linking bars, like a twisted rope ladder.

> **...FASCINATING FACT...**
> There are more than 30,000 individual genes inside every single cell of your body.

- **The bars of DNA** are four special chemicals called bases – guanine, adenine, cytosine and thymine.

- **The bases in DNA** are set in groups of three called codons, and the order of the bases in each codon varies to provide a chemical code for the cell to make a particular amino acid.

365

Heredity

▲ *Sisters tend to look alike, as they have inherited similar genes from their parents.*

- **Your heredity** is all the body characteristics you inherit from your parents, whether it is your mother's black hair or your father's knobbly knees.

- **Characteristics** are passed on by the genes carried on your chromosomes.

- **The basic laws** of heredity were discovered by the Austrian monk Gregor Mendel 150 years ago.

- **Your body characteristics** are a mix of two sets of instructions – one from your mother's chromosomes and the other from your father's.

- **Each characteristic** is the work of only one gene – either your mother's or your father's. This gene is said to be 'expressed'.

- **A gene that is not expressed** does not vanish. Instead, it stays dormant (inactive) in your chromosomes, possibly to pass on to your children.

- **A gene** that is always expressed is called a dominant gene.

- **A recessive gene** is one that loses out to a dominant gene and stays dormant.

- **A recessive gene** may be expressed when there is no competition – that is, when the genes from both of your parents are recessive.

▲ *The gene for blue eyes is recessive, but if a girl gets a blue-eye gene from both of her parents, she may have blue eyes.*

Hormones

- **Hormones are** the body's chemical messengers, released from stores at times to trigger certain reactions in different parts of the body.

- **Most hormones** are endocrine hormones which are spread around your body in your bloodstream.

- **Each hormone** is a molecule with a certain shape that creates a certain effect on target cells.

- **Hormones are controlled** by feedback systems. This means they are only released when their store gets the right trigger – which may be a chemical in the blood or another hormone.

- **Major hormone sources** include: the pituitary gland just below the brain; the thyroid gland; the adrenal glands; the pancreas; a woman's ovaries; a man's testes.

▶ *During an exhilarating moment, adrenalin boosts your breathing and heartbeat, and makes your skin sweat and eyes widen.*

- **The pituitary** is the source of many important hormones, including growth hormones which spur growing.

- **Adrenaline** is released by the adrenals to ready your body for action.

- **Endorphins and enkephalins** block or relieve pain.

- **Oestrogen and progesterone** are female sex hormones that control a woman's monthly cycle.

- **Testosterone** is a male sex hormone which controls the workings of a man's sex organs.

▲ *Women over the age of around 45 to 55 stop producing some female hormones.*

Sex hormones

- **The sexual development** of girls and boys depends on the sex hormones (see reproduction).

- **Sex hormones** control the development of primary and secondary sexual characteristics, and regulate all sex-related processes such as sperm and egg production.

- **Primary sexual characteristics** are the major sexual organs, in particular the genitals.

- **Secondary sexual characteristics** are other differences between the sexes, such as men's beards.

- **There are three main types of sex hormone** – androgens, oestrogen and progesterone.

▶ *A girl's sexual development depends on female sex hormones.*

▶ *Men grow facial hair due to the male sex hormone, testosterone.*

- **Androgens** are male hormones such as testosterone. They make a boy's body develop features such as a beard, deepen his voice and make his penis grow.

- **Oestrogen** is the female hormone made mainly in the ovaries. It not only makes a girl develop her sexual organs, but controls her monthly menstrual cycle.

- **Progesterone** is the female hormone that prepares a girl's uterus (womb) for pregnancy every month.

- **Some contraceptive pills** have oestrogen in them to prevent the ovaries releasing their egg cells.

> **. . . FASCINATING FACT . . .**
> Boys have female sex hormones and girls male
> sex hormones, but they usually have no effect.

Puberty

- **Puberty** is the time of life when girls and boys mature sexually.

- **The age of puberty varies hugely,** but on average it is between 10 and 13 years for girls, and between 11 and 15 years for boys.

- **Puberty is started** by two hormones sent out by the pituitary gland (see the brain) – the follicle-stimulating hormone and the luteinizing hormone.

- **During puberty, a girl** will develop breasts and grow hair under her arms and around her genitals.

- **Inside her body,** a girl's ovaries grow ten times as big and release sex hormones (see reproduction – female).

- **The sex hormones** oestrogen and progesterone spur the development of a girl's

▶ *In their early teens, girls go through puberty and begin to develop the sexual characteristics*

▲ *Puberty is part of the longer and more complex time called adolescence, when young people start to change, not only physically, but in the way they think and behave as well.*

- **A year or so after puberty begins,** a girl has her menarche (the first menstrual period). When her periods come regularly, she will be able to have a baby.

- **For a boy during puberty,** his testes grow and hair sprouts on his face, under his arms and around his genitals (see reproduction - male).

- **Inside his body,** a boy's testes begin to make sperm.

Reproduction– female

- **A woman's reproductive system** is where her body stores, releases and nurtures the egg cells (ova – singular, ovum) that create a new human life when joined with a male sperm cell.

- **All the egg cells** are stored from birth in the ovaries – two egg-shaped glands inside the pelvic region. Each egg is stored in a tiny sac called a follicle.

- **One egg cell** is released every monthly menstrual cycle by one of the ovaries.

- **A monthly menstrual cycle starts** when follicle-stimulating hormone (FSH) is sent by the pituitary gland in the brain to spur follicles to grow.

- **As follicles grow,** they release the sex hormone oestrogen. Oestrogen makes the lining of the uterus (womb) thicken.

- **When an egg is ripe,** it slides down a duct called a Fallopian tube.

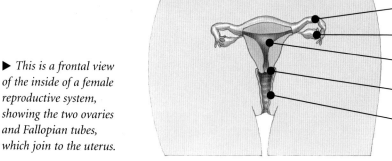

▶ *This is a frontal view of the inside of a female reproductive system, showing the two ovaries and Fallopian tubes, which join to the uterus.*

Fallopian tube
Ovary
Uterus
Cervix
Vagina

- **If a woman** has sexual intercourse at this time, sperm from the man's penis may swim up her vagina, enter her womb and fertilize the egg in the Fallopian tube.

- **If the egg is fertilized,** the womb lining goes on thickening ready for pregnancy, and the egg begins to develop into an embryo.

- **If the egg is not fertilized,** it is shed with the womb lining in a flow of blood from the vagina. This shedding is called a menstrual period.

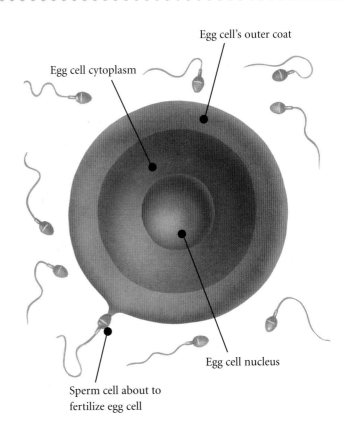

Egg cell's outer coat

Egg cell cytoplasm

Egg cell nucleus

Sperm cell about to fertilize egg cell

▲ *The female egg cell passes along the woman's Fallopian tube. At fertilization, tiny sperm cells swarm around the egg until one sperm manages to push its head on to the surface of the egg. The sperm head and egg membrane join, and fertilization takes place.*

375

Reproduction – male

- **A man's reproductive system** is where his body creates the sperm cells that combine with a female egg cell to create a new human life.

- **Sperm cells** look like microscopically tiny tadpoles. They are made in the testes, which is inside the scrotum.

- **The testes and scrotum** hang outside the body where it is cooler, because this improves sperm production.

- **At 15**, a boy's testes can make 200 million sperm a day.

- **Sperm leave** the testes via the epididymis – a thin, coiled tube, about 6 m long.

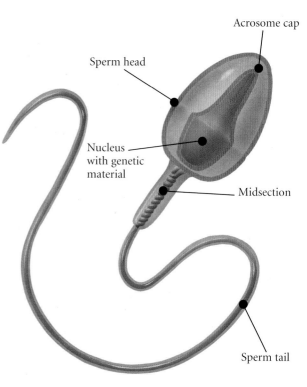

Acrosome cap

Sperm head

Nucleus with genetic material

Midsection

Sperm tail

▲ *A mature sperm cell consists of a head, where the genetic information is stored, a midsection and a tadpole-like tail, which allows it to swim rapidly towards the female egg cell.*

- **When the penis** is stimulated during sexual intercourse, sperm are driven into a tube called the vas deferens and mix with a liquid called seminal fluid to make semen.

- **Semen** shoots through the urethra (the tube inside the penis through which males urinate) and is ejaculated into the female's vagina.

- **The male sex hormone** testosterone is also made in the testes.

- **Testosterone** stimulates bone and muscle growth.

- **Testosterone** also stimulates the development of male characteristics such as facial hair and a deeper voice.

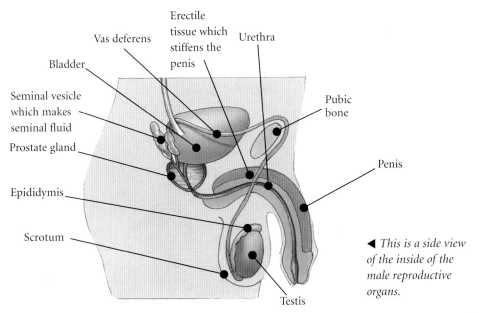

Vas deferens

Erectile tissue which stiffens the penis

Urethra

Bladder

Seminal vesicle which makes seminal fluid

Prostate gland

Epididymis

Scrotum

Pubic bone

Penis

Testis

◀ This is a side view of the inside of the male reproductive organs.

Pregnancy

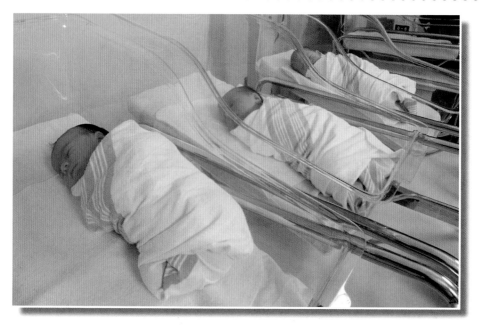

▲ *Newborn babies are sometimes cared for in nurseries. This gives the new mother a chance to sleep.*

- **Pregnancy** begins when a woman's ovum (egg cell) is fertilized by a man's sperm cell. Usually this happens after sexual intercourse, but it can begin in a laboratory.

- **When a woman becomes pregnant** her monthly menstrual periods stop. Tests on her urine show whether she is pregnant.

- **During pregnancy,** the fertilized egg divides again and again to grow rapidly – first to an embryo (the first eight weeks), and then to a foetus (from eight weeks until birth).

▶ *These are the various stages of development of an embryo and then foetus inside the mother's womb. After fertilization, the egg cell divides and develops into an embryo. After eight weeks, the embryo is called a foetus.*

5 weeks

8 weeks

12 weeks

20 weeks

40 weeks

30 weeks

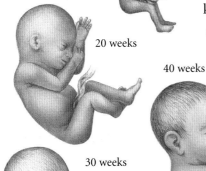

● **Unlike an embryo,** a foetus has grown legs and arms, as well as internal organs such as a heart.

● **Pregnancy lasts nine months,** and the time is divided into three trimesters (periods of about 12 weeks).

● **The foetus** lies cushioned in its mother's uterus (womb) in a bag of fluid called the amniotic sac.

● **The mother's blood** passes food and oxygen to the foetus via the placenta, also known as the afterbirth.

● **The umbilical cord** runs between the foetus and the placenta, carrying blood between them.

● **During pregnancy** a woman gains 30% more blood, and her heart rate goes up.

● **During pregnancy** a woman's breasts grow and develop milk glands to produce milk for feeding the baby.

379

Birth

- **Babies are usually born** 38–42 weeks after the mother becomes pregnant.

- **A few days or weeks before a baby is born,** it usually turns in the uterus (womb) so its head is pointing down towards the mother's birth canal (her cervix and vagina).

- **Birth begins** as the mother goes into labour – when the womb muscles begin a rhythm of contracting (tightening) and relaxing in order to push the baby out through the birth canal.

- **There are three stages** of labour. In the first, the womb muscles begin to contract or squeeze, bursting the bag of fluid around the baby. This is called breaking the waters.

▼ *A mother makes a special bond with her baby.*

▶ *Babies that weigh less than 2.4 kg when they are born are known as premature. They are nursed in special care units.*

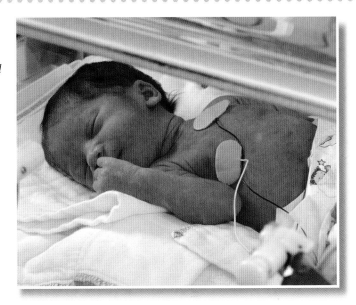

- **In the second stage** of labour, the baby is pushed out through the birth canal, usually by its head first, the body following quite quickly.

- **In the third stage** of labour, the placenta, which passed oxygen and nutrients from the mother's blood, is shed and comes out through the birth canal.

- **The umbilical cord** is the baby's lifeline to its mother. It is cut after birth.

- **A premature baby** is one born before it is fully developed.

- **A miscarriage** is when the developing baby is 'born' before the 28th week of pregnancy and cannot survive.

- **A Caesarian section** is an operation that happens when a baby cannot be born through the birth canal and emerges from the womb through a surgical cut made in the mother's belly.

381

Babies

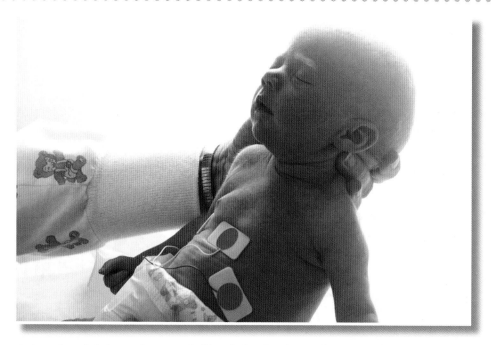

▲ *A newborn baby's muscles cannot hold up its head, so it must be supported.*

- **A baby's head** is three-quarters of the size it will be as an adult – and a quarter of its total body height.

- **The bones** of a baby's skeleton are fairly soft, to allow for growth. They harden over time.

- **Baby boys grow faster** than baby girls during the first seven months.

- **A baby** has a highly developed sense of taste, with taste buds all over the inside of its mouth.

> **. . . FASCINATING FACT . . .**
> A baby's brain is one of the fastest-
> growing parts of its body.

- **Babies have** a much stronger sense of smell than adults – perhaps to help them find their mother.

- **There are two gaps** called fontanelles between the bones of a baby's skull, where there is only membrane (a 'skin' of thin tissue), not bone. The gaps close and the bones join together by about 18 months.

- **A baby is born** with primitive reflexes (things it does automatically) such as grasping or sucking a finger.

- **A baby's body weight** usually triples in the first year of its life.

- **A baby seems to learn** to control its body in stages, starting first with its head, then moving on to its arms and legs.

▶ *Babies start to crawl when their leg muscles grow strong enough, after nine months or so.*

383

Ageing

▲ *People in Japan have a long life expectancy. This is probably due to a combination of factors including a healthy diet and certain social customs, which tend to favour the elderly.*

- **Most people live** for between 60 and 100 years, although a few live even longer than this.

- **The longest officially confirmed age** is that of Frenchwoman Jeanne Calment, who died in 1997, aged 122 years and 164 days.

- **Life expectancy** is how long statistics suggest you are likely to live.

- **On average in Europe**, men can expect to live about 75 years and women about 80. However, because health is improving generally, people are now living longer.

- **As adults grow older**, their bodies begin to deteriorate (fail). Senses such as hearing, sight and taste weaken.

- **Hair goes grey** as pigment (colour) cells stop working.

- **Muscles weaken** as fibres die.

- **Bones become more brittle** as they lose calcium. Cartilage shrinks between joints, causing stiffness.

- **Skin wrinkles** as the rubbery elastin and collagen fibres that support it sag. Exposure to sunlight speeds this up, which is why the face and hands get wrinkles first.

- **Circulation and breathing weaken**. Blood vessels may become stiff and clogged, forcing the heart to work harder and raising blood pressure.

▲ *Changes in health standards mean that more and more people than ever before are remaining fit in old age.*

Anatomy

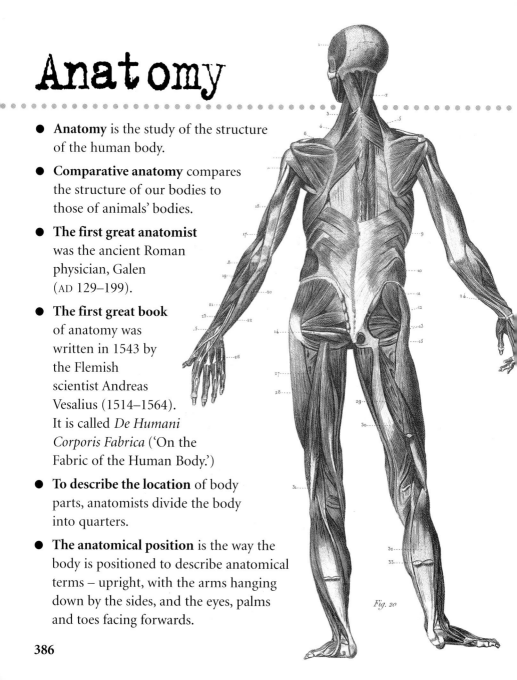

- **Anatomy** is the study of the structure of the human body.

- **Comparative anatomy** compares the structure of our bodies to those of animals' bodies.

- **The first great anatomist** was the ancient Roman physician, Galen (AD 129–199).

- **The first great book** of anatomy was written in 1543 by the Flemish scientist Andreas Vesalius (1514–1564). It is called *De Humani Corporis Fabrica* ('On the Fabric of the Human Body.')

- **To describe the location** of body parts, anatomists divide the body into quarters.

- **The anatomical position** is the way the body is positioned to describe anatomical terms – upright, with the arms hanging down by the sides, and the eyes, palms and toes facing forwards.

Fig. 20

- **The central coronal plane** divides the body into front and back halves. Coronal planes are any slice across the body from side to side, parallel to the central coronal plane.

- **The ventral or anterior** is the front half of the body.

- **The dorsal or posterior** is the back half of the body.

- **Every part of the body** has a Latin name, but anatomists use a simple English name if there is one.

◀ ▶ *Much of our basic knowledge of human anatomy comes from the anatomists of the 16th and 17th centuries, who meticulously cut up corpses and then accurately drew what they saw.*

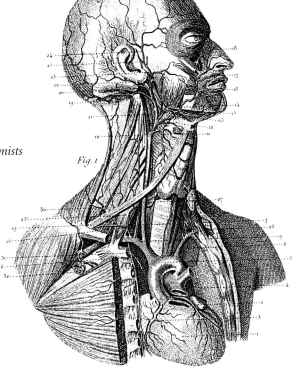

Fig. 1

Fitness

- **Fitness** is about how much and what kind of physical activity you can do without getting tired or strained.

- **Fitness depends** on your strength, flexibility (bendiness) and endurance (staying power).

- **One key to fitness** is cardiovascular fitness – that is, how well your heart and lungs respond to the extra demands of exercise.

- **One measure of cardiovascular fitness** is how quickly your pulse rate returns to normal after exercise – the fitter you are, the quicker it returns.

- **Another measure of cardiovascular fitness** is how slowly your heart beats during exercise – the fitter you are, the slower it beats.

◄ *Skiing is one of the most demanding of all sports, and top skiers need to be extremely fit to cope with the extra strain on their bodies.*

- **Being fit** improves your physical performance.

- **Being fit** can often protect against illness.

- **Being fit** can slow down the effects of ageing.

- **Cardiovascular fitness** reduces the chances of getting heart disease.

- **Fitness tests** involve comparing such things as height, weight and body fat, and measuring blood pressure and pulse rate before and after exercise.

◀ *Many people keep fit by attending exercise classes.*

389

Exercise

- **When you exercise,** your muscles have to work much harder than normal, so need much more oxygen and glucose (a kind of sugar) from the blood.

- **To boost oxygen,** your heart beats twice as fast and pumps twice as much blood, and your lungs take in ten times more air with each breath.

- **To boost glucose,** adrenalin triggers your liver to release its store of glucose.

- **If oxygen delivery** to muscles lags, the muscles fill up with lactic acid, affecting your body for hours and sometimes causing cramp.

- **The fitter you are,** the quicker your body returns to normal after exercise.

- **Aerobic exercise** is exercise that is long and hard enough for the oxygen supply to the muscles to rise enough to match the rapid burning of glucose.

◀ *A sportsman such as a football player builds up his body's ability to supply oxygen to his muscles by regular aerobic training.*

▲ *Swimming is good for improving overall fitness without putting strain on the muscles and joints.*

- **Regular aerobic exercise** strengthens your heart and builds up your body's ability to supply extra oxygen through your lungs to your muscles.

- **Regular exercise** multiplies muscle fibres and strengthens tendons.

- **Regular exercise** helps to reduce weight when it is combined with a controlled diet.

Tissue and organs

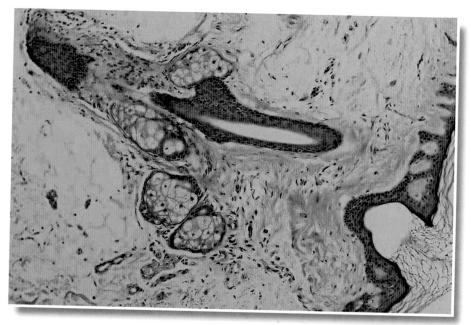

▲ *Skin, shown here in this highly-magnified photograph, is a complex form of ephithelial tissue.*

- **A tissue is a body substance** made from many of the same type of cell. Muscle cells make muscle tissue, nerve cells form nerve tissue, and so on.

- **As well as cells**, some tissues include other materials.

- **Connective tissues** are made from particular cells (such as fibroblasts), plus two other materials – long fibres of protein (such as collagen) and a matrix. Matrix is a material in which the cells and fibres are set like the currants in a bun.

392

▶ *Lungs are largely made from special lung tissues (see right), but the mucous membrane that lines the airways is epithelial tissue.*

- **Connective tissue** holds all the other kinds of tissue together in various ways. The adipose tissue that makes fat, tendons and cartilage is connective tissue.

- **Bone and blood** are both connective tissues.

- **Epithelial tissue** is good lining or covering material, making skin and other parts of the body.

- **Epithelial tissue** may combine three kinds of cell to make a thin waterproof layer – squamous (flat), cuboid (box-like) and columnar (pillar-like) cells.

- **Nerve tissue** is made mostly from neurons (nerve cells), plus the Schwann cells that coat them.

- **Organs** are made from combinations of tissues. The heart is made mostly of muscle tissue, but also includes epithelial and connective tissue.

... FASCINATING FACT ...
All your body is made from tissue and tissue fluid (liquid that fills the space between cells).

Microscopes

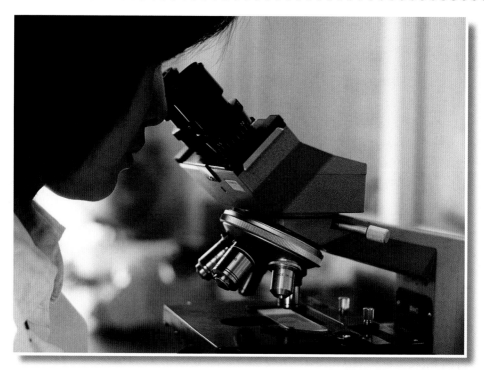

▲ *This optical microscope has several lenses so that it can give different magnifications. The lenses bend the light shining through the object before it reaches the eye.*

- **Optical microscopes** use lenses and light to magnify things (make them look bigger). By combining two or more lenses, they can magnify specimens up to 2000 times and reveal individual blood cells.

- **To magnify things more,** scientists use electron microscopes – microscopes that fire beams of tiny charged particles called electrons.

▶ *In this picture, a drop of blood has been placed between two glass slides. The slides will then be placed under an optical microscope to be viewed at a higher magnification.*

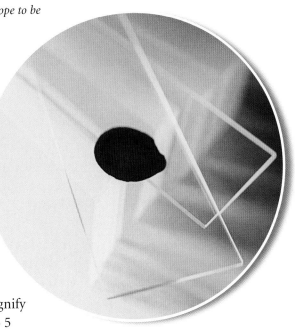

- **Electrons** have wavelengths 100,000 times smaller than light and so can give huge magnifications.

- **Scanning electron microscopes** (SEMs) are able to magnify things up to 100,000 times.

- **SEMs** show such things as the structures inside body cells.

- **Transmission electron microscopes** (TEMs) can magnify even more than SEMs – up to 5 million times.

- **TEMs** can reveal the individual molecules in a cell.

- **SEM specimens** (things studied) must be coated in a special substance such as gold. They give a three-dimensional view.

- **Optical microscope specimens** are thinly sliced and placed between two glass slides. They give a cross-sectional view.

- **Microscopes help** to identify germs.

Cells

- **Cells** are the basic building blocks of your body. Most are so tiny you would need 10,000 to cover a pinhead.

- **There are over 200 different kinds** of cell in your body, including nerve cells, skin cells, blood cells, bone cells, fat cells, muscle cells and many more.

- **A cell is basically** a little parcel of organic (life) chemicals with a thin membrane (casing) of protein and fat. The membrane holds the cell together, but lets nutrients in and waste out.

- **Inside the cell** is a liquid called cytoplasm, and floating in this are various minute structures called organelles.

- **At the centre** of the cell is the nucleus – this is the cell's control centre and it contains the amazing molecule DNA (see genes). DNA not only has all the instructions the cell needs to function, but also has the pattern for new human life.

- **Each cell** is a dynamic chemical factory, and the cell's team of organelles is continually busy – ferrying chemicals to and fro, breaking up unwanted chemicals, and putting together new ones.

- **The biggest cells** in the body can be nerve cells. Although the main nucleus of nerve cells is microscopic, the tails of some cells can extend for a metre or more through the body, and be seen even without a microscope.

- **Among the smallest cells** in the body are red blood cells. These are just 0.0075 mm across and have no nucleus, since nearly their only task is ferrying oxygen.

- **Most body cells** live a very short time and are continually being replaced by new ones. The main exceptions are nerve cells – these are long-lived, but rarely replaced.

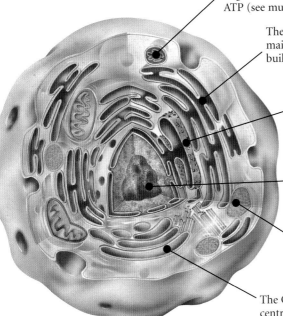

Mitochondria are the cell's power stations, turning chemical fuel supplied by the blood as glucose into energy packs of the chemical ATP (see muscle movement)

The endoplasmic reticulum is the cell's main chemical factory, where proteins are built under instruction from the nucleus

The ribosomes are the individual chemical assembly lines, where proteins are put together from basic chemicals called amino acids (see diet)

The nucleus is the cell's control centre, sending out instructions via a chemical called messenger RNA whenever a new chemical is needed

The lysosomes are the cell's dustbins, breaking up any unwanted material

The Golgi bodies are the cell's despatch centre, where chemicals are bagged up inside tiny membranes to send where they are needed

▲ *This illustration shows a typical cell, and some of the different organelles (special parts of a cell) that keep it working properly. The instructions come from the nucleus in the cell's control centre, but every kind of organelle has its own task.*

... **FASCINATING FACT** ...
There are 75 trillion cells in your body!

The immune system

The adenoids in the nose are one of the body's defence centres, releasing cells to fight infections

If you get a throat infection the tonsils release cells to fight it

The thymus is a gland in the chest which turns ordinary white blood cells into special T-cells that fight harmful microbes

During an infection, lymph nodes may swell up with white blood cells that have swallowed up germs

The spleen not only destroys worn-out red blood cells, but also helps make antibodies and phagocytes

◄ *The body's range of interior defences against infection is amazingly complex. The various kinds of white blood cells and the antibodies the defences make are particularly important.*

Lymph glands in the groin often swell up as the body fights an infection

Sebaceous glands in the skin ooze an oil that is poisonous to many bacteria

▶ *The AIDS virus, HIV, attacks the body's immune cells and prevents them from dealing with infections.*

- **The immune system** is the complicated system of defences that your body uses to prevent or fight off attack from germs and other invaders.

- **Your body** has a variety of barriers, toxic chemicals and booby traps to stop germs entering it. The skin is a barrier that stops many germs getting in, as long as it is not broken.

- **Mucus is a thick, slimy fluid** that coats vulnerable, internal parts of your body such as your stomach and nose. It also acts as a lubricant (oil), making swallowing easier.

- **Mucus lines your airways** and lungs to protect them from smoke particles as well as from germs. Your airways may fill up with mucus when you have a cold, as your body tries to minimize the invasion of airborne germs.

- **Itching, sneezing, coughing and vomiting** are your body's ways of getting rid of unwelcome invaders. Small particles that get trapped in the mucous lining of your airways are wafted out by tiny hairs called cilia.

- **The body** has many specialized cells and chemicals which fight germs that get inside you.

- **Complement** is a mixture of liquid proteins found in the blood which attacks bacteria.

- **Interferons** are proteins which help the body's cells to attack viruses and also stimulate killer cells (see lymphocytes).

- **Certain white blood cells** are cytotoxic, which means that they are poisonous to invaders.

- **Phagocytes** are big white blood cells that swallow up invaders and then use an enzyme to dissolve them (see antibodies). They are drawn to the site of an infection whenever there is inflammation.

Lymphocytes

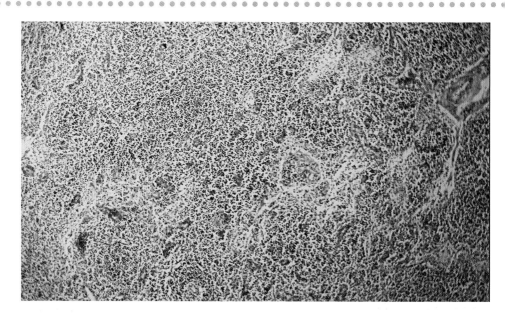

▲ *A lymph node packed with lymphocytes fighting infection.*

- **Lymphocytes** are white blood cells that play a key role in the body's immune system, which targets invading germs.

- **There are two kinds of lymphocyte** – B lymphocytes (B-cells) and T lymphocytes (T-cells).

- **B-cells** develop into plasma cells that make antibodies to attack bacteria such as those which cause cholera, as well as some viruses (see antibodies).

- **T-cells** work against viruses and other micro-organisms that hide inside body cells. T-cells help identify and destroy these invaded cells or their products. They also attack certain bacteria.

- **There are two kinds of T-cell** – killers and helpers.

- **Helper T-cells** identify invaded cells and send out chemicals called lymphokines as an alarm, telling killer T-cells to multiply.

- **Invaded cells** give themselves away by abnormal proteins on their surface.

- **Killer T-cells** lock on to the cells that the helpers have identified, then move in and destroy them.

- **Some B-cells**, called memory B-cells, stay around for a long time, ready for a further attack by the same organism.

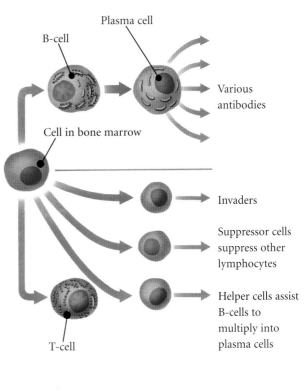

Plasma cell

B-cell

Various antibodies

Cell in bone marrow

Invaders

Suppressor cells suppress other lymphocytes

Helper cells assist B-cells to multiply into plasma cells

T-cell

▲ *Our bodies are constantly under attack from harmful bacteria and viruses. Lymphocytes are key defenders, producing special cells to either identify, alert, suppress or kill.*

. . . **FASCINATING FACT** . . .
If you get flu, it is your T lymphocytes that come to the rescue and fight off the virus.

401

Antibodies

- **Antibodies** are tiny proteins that make germs vulnerable to attack by white blood cells called phagocytes (see the immune system).

- **Antibodies are produced** by white blood cells derived from B lymphocytes (see lymphocytes).

- **There are thousands** of different kinds of B-cell in the blood, each of which produces antibodies against a particular germ.

- **Normally, only a few B-cells** carry a particular antibody. But when invading germ is detected, the correct B-cell multiplies rapidly to cause the release of antibodies.

- **Invaders** are identified when your body's immune system recognizes proteins on their surface as foreign. Any foreign protein is called an antigen.

▲ *Pollen from plants can often cause allergies such as hayfever. Your body's immune system mistakenly produces antibodies to fight the harmless pollen grains, which causes an allergic reaction.*

▶ *Bacteria, viruses and many other micro-organisms have antigens which spur B-cells into action to produce antibodies, as this artist's impression shows.*

● **Your body was armed** from birth with antibodies for germs it had never met. This is called innate immunity.

● **If your body comes across** a germ it has no antibodies for, it quickly makes some. It then leaves memory cells ready to be activated if the germ invades again. This is called acquired immunity.

● **Acquired immunity** means you only suffer once from some infections, such as chickenpox. This is also how vaccination works.

● **Allergies** are sensitive reactions that happen in your body when too many antibodies are produced, or when they are produced to attack harmless antigens.

● **Autoimmune diseases** are ones in which the body forms antibodies against its own tissue cells.

Vaccination

- **Vaccination** helps to protect you against an infectious disease by exposing you to a mild or dead version of the germ in order to make your body build up protection in the form of antibodies.

- **Vaccination** is also called immunization, because it builds up your resistance or immunity to a disease.

- **In passive immunization** you are injected with substances such as antibodies which have already been exposed to the germ. This gives instant but short-lived protection.

▲ *Vaccinations are crucial in many tropical regions where diseases are more widespread.*

- **In active immunization** you are given a killed or otherwise harmless version of the germ. Your body makes the antibodies itself for long-term protection.

- **Children in many countries** are given a series of vaccinations as they grow up, to protect them against diseases such as polio, diphtheria and tetanus.

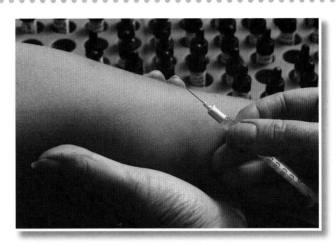

▲ *Diseases such as diphtheria, rubella and whooping cough are now rare in many countries thanks to vaccination. The dangerous disease smallpox – once very common – has been wiped out.*

- **The measles vaccine** carries a 1-in-87,000 chance of causing encephalitis (brain inflammation).

- **In cholera, typhoid, rabies and flu vaccines,** the germ in the vaccine is killed to make it harmless.

- **In measles, mumps, polio and rubella vaccines,** the germ is live attenuated – this means that its genes or other parts have been altered in order to make it harmless.

- **In diphtheria and tetanus vaccines,** the germ's toxins (poisons) are removed to make them harmless.

- **The hepatitis B** vaccine can be prepared by genetic engineering.

Diagnosis

- **Diagnosis** is when a doctor works out what a patient is suffering from – the illness and perhaps its cause.
- **The history** is the patient's own account of their illness. This provides the doctor with a lot of clues.
- **The prognosis** is the doctor's assessment of how the illness will develop in the future.
- **Symptoms** are changes which the patient or others notice and report.
- **Signs** are changes the doctor detects on examination and maybe after tests.
- **After taking a history** the doctor may carry out a physical examination, looking at the patient's body for symptoms such as swelling and tenderness.

▼ *A doctor examines her patient to check for any swelling or abnormalities that will help her make a diagnosis.*

◀ To make a diagnosis, a doctor may need to carry out a number of different tests. This test, using an ECG machine, measures the patient's heartrate.

▼ By listening to the heartbeat through a stethoscope, doctors can tell a lot about a patient's health.

- **A stethoscope** is a set of ear tubes which allows the doctor to listen to sounds made by the body, such as breathing and the heart beating.

- **With certain symptoms,** a doctor may order laboratory tests of blood and urine samples. Devices such as ultrasounds and X-rays may also be used to take special pictures.

- **Doctors** nowadays may use computers to help them make a diagnosis.

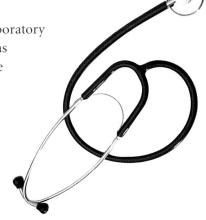

. . . FASCINATING FACT . . .
In future, many illnesses will be diagnosed entirely by computer.

407

Disease

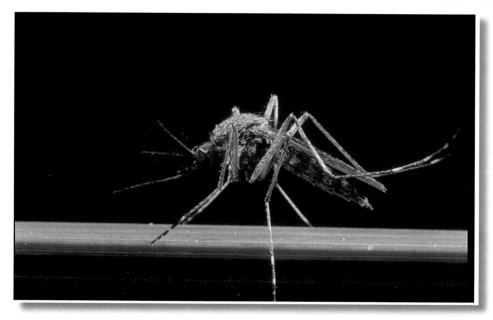

▲ *Mosquitos spread deadly diseases by transferring infected blood from one person to another.*

- **A disease** is something that upsets the normal working of any living thing. It can be acute (sudden, but short-lived), chronic (long-lasting), malignant (spreading) or benign (not spreading).

- **Some diseases** are classified by the body part they affect (such as heart disease), or by the body activity they affect (such as respiratory, or breathing, disease).

- **Heart disease** is the most common cause of death in the USA, Europe and also Australia.

- **Some diseases** are classified by their cause. These include the diseases caused by the staphylococcus bacteria – pneumonia is one such disease.

- **Diseases can be** either contagious (passed on by contact) or non-contagious.

- **Contagious diseases** are caused by germs such as bacteria and viruses (see germs). They include the common cold, polio, flu and measles. Their spread can be controlled by good sanitation and hygiene, and also by vaccination programmes.

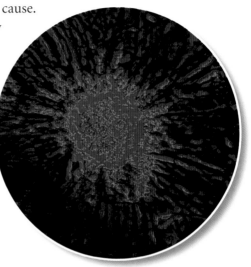

▲ *This is a microscope photograph of a cancer cell.*

- **Non-contagious diseases** may be inherited or they may be caused by such things as eating harmful substances, poor nutrition or hygiene, getting old or being injured.

- **Endemic diseases** are diseases that occur in a particular area of the world, such as sleeping sickness in Africa.

- **Cancer** is a disease in which malignant cells multiply abnormally, creating growths called tumours.

- **Cancer kills** 6 million people a year around the world. The risk increases as you get older.

409

Germs

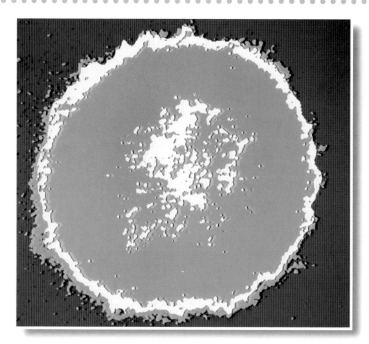

◄ *The disease AIDS (Acquired Immune Deficiency Syndrome) is caused by a virus called HIV (Human Immunodeficiency Virus). This virus gets inside vital cells of the body's immune system and weakens its ability to fight against other infections.*

- **Germs** are microscopic organisms that enter your body and cause harm.

- **The scientific word** for germ is 'pathogen'.

- **When germs** begin to multiply inside your body, you are suffering from an infectious disease.

- **An infection** that spreads throughout your body (flu or measles, for example) is called a systemic infection.

- **An infection** that affects only a small area (such as dirt in a cut) is called a localized infection.

- **It is often the reaction** of your body's immune system to the germ that makes you feel ill.

- **Bacteria** are single-celled organisms. They are found almost everywhere in huge numbers, and multiply rapidly.

- **Most bacteria are harmless,** but there are three harmful groups – cocci are round cells, spirilla are coil-shaped, and bacilli are rod-shaped. These harmful bacteria cause diseases such as tetanus and typhoid.

- **Viruses** can only live and multiply by taking over other cells – they cannot survive on their own. They cause diseases such as colds, flu, mumps and AIDS.

- **Parasites** are animals such as tapeworms that may live in or on your body, feeding on it and making you ill.

- **Fungal spores** and tiny organisms called protozoa can also cause illness.

▶ *When germs attack our immune system, our bodies react by fighting back strongly. This often makes us feel unwell.*

X-rays

▲ *Doctors have been using X-rays in their diagnosis since the end of the nineteenth century.*

- **X-rays** are a form of electromagnetic radiation, as are radio waves, microwaves, visible light and ultraviolet. They all travel as waves, but have different wavelengths.

- **X-ray waves** are much shorter and more energetic than visible light waves. X-rays are invisible because their waves are too short for our eyes to see.

- **X-rays are made** when negatively charged particles called electrons are fired at a heavy plate made of the metal tungsten. The plate bounces back X-rays.

- **Even though they are invisible** to our eyes, X-rays register on photographic film.

- **X-rays are so energetic** that they pass through some body tissues like a light through a net curtain.

- **To make an X-ray photograph,** X-rays are shone through the body. The X-rays pass through some tissues and turn the film black, but are blocked by others, leaving white shadows on the film.

- **Each kind of tissue** lets X-rays through differently. Bones are dense and contain calcium, so they block X-rays and show up white on film. Skin, fat, muscle and blood let X-rays through and show up black on film.

- **X-ray radiation** is dangerous in high doses, so the beam is encased in lead, and the radiographer who takes the X-ray picture stands behind a screen.

- **X-rays are** very good at showing up bone defects. So if you break a bone, it will probably be X-rayed.

- **X-rays also** reveal chest and heart problems.

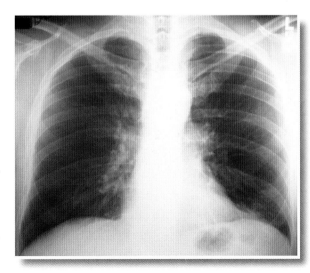

▶ *An X-ray gives a clear picture of the inside of the chest, showing the ribs, the spine and the branching airways in the lung. Any lung problems and blockages show up as white shadows.*

413

Scans

▲ *MRI scans are particularly valuable for providing clear images of the brain and spinal cord.*

- **Diagnostic imaging** means using all kinds of complex machinery to make pictures or images of the body to help diagnose and understand a problem.

- **Many imaging techniques** are called scans, because they involve scanning a beam around the patient, to and fro in lines or waves.

- **CT scans** rotate an X-ray beam around the patient while moving him or her slowly forward. This gives a set of pictures showing different slices of the patient's body.

- **CT** stands for computerized tomography.

- **MRI scans** surround the patient with such a strong magnet that all the body's protons (tiny atomic particles) turn the same way. A radio pulse is then used to knock the protons in and out of line, sending out radio signals that the scanner picks up to give the picture.

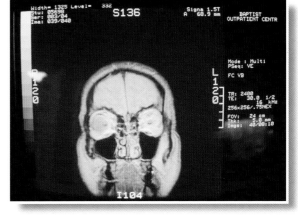

▲ *One of a series of CT scans of the head and brain.*

- **MRI** stands for magnetic resonance imaging.

- **PET scans** involve injecting the patient with a mildly radioactive substance, which flows around with the blood and can be detected because it emits (gives out) particles called positrons.

- **PET** stands for positron emission tomography.

- **PET scans** are good for seeing how blood flow alters to a particular part of the body.

... **FASCINATING FACT** ...
PET scans allow scientists to track blood through
a live brain and see which areas are in action.

Operations

- **A surgical operation** is when a doctor cuts or opens up a patient's body to repair or remove a diseased or injured body part.

- **An anaesthetic** is a drug or gas that either sends a patient completely to sleep (a general anaesthetic), or numbs part of the body (a local anaesthetic).

- **Minor operations** are usually carried out with just a local anaesthetic.

- **Major operations** such as transplants are done under a general anaesthetic.

- **Major surgery** is performed by a team of people in a specially equipped room called an operating theatre.

- **The surgical team** is led by the surgeon. There is also an anaesthetist to make sure the patient stays asleep, as well as surgical assistants and nurses.

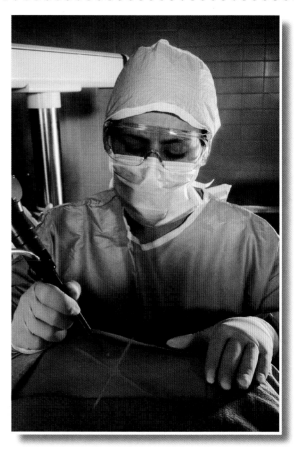

▲ *In some operations, laser beams are used instead of the standard surgical knife, as they allow more control and precision, and reduce the risk of damage or bleeding.*

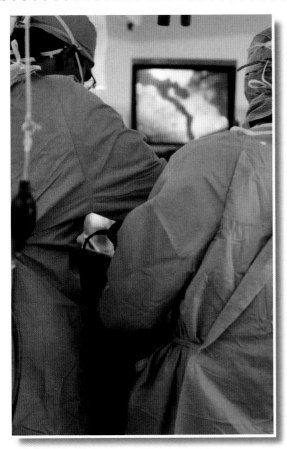

- **The operating theatre** must be kept very clean to prevent an infection entering the patient's body during the operation.

- **In microsurgery,** a microscope is used to help the surgeon work on very small body parts such as nerves or blood vessels.

- **In laser surgery**, the surgeon cuts with a laser beam instead of a scalpel, and the laser seals blood vessels as it cuts. It is used for delicate operations such as eye surgery.

- **An endoscope is** a tube-like instrument with a TV camera at one end. It can be inserted into the patient's body during an operation to allow surgeons to look more closely at body parts.

▲ *Many tricky operations are now performed using miniature cameras which help the surgeon see tiny details inside the body.*

417

Drugs

- **Antibiotic drugs** are used to treat bacterial infections such as tuberculosis (TB) or tetanus. They were once grown as moulds (fungi) but are now made artificially.

- **Penicillin** was the first antibiotic drug, discovered in a mould in 1928 by Alexander Fleming (1881–1955).

- **Analgesic drugs** such as aspirin relieve pain, working mainly by stopping the body making prostaglandin, the chemical that sends pain signals to the brain.

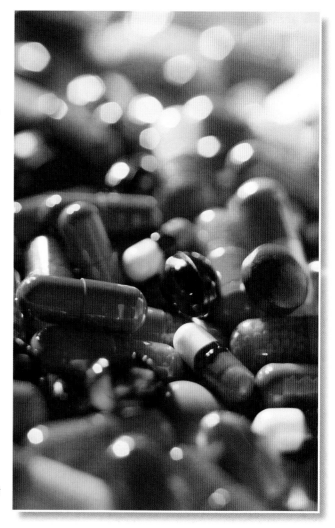

▶ *Today, thousands of different drugs are used to treat illness.*

- **Tranquillizers** are drugs that calm. Minor tranquillizers are drugs such as prozac, used to relieve anxiety.

- **Major tranquillizers** are used to treat mental illnesses such as schizophrenia.

- **Psychoactive drugs** are drugs that change your mood. Many, including heroin, are dangerous and illegal.

- **Stimulants** are drugs that boost the release of the nerve transmitter noradrenaline, making you more lively and awake. They include the caffeine in coffee.

- **Narcotics,** such as morphine, are powerful painkillers that mimic the body's own natural painkiller, endorphin.

- **Depressants** are drugs such as alcohol which do not depress you, but instead slow down the nervous system.

▲ *Alexander Fleming was a British bacteriologist. His discovery in 1928 of the life-saving antibiotic, penicillin, opened a new era for medicine.*

. . . FASCINATING FACT . . .
In future, more drugs may be made by microbes or animals with altered genes. Insulin is already made in the pancreas of pigs.

419

Transplants

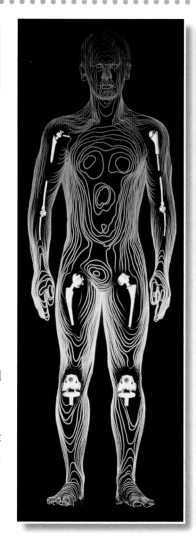

- **More and more body parts** can now be
  replaced, either by transplants (parts taken
  from other people or animals) or by implants
  (artificial parts).

- **Common transplants include:** the kidney, the
  cornea of the eye, the heart, the lung, the liver
  and the pancreas.

- **Some transplant organs** (such as the heart,
  lungs and liver) are taken from someone who
  has died.

- **Other organs** (such as the kidney) may be
  taken from living donors.

- **After the transplant organ** is taken from the
  donor, it is washed in an oxygenated liquid and
  cooled to preserve it.

- **One problem** with transplants is that the
  body's immune system identifies the transplant
  as foreign and attacks it. This is called rejection.

▶ *These are just some of the artificial implants now put in
place – hip, knee, shoulder and elbow. Old people often need
implants to replace joints that have deteriorated.*

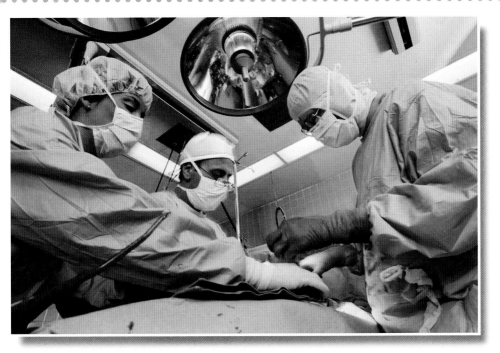

▲ *Most organ transplant operations last for several hours. The patient must then remain in the hospital for up to four weeks, depending on the particular organ that has been transplanted.*

- **To cut down** the chance of rejection, patients may be given drugs such as cyclosporin to suppress their immune system.

- **Heart transplant** operations last 4 hours.

- **During a heart transplant**, the patient is connected to a heart-lung machine which takes over the heart's normal functions.

421

The first railways

- **Railways** were invented long before steam power.

- **The Diolkos** was a 6 km-long railway that transported boats across the Corinthisthmus in Greece in the 6th-century BC. Trucks pushed by slaves ran in grooves in a limestone track.

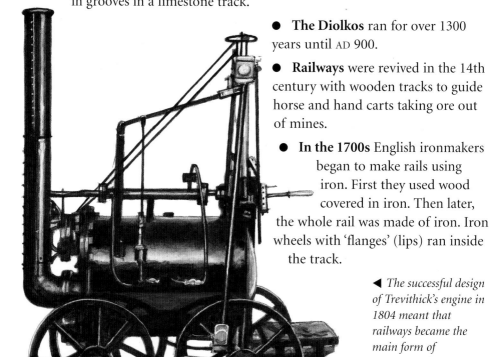

- **The Diolkos** ran for over 1300 years until AD 900.

- **Railways** were revived in the 14th century with wooden tracks to guide horse and hand carts taking ore out of mines.

- **In the 1700s** English ironmakers began to make rails using iron. First they used wood covered in iron. Then later, the whole rail was made of iron. Iron wheels with 'flanges' (lips) ran inside the track.

◀ *The successful design of Trevithick's engine in 1804 meant that railways became the main form of transportation.*

- **In 1804** Cornish engineer Richard Trevithick built the first successful steam railway locomotive.

- **Trevithick's** engine pulled a train of five wagons with 9 tonnes of iron and 70 men along 15 km of track at the Pendarren ironworks in Wales.

- **On 27 September 1825** George and Robert Stephenson opened the world's first steam passenger railway, the Stockton and Darlington in England.

- **The gauge (track width)** used for the Stockton and Darlington was 1.44 m, the same length as axles on horse-wagons. This became the standard gauge in the USA and much of Europe.

- **The English-built *Stourbridge Lion*** was the first full-size steam locomotive to run in the USA. It ran on wooden track in Pennsylvania in 1829.

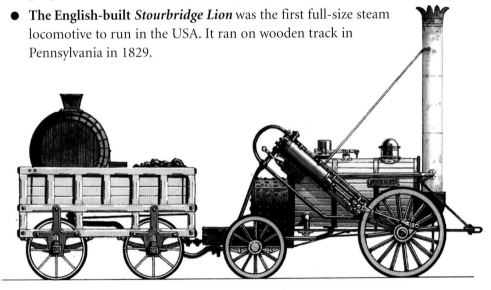

▲ *The Stephensons'* Rocket *was the most famous early locomotive, winning the first locomotive speed trials at Rainhill in England in 1829.*

423

Steam locomotives

▶ *The biggest and strongest steam locomotives ever were nicknamed 'Big Boy'. They were designed to haul 3000-tonne freight trains over the Rocky Mountains.*

- **Steam locomotives** get their power by burning coal in a firebox. This heats up water in a boiler, making steam. The steam drives a piston to and fro and the piston turns the wheels via connecting rods and cranks.

- **It takes about three hours** for the crew to get up enough steam to get a locomotive moving.

- **Coal and water** are often stored in a wagon called a tender, towed behind the locomotive.

- **A tender** holds 10 tonnes of coal and 30,000 litres of water.

- **Loco classes** are described by their wheel layout.

- **A 4-6-2** has four small leading 'bogie' wheels, six big driving wheels and two small trailing wheels. The small bogie wheels carry much of the weight.

- **The greatest** Victorian loco designer was James Nasmyth.

- **In the American Civil War** (1861–65) the loco *The General* was recaptured by Confederates after an epic chase in another loco.

> ....**FASCINATING FACT**....
> The first loco to hit 100 mph (160 km/h) was in the City of Truro in 1895.

- **The Flying Scotsman** was a famous loco designed by Sir Nigel Gresley (1876–1941). It pulled trains non-stop the 630 km from London to Edinburgh in under six hours.

◄ *An American locomotive dating from the 1890s.*

Diesel trains

- **The diesel engine** was invented by Rudolf Diesel in 1892 and experiments with diesel locomotives started soon after. The first great success was the *Flying Hamburger* which ran from Berlin to Hamburg in the 1930s at speeds of 125 km/h. Diesel took over from steam in the 1950s and 1960s.

- **Diesel locomotives** are really electric locomotives that carry their own power plant. The wheels are driven by an electric motor which is supplied with electricity by the locomotive's diesel engine.

Diesel engine in which diesel fuel is squeezed inside cylinders until it bursts into flame. The expansion of the fuel as it burns provides the

Locomotive driving wheel turned by the power of the electricity generator

Direct Current electricity generator turned by the power of the diesel engine

Driver's cab

● **The power output of a diesel** engine is limited, so high-speed trains are electric – however diesels can supply their own electricity so need no trackside cables.

Fuel tank carrying diesel fuel. Because a diesel train

● **There are two other kinds** of diesel apart from diesel-electrics: diesel-hydraulic and diesel-mechanical.

● **In diesel-hydraulics,** the power from the diesel engine is connected to the wheels via a torque converter, which is a turbine driven round by fluid.

● **In diesel-mechanicals,** the power is transmitted from the diesel engine to the wheels via gears and shafts. This only works for small locomotives.

● **Diesel locomotives** are made up from one or more separate units. An A unit holds the driver's cab and leads the train. A B unit simply holds an engine.

▲ *This is a typical British diesel-electric locomotive from the 1960s. It has a cab at both ends so that it can be operated in either direction. This is one of the older generation of diesel-electrics that use DC (Direct Current) generators. DC generators give a current that flows in only one direction. Most newer engines take advantage of rectifiers to use the current from an AC (Alternating Current) generator. An AC generator gives a current that swaps direction many times a second. The rectifiers convert this into a direct current. AC generators are far more powerful and efficient.*

● **A typical diesel locomotive** for fast, heavy trains may consist of one A unit and six B units.

● **The usual maximum** power output from a single diesel locomotive is about 3500–4000

427

Electric trains

▲ *Electric current flows from the power line through conductors to the locomotive's motor.*

- **The first practical electric** trains date from 1879, but they only became widespread in the 1920s.

- **Electric locos** pick up electric current either from a third 'live' rail or from overhead cables.

- **To pick up** power from overhead cables, locos need a spring-loaded frame or pantograph to keep in contact.

- **Electric trains** are clean and powerful and are also able to travel faster than other trains.

- **Older systems** mostly used Direct Current (DC) motors, operating at 1500–3000 volts for overhead cables and 700 volts for live rails.

▶ *Japan's Shinkansen 'bullet train' was the first of the modern high-speed electric trains, regularly operating at speeds of over 400 km/h.*

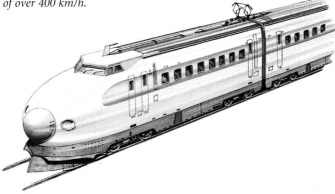

- **High-speed trains** like France's TGV and Japan's Shinkansen use 'three-phase' Alternating Current (AC) motors operating at 25,000 volts.

- **The Paris--London** Eurostar train works on 25,000 volt AC overhead cables in France, and 750 volt live rails after it comes out of the Channel Tunnel in England.

- **Magnetic levitation** or maglev trains do not have wheels but glide along supported by electromagnets.

- **In electrodynamic maglevs**, the train rides on repulsing magnets. In electromagnetic maglevs, they hang from attracting magnets.

- **Maglevs** are used now only for short, low-speed trains, but they may one day be the fastest of all. High-speed maglev developments now use 'superconducting' electromagnets which are costly to make. But a new idea is to use long strings of ordinary permanent magnets.

Record-breaking trains

▶ *TGV Atlantiques often hit 300 km/h on the French part of the Eurostar run from Paris to London.*

- **The fastest steam train** ever was the *Mallard* designed by Gresley (see steam locomotives). It pulled seven coaches at a speed of 201 km/hr on 3 July 1938.

- **The most powerful** steam loco was the US Virginian Railway's No. 700. It pulled with a force of over 90,000 kg.

- **The heaviest trains** ever pulled by a single locomotive were 250-truck trains that ran on the Erie Railroad in the USA from 1914 to 1929. They weighed over 15,000 tonnes.

- **The longest train** was a 7.3 km 660-truck train that ran from Saldanha to Sishen in South Africa on 26 August 1989.

- **The longest passenger train** was a 1732 m 70-coach train that travelled from Ghent to Ostend in Belgium on 27 April 1991.

- **The fastest speed recorded by a diesel train** was 248 km/h, achieved by a British Rail Intercity 125 travelling between Darlington and York on 1 November 1987.

▲ *Bullet trains in a Tokyo train station.*

- **The fastest scheduled service** is the Hiroshima to Kokura bullet train in Japan which covers 192 km in 44 minutes at an average 261.8 km/h.

- **The TGV** from Lille to Roissy in France covers 203 km in 48 mins at an average 254.3 km/h.

- **The fastest train speed ever** was 515.3 km/h by the TGV between Courtalain and Tours, France on 18 May 1990.

- **The fastest speed on rail** was 9851 km/h by a rocket sled on White Sands Missile Range, New Mexico in October 1982.

431

Trains of the future

- **Monorails** are single-beam tracks raised over city streets.

- **The first monorail** was built in Wuppertal in Germany as long ago as 1901 and monorails have been seen as trains of the future ever since.

- **Monorails** of the future may be air-cushion trains or maglevs, as at Birmingham airport.

- **A maglev** is proposed in Japan to take passengers the 515 km from Tokyo to Osaka in under 60 minutes. Germany is planning a system called Transrapid.

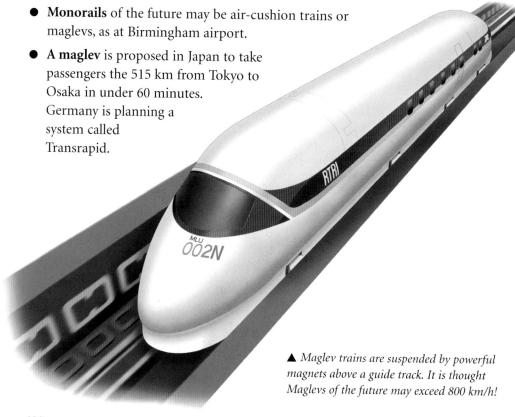

▲ *Maglev trains are suspended by powerful magnets above a guide track. It is thought Maglevs of the future may exceed 800 km/h!*

- **PRT** or Personalized Rapid Transport is a system of small vehicles that run on elevated tracks at high speed and are operated electrically.

- **300 km/h plus** High Speed Train (HST) systems such as the French TGV are being built in many countries. A line from Moscow to St Petersburg was opened in 2000.

- **In 2004** the 320 km/h Tampa-Miami Florida Overland Express opens. The same year a 4500 km 300 km/h line may also open from Melbourne to Darwin, Australia.

- **Most HSTs** run on special straight tracks. Tilting trains lean into bends to give high speeds on winding old tracks.

- **Tilting trains** include the 300 km/h Italian Fiat Pendolini and the Swedish-built X2000.

- **In 2000** the 240 km/h tilting train *The American Flyer* – Washington to Baltimore – became the USA's fastest train.

▶ *Many cities now have short monorails, but they seem unlikely to get much bigger because of the disruption the building work would cause.*

Early cars

- **In 1890** Frenchman Emile Levassor made the first real car, with an engine at the front. He laughed about his invention, saying, 'C'est brutal, mais ca marche' ('It's rough, but it goes.').

- **The Duryea** brothers made the first successful American car in 1893.

- **Early accidents** made cars seem dangerous. Until 1896 in Britain and 1901 in New York cars had to be preceded by a man on foot waving a red flag.

- **In 1895** the French Panhard-Levassor company made the first covered 'saloon' car.

- **In 1898** Renault drove the wheels with a shaft not a chain.

- **The Oldsmobile** Curved Dash of 1900 was the first car to sell in thousands.

- **On early cars** speed was controlled by moving a small ignition advance lever backwards or forwards.

▼ *Frederick Lanchester designed some of the world's earliest motor-cars. He built his first automobile in 1896.*

▲ *By 1904, many cars were starting to have the familiar layout of cars today – engine at the front, driver on one side, steering wheel, petrol tank at the back, a shaft to drive the wheels and so on.*

- **Dirt roads**, oil spray and noise meant early motorists needed protective clothing such as goggles.

- **The first cars** had wooden or wire-spoked wheels. Pressed-steel wheels like today's came in after 1945.

- **In 1906** an American steam-driven car, the Stanley Steamer, broke the Land Speed Record at over 205 km/h.

435

Supercars

◀ *The Porsche 911 is one of the classic supercars, first introduced in 1964, but still looking sleek many years later.*

- **The Mercedes Benz 300SL** of 1952 was one of the first supercars of the post-war years, famous for its stylish flip-up 'Gullwing' doors.

- **The Jaguar E-type** was the star car of the early 1960s with incredibly sleek lines and 250 km/h performance.

- **The Ford Mustang** was one of the first young and lively 'pony' cars, introduced in 1964.

- **The Aston Martin DB6** was the classic supercar of the late 1960s, driven by film spy James Bond.

- **The Porsche 911 turbo** was the fastest accelerating production car for almost twenty years after it was launched in 1975, scorching from 0 to 100 km/h in just 5.4 seconds.

- **The Lamborghini** Countach was the fastest supercar of the 1970s and 1980s, with a top speed of 295 km/h.

- **The Maclaren F1** can accelerate from 0 to 160 km/h in less time than it takes to read this sentence.

- **The Maclaren F1** is capable of going from 0 to 160 km/h and back to 0 again in under 20 seconds.

- **A tuned version** of the Chevrolet Corvette, the Callaway Sledge Hammer, can hit over 400 km/h.

. . . FASCINATING FACT . . .
The Ford GT-90 has a top speed of
378 km/h and zooms from 0 to 100 km/h
in 3.2 seconds.

▲ *Mercedes wins the Fomula One World Championship in 1954.*

Record-breaking cars

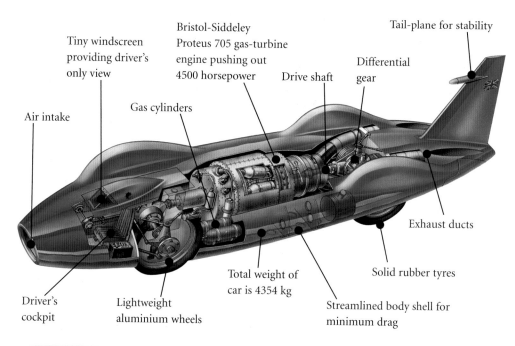

Tiny windscreen providing driver's only view

Bristol-Siddeley Proteus 705 gas-turbine engine pushing out 4500 horsepower

Drive shaft

Tail-plane for stability

Differential gear

Air intake

Gas cylinders

Exhaust ducts

Driver's cockpit

Lightweight aluminium wheels

Total weight of car is 4354 kg

Solid rubber tyres

Streamlined body shell for minimum drag

···· FASCINATING FACT ····

On 13 October 1997, a British jet car called *Thrust SSC* driven by British fighter pilot Andy Green broke the sound barrier for the first time. In two runs across Nevada's Black Rock desert it hit over 1220 km/h.

▲ *Donald Campbell took on the record-breaking mantle of his father – and the Bluebird name for his car. On 17 July 1964, Campbell's Bluebird hit a world record 690.909 km/h on the salt flats at Lake Eyre in South Australia. At one moment he hit over 716 km/h – faster than any wheel-driven car has ever been.*

- **The first car speed record** was achieved by an electric Jentaud car in 1898 at Acheres near Paris. Driven by the Comte de Chasseloup-Laubat, the car hit 63.14 km/h. Camille Jenatzy vied with de Chasseloup-Laubat for the record, raising it to 105.85 km/h in his car *Jamais Contente* in 1899.

- **Daytona Beach** in Florida became a venue for speed trials in 1903.

- **The biggest engine** ever to be raced in a Grand Prix was the 19,891 cc V4 of American Walter Christie, which he entered in the 1907 French Grand Prix. Later the Christie was the first front-wheel-drive car to win a major race – a 400 km race on Daytona Beach.

- **The record** for the circuit at Brooklands in England was set in 1935 by John Cobb in a Napier-Railton at 1 min 0.41 sec (230.79 km/h) and never beaten.

- **In 1911** the governing body for the Land Speed Record said that cars had to make two runs in opposite directions over a 1 km course to get the record.

- **In 1924** Sir Malcolm Campbell broke the Land Speed Record for the first of many times in a Sunbeam at 235.17 km/h. In 1925 he hit 150 mph (242 km/h) for the first time. But his most famous record-breaking runs were in the 1930s in his own *Bluebird* cars.

- **In 1947** John Cobb drove with tremendous skill to reach 634.27 km/h in his Railton-Mobil. This stood as the record for 17 years.

- **In 1964** the rules were changed to allow jet and rocket-propelled cars to challenge for the Land Speed Record. The next year Craig Breedlove drove his three-wheeler jet *Spirit of America* to over 500 mph (846.78 km/h).

- **In 1970** Gary Gabelich set the record over 1000 km/h with his rocket-powered *Blue Flame*. This record wasn't beaten until Richard Noble roared to 1019.37 km/h in his Rolls-Royce jet-powered *Thrust 2* in 1983.

Balloons

- **Balloons** are bags filled with a light gas or hot air – both so light that the balloon floats in the air.

- **Balloons** designed to carry people into the air are of two types: hot-air balloons and gas balloons filled with hydrogen or helium.

- **Hot-air balloons** have a burner that continually fills the balloon with warm air to keep it afloat.

- **To carry two people** a hot-air balloon must have a bag of about 1700 cubic metres in volume.

- **Balloons** are normally launched at dusk or dawn when the air is quite calm.

◀ *Hot-air ballooning has become a popular sport since Ed Yost, Tracy Barnes and other Americans began to make the bags from polyester in the 1960s.*

- **As the air in the bag cools** the balloon gradually sinks. To maintain height, the balloonist lights the burner to add warm air again.

- **To descend quickly** the balloonist pulls a cord to let air out through a vent in the top of the bag.

- **The first flight** in a hot-air balloon was made in Paris on 15 October 1783 by French scientist Jean de Rozier in a balloon made by the Montgolfier brothers.

- **The first hydrogen gas balloon flight** was made in Paris on 1 December 1783 by Jacques Charles and one of the two brothers Robert who built the balloon.

- **On 20 March 1999** Swiss Bertran Piccard and British Brian Jones completed the first round-the-world hot-air balloon flight.

▶ *The Montgolfier balloon was built from paper and silk.*

441

The Wright brothers

▲ *One of the five who witnessed the flight took this picture. But apart from a report in 'Popular Science' the Wrights' success was little known about for five years.*

- **The Wright brothers**, Orville and Wilbur, built the world's first successful plane, the *Flyer*.
- **On 17 December 1903** the Wright brothers made the first powered, long and controlled aeroplane flight at Kitty Hawk, USA.

- **Wilbur Wright** was born in 1867 on a farm near New Castle, Indiana; Orville was born in 1871 in Dayton, Ohio.

- **The Wright brothers** began as bicycle-makers but became keen on flying after hearing about the death of pioneer glider Otto Lilienthal in 1896.

- **From 1899 to 1903** they worked at Kitty Hawk methodically improving their design and flying skill.

- **Many early planes** took off but lacked control. The key to the Wrights' success was stopping the plane rolling, using wires to 'warp' (twist) the wings to lift one side or the other.

- **The *Flyer*'s** wing warp meant it could not only fly level but make balanced, banked turns (like a bicycle cornering).

- **For the first flight** Orville was at the controls.

- **The historic first flight** lasted 12 seconds, in which the *Flyer* travelled 37 m and landed safely.

- **On 5 October 1905** the Wrights flew 38.9 km in 38 minutes.

▶ *Orville and Wilbur Wright's first aeroplane cost less than $1000 to build.*

Taking off

▶ *An F-15 preparing for take-off.*

- **An aircraft's wings** or 'foils' are lifted by the air flowing above and beneath them as they slice through the air.

- **Because the top** of the wing is curved, air pushed over the wing speeds up and stretches out. The stretching of the air reduces its pressure.

- **Underneath the wing** air slows down and bunches up, the air pressure in this area rises.

- **The wing gains 'lift'** as the air around the wing is sucked from above and pushed from below.

- **The amount of lift** depends on the angle of the wing – called the angle of attack – and its shape, and also how fast it is moving through the air.

- **Aircraft** get extra lift for climbing by increasing their speed through the air and by dropping the tail so that the main wings cut through the air at a steeper angle.

- **If the angle of attack** becomes too steep, the airflow breaks up and the wing loses lift. This is called a stall.

- **Planes** take off when air is moving fast enough over the wing to provide enough lift.

- **Airliners** have 'high-lift' slots and flaps on the wings to give extra lift for slow take-off and landing speeds.

. . . FASCINATING FACT . . .
Slots on the wing's leading edge smooth
airflow to increase the safe angle of attack.

▲ *The high-lift flaps are down to give extra lift on a climb.*

Warplanes

- **The 870 km/h** German Messerschmitt Me 262 was the first jet fighter. It had straight wings like propeller planes.

- **The Lockheed Shooting Star** was the first successful US jet fighter.

- **The Korean War** of the 1950s saw the first major combat between jet fighters. Most now had swept-back wings, like the Russian MiG-15 and the US F-86 Sabre.

- **In 1954** Boeing introduced the B-52 Superfortress, still the USAF's main bomber because of its huge bomb-carrying capacity.

- **In the 1950s** aircraft began flying close to the ground to avoid detection by radar. On modern ground-hugging planes like the Lockheed F-111 a computer radar system flies the plane automatically at a steady height over hills and valleys. If the system fails, the plane climbs automatically.

▲ *Pilots fly modern jets at supersonic speeds aided by laser-guided weapons, night-vision goggles and other high-tech equipment.*

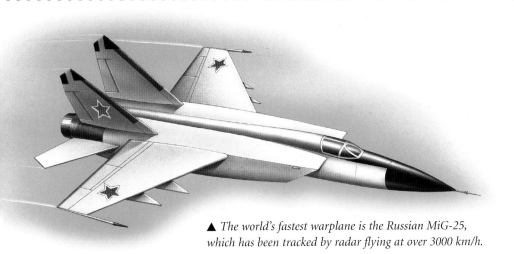

▲ *The world's fastest warplane is the Russian MiG-25,*
which has been tracked by radar flying at over 3000 km/h.

- **The Hawker Harrier** of 1968 was the only successful 'jump jet' with swivelling jets for vertical take-off (VTOL).

- **Airborne Early Warning** systems (AEWs) look down from above and detect low-flying aircraft. To evade them the Americans began developing 'stealth' systems like RCS and RAM.

- **RCS** or Radar Cross Section means altering the plane's shape to make it less obvious to radar. RAM (Radar Absorbent Material) is a coating that doesn't reflect radar.

- **In 1988** the US unveiled its first 'stealth' bomber, the B-2, codenamed Have Blue. The F117 stealth fighter followed.

- **The 2500 km/h Russian Sukhoi S-37** Berkut ('golden eagle') of 1997 uses Forward Swept Wings (FSW) for maximum agility, rather than stealth technology.

Missiles

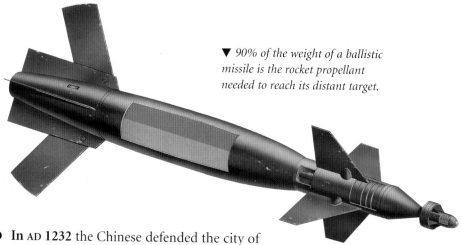

▼ *90% of the weight of a ballistic missile is the rocket propellant needed to reach its distant target.*

- **In AD 1232** the Chinese defended the city of K'ai-feng against the Mongols with gunpowder rockets.

- **In the early 1800s** British army officer William Congreve developed metal rockets carrying explosives.

- **In World War II** the Germans developed the first guided missiles – missiles steered to their target in flight.

- **The most frightening** German guided missiles were the V-1 flying bombs or 'doodlebugs' and the V-2 supersonic rockets. The V-2s flew at 5300 km/h.

- **Ballistic missiles** arch through the air like a thrown ball. Rockets propel them on the upward trajectory (path). They then coast down on their target. Cruise missiles are propelled by jet on a low flat path all the way.

- **In the 1950s** the USA and Soviet Union competed to develop long-range ICBMs (Intercontinental Ballistic Missiles) usually armed with nuclear warheads.

448

· · · **FASCINATING FACT** · · ·
American Tomahawk cruise missiles could
be aimed through goalposts at both ends
of a football field 500 km away.

- **In the 1960s** antiballistic missiles
  were developed to shoot down
  missiles.

- **Some ICBMs** have a range of over
  5000 km. Short-range missiles
  (SRBMs) like Pershings reach up to
  500 km.

- **SAMs** (surface-to-air missiles) like
  Redeye are fired from the ground at
  aircraft. Some can be fired by a
  soldier with a backpack. AAMs
  (air-to-air missiles) like
  Sidewinders are fired from planes
  for use against other planes.

▶ *Rocket missiles can carry nuclear
warheads or other weapons halfway
around the world.*

Record-breaking flights

- **On 25 July 1909** Louis Blériot made the first flight across the English Channel in a plane he built himself.

- **On 8–31 May 1919** (with stops) Capt A.C. Read and his crew made the first flight across the Atlantic in a Curtiss flying boat.

- **On 14–15 June 1919** John Alcock and Arthur Brown made the first non-stop flight across the Atlantic in an open cockpit Vickers Vimy biplane.

- **On 12 November–10 December 1921** brothers Keith and Ross Smith made the first flight from England to Australia.

- **In February 1921** William Corey was the first person to fly solo across the United States.

- **In 1927** Frenchman Louis Breguet made the first flight across the South Atlantic.

▼ *Alcock and Brown's 3138 km flight from Newfoundland to Ireland took 15 hours 57 minutes.*

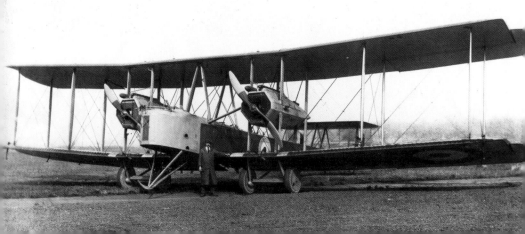

> **FASCINATING FACT**
> In December 1986, the American plane *Voyager* flew round the world non-stop in nine days.

▲ *Louis Bleriot's first flight across the English Channel in 1909.*

- **On 21 May 1927** American Charles Lindbergh made the first solo flight across the Atlantic in the *Spirit of St Louis*.

- **In July 1931** Wiley Post made the fastest round-the-world flight yet.

- **The story of Post's epic flight** was recorded in the book *Round the World in Eight Days*.

Helicopters

Without a tail rotor, the helicopter would spin round the opposite way to the main rotors. This is called torque reaction. The tail rotor also acts as a rudder to swing the tail left or right

To fly up or down, the pilot alters the angle or 'pitch' of the main rotor blades with the 'collective pitch' control. When the blades cut through the air almost flat, they give no lift and the helicopter sinks. To climb, the pilot steepens the pitch to increase lift

The angle of the blades is changed via rods linked to a sliding collar round the rotor shaft, called the swashplate

To fly forwards or back, or for a banked turn, the pilot tilts the whole rotor with the 'cyclic pitch' control

Rockets

Tail rotor drive shaft

Engine

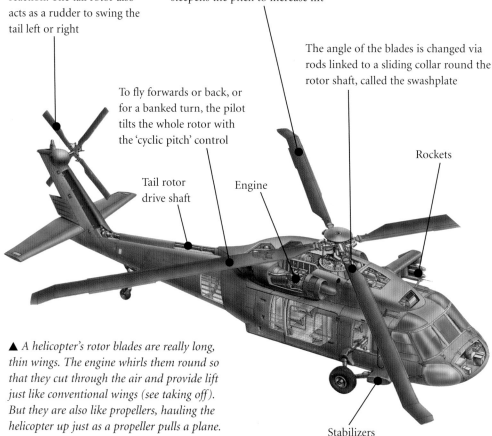

▲ A helicopter's rotor blades are really long, thin wings. The engine whirls them round so that they cut through the air and provide lift just like conventional wings (see taking off). But they are also like propellers, hauling the helicopter up just as a propeller pulls a plane.

Stabilizers

- **Toy helicopters** have been around for centuries, and those made by air pioneer Sir George Cayley in the early 19th century are the most famous.

- **On 13 November 1907** a primitive helicopter with two sets of rotors lifted French mechanic Paul Cornu off the ground for 20 seconds.

- **The problem** with pioneer helicopters was control. The key was to vary the pitch of the rotor blades.

- **In 1937** German designer Heinrich Focke built an aircraft with two huge variable pitch rotors instead of wings and achieved a controlled hover. Months later, German Anton Flettner built the first true helicopter.

- **Focke and Flettner's** machines had two rotors turning in opposite directions to prevent torque reaction. In 1939, Russian-born American Igor Sikorsky solved the problem by adding a tail rotor.

- **The Jesus nut** that holds the main rotor to the shaft got its name because pilots said, "Oh Jesus, if that nut comes off…".

- **The biggest helicopter** was the Russian Mil Mi-12 Homer of 1968 which could lift 40,204 kg up to 2255 m.

- **The fastest helicopter** is the Westland Lynx, which flew at 402 km/h on 6 August 1986.

- **The Boeing/Sikorsky RAH-66** Comanche unveiled in 1999 is the first helicopter using stealth technology (see warplanes). It is made of carbon-fibre and other composite materials, and the rotor hub is hidden.

▶ *The Vietnam War saw the rise of heavily armed helicopter gunships designed to hit targets such as tanks.*

Boat building

- **For much of history** ships were built and designed by shipwrights.

- **Shipwrights** worked from experience and rarely drew plans. But in the 17th and 18th centuries, they often made models.

- **Nowadays** ships are designed by 'naval architects' and built by shipbuilders.

- **Wooden ships** were built on a building berth. Timbers and planks were cut and shaped around, then fitted together on, the berth to form the hull.

- **First the long spine** or keel of the boat was laid down. Thick wooden ribs were added to make a strong frame.

- **In the Middle Ages** in the Mediterranean, wooden ships were carvel-built, meaning the planks were fitted together edge to edge onto the ribs of the structure.

- **In the Middle Ages** in northern Europe, wooden ships were clinker-built. This means the planks overlapped, as in Viking ships.

- **Ships** are launched down a slope called a slipway.

- **After launching,** a ship has just the bare bones of a hull and main structures. It is finished in a fitting-out basin.

◀ *The method for constructing a wooden-hulled boat has changed little over the centuries.*

455

Submersibles

- **Submersibles** are small underwater craft. Some are designed for very deep descents for ocean research. Others are designed for exploring wrecks.

- **One early submersible** was a strong metal ball or bathysphere, lowered by cables from a ship.

- **The bathysphere** was built by Americans William Beebe and Otis Barton. On 11 June 1931 they used it to descend 900 m off the coast of Bermuda.

- **The bathyscaphe** was a diving craft that could be controlled underwater, unlike the bathysphere. Its strong steel hull meant it could descend 4000 m.

- **The first bathyscaphe**, the FNRS 2, was developed by Swiss scientist August Piccard between 1946 and 1948. An improved version, the FNRS 3, descended 4000 m off Senegal on 15 February 1954.

- **In the 1960s** the Woods Hole Oceanographic Institute in the USA began to develop a smaller, more manoeuvrable submersible, called Alvin.

- **ROVs** or Remote Operated Vehicles are small robot submersibles. ROVs are controlled from a ship with video cameras and computer virtual reality systems. Using the ROV *Argo-Jason*, Robert Ballard found the wreck of the liner Titanic in 1985.

> **... FASCINATING FACT ...**
> On 23 January 1960, the bathyscaphe *Trieste*, controlled by August Piccard's son Jacques, descended a record 10,916 m in the Marianas Trench in the Pacific.

- *Deep Flight* is a revolutionary submersible with wings that can fly underwater like an aeroplane, turning, diving, banking and rolling.

- **A new breed** of small submersibles, like the *Sea Star* and *Deep Rover*, cost about the same as a big car and are designed for sports as well as research.

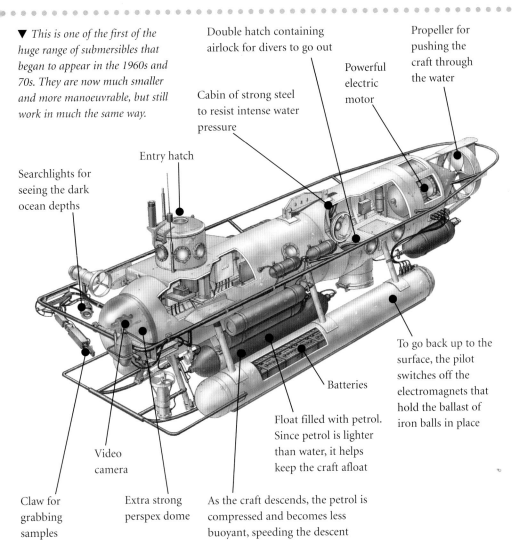

▼ *This is one of the first of the huge range of submersibles that began to appear in the 1960s and 70s. They are now much smaller and more manoeuvrable, but still work in much the same way.*

Double hatch containing airlock for divers to go out

Propeller for pushing the craft through the water

Powerful electric motor

Cabin of strong steel to resist intense water pressure

Entry hatch

Searchlights for seeing the dark ocean depths

To go back up to the surface, the pilot switches off the electromagnets that hold the ballast of iron balls in place

Batteries

Float filled with petrol. Since petrol is lighter than water, it helps keep the craft afloat

Video camera

Claw for grabbing samples

Extra strong perspex dome

As the craft descends, the petrol is compressed and becomes less buoyant, speeding the descent

457

Submarines

▲ *Nuclear submarines can stay submerged for months at a time.*

- **The first workable submarine** was a rowing boat covered with waterproofed skins, built by Dutch scientist Cornelius Van Drebbel in 1620.

- **In 1776** David Bushnell's one-man submarine, the *Turtle*, attacked British ships in America's War of Independence.

- **Petrol engines** and electric batteries were combined to make the first successful subs in the 1890s.

- **Powerful**, less fumy diesel engines took over from 1908.

- **In 1954** the US launched the *Nautilus*, the first nuclear powered sub. Now all subs are nuclear-powered.

- **U-boats** were German submarines that attack Allied convoys of ships in World Wars I and II.

The tower on top of a submarine is called the sail or conning tower.

- **In a modern sub** a strong hull of steel or titanium stops it from being crushed by the pressure of water.

- **Most subs** are designed for war and have long missiles called torpedoes to fire at enemy ships.

- **Attack** subs have torpedoes and guided missiles for attacking ships. Ballistic subs have missiles with nuclear warheads for firing at land targets.

▶ *To gain weight for a dive, submarines fill their 'ballast' tanks with water. To surface, they empty the tanks.*

459

Hovercraft

- **A hovercraft** or air cushion vehicle floats on a layer of compressed air just above the ground. It is also called a ground-effect machine. The air means there is very little friction between the craft and the ground.

- **A hovercraft** has one or more big fans that suck air into the craft, then blow it down underneath. The air is trapped underneath by a flexible rubber skirt.

▼ *Hovercraft vary in speed, size and power, but they are used essentially for one of two purposes – as ferries across short stretches of water, like this one, or by the army and navy.*

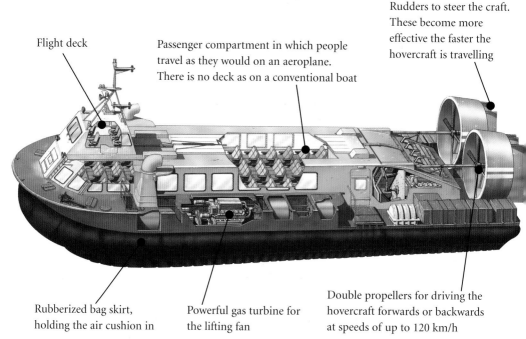

Flight deck

Passenger compartment in which people travel as they would on an aeroplane. There is no deck as on a conventional boat

Rudders to steer the craft. These become more effective the faster the hovercraft is travelling

Rubberized bag skirt, holding the air cushion in

Powerful gas turbine for the lifting fan

Double propellers for driving the hovercraft forwards or backwards at speeds of up to 120 km/h

- **The idea began with** Sir John Thornycroft in the 1870s. He thought the drag on a ship's hull could be reduced if an indent allowed it to ride on a cushion of air. But no-one could work out how to contain the air.

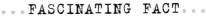

FASCINATING FACT
Hospitals may use special hoverbeds to support badly burned patients on air.

- **In the 1950s** Christopher Cockerell cracked the problem by pumping air down around the edge of a curtain-like skirt. The air itself then sealed the cushion of air inside the curtain.

- **In 1959** the world's first practical hovercraft, the SRN1, was built using Cockerell's system. It crossed the English Channel on the 50th anniversary of Blériot's first flight across the Channel.

- **In the late 1960s** the US army and navy began using hovercraft in the Vietnam War for patrol and rescue missions because of their ability to go over land, water and swampy ground equally easily. The Russian and US armies are still the biggest users of hovercraft.

- **In 1968** big hovercraft able to carry scores of cars and lorries were introduced as ferries across the English Channel, but elsewhere they have not lived up to expectations. The biggest cross-Channel hovercraft was the 56 m-long SRN4 MkIII which carried 418 passengers and 60 cars.

- **In the late 1950s** French engineer Jean Bertin developed a train called a tracked air cushion vehicle. This is basically a hovercraft on rails. Trains like this could swish between cities almost silently at speeds of 500 km/h.

- **On 25 January 1980** a 100 tonne US Navy hovercraft, the SES 100-B, reached a record speed of 170 km/h – faster than any warship has ever travelled.

Hydrofoils

- **Hydrofoils** are boats with hulls that lift up above the water when travelling at high speeds.

- **The hydrofoils** are wings attached to the hull by struts that move underwater like aeroplane wings and lift the boat up.

- **Because only the foils** dip in the water, hydrofoils avoid water resistance, so can travel faster with less power.

- **Surface-piercing hydrofoils** are used in calm inland waters and skim across the surface.

- **Fully submerged hydrofoils** dip deep into the water to provide stability in seagoing boats.

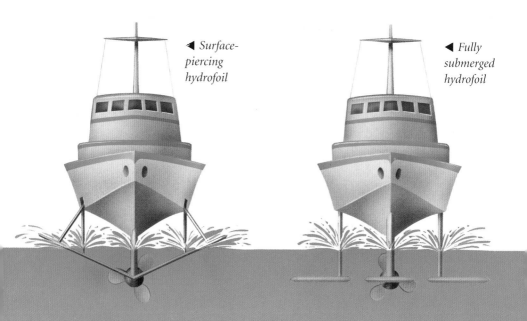

◀ *Surface-piercing hydrofoil*

◀ *Fully submerged hydrofoil*

▲ *By lifting themselves out of the water and almost flying across the surface, hydrofoils can achieve very fast speeds.*

- **The foils** are usually in two sets, bow and stern.

- **The bow and stern foils** are in one of three arrangements. 'Canard' means the stern foil is bigger. 'Airplane' means the bow foil is bigger. 'Tandem' means they are both the same size.

- **The first successful hydrofoil** was built by Italian Enrico Forlanini in 1906.

- **In 1918** Alexander Graham Bell, inventor of the telephone, built a hydrofoil that set a world water speed record at 61.6 knots (114 km/h). The record was not beaten until the American *Fresh 1*, another hydrofoil, set a new record of 84 knots (155 km/h) in 1963.

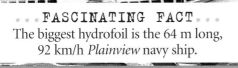

... FASCINATING FACT ...
The biggest hydrofoil is the 64 m long,
92 km/h *Plainview* navy ship.

463

Powerboats

▲ *The engine of a jet ski sucks in water and pumps it out of the back pushing the ski forwards.*

- **Powerboating** began in 1863 when Frenchman Jean Lenoir installed a petrol engine in a small boat.

- **The first major race** was in 1903 across the English Channel. The Gold Cup, organised by the American Power Boat Association (APBA), started on the Hudson in 1904.

- **In about 1910** motor makers such as Evinrude introduced detachable 'outboard' motors that clamp to the stern. Inboard motors have the engine built into the hull.

- **In the 1920s** racing boats adopted 'planing hulls' for skimming across the water at high speeds, rather than traditional deep v-shaped 'displacement' hulls. After World War II hulls were made more and more, not from wood, but metals and fibreglass.

- **Most powerboats** are driven by a high-speed jet of wate as opposed to by a propeller screw.

- **In 1994** American Tom Gentry set the offshore Class 1 record of 253.35 km/h in Skater powerboats.

- **In 1996** Gentry's *Gentry Eagle* crossed the Atlantic in 2 days 14 hours 7 mins. In 1997, the skipper *Destriero* made it in 2 days 6 hours 34 minutes.

- **The official water speed** record is 511.11 km/h by Kenneth Warby in his hydroplane *Spirit of Australia* on Blowering Lake, New South Wales on 8 October 1978.

- **Jet skis** are like motorboats that skim across the water on a ski. They were developed by the American Clayton Jacobsen back in the 1960s.

- **The jet ski** speed record is 69 km/h by French D. Condemine in 1994 on a Yahama.

▲ *Powerboat racing has become hugely competitive like motor racing, and Formula One boats roar round at speeds over 200 km/h.*

Navigation

- **Early sailors** found their way by staying near land, looking for 'landmarks' on shore. Away from land they steered by stars, so had only a vague idea of direction in the day.

- **After** c **1100** European sailors used a magnetic compass needle to find North.

- **A compass** only gives you a direction to steer in; it does not tell you where you are.

- **The astrolabe** was used for navigation from about 1350. This measured the angle of a star above the horizon, or the Sun at noon, and so gave a rough idea of a sailor's latitude (how far north or south of the Equator they were).

GPS satellite

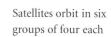

GPS receiver

Satellites orbit in six groups of four each

▲▶ *In the the Global Positioning System, sometimes known as 'satellite navigation', 24 satellites in orbit around the Earth send out radio signals to the surface. At any place on the planet, signals from at least three satellites can be detected and compared by a hand-held receiver, to fix a location within 10 to 50 metres.*

- **From the 1500s** the cross-staff gave a more accurate measure of latitude at night from the angle between the Pole Star and the horizon.

- **From the mid-1700s** until the 1950s, sailors measured latitude with a mirror sextant. This had two mirrors. It gave the angle of a star (or the Sun) when one mirror was adjusted until the star was at horizon height in the other.

- **For centuries** the only way to find longitude – how far east or west – was by dead reckoning. This meant trailing a knotted rope in the water to keep track of speed, and so estimate how far you had come.

- **You can find longitude** by comparing the Sun's height with its height at the same time at a longitude you know. But early pendulum clocks did not work well enough aboard ship to give the correct time.

- **The longitude problem** was solved in the 1700s when John Harrison made a very accurate spring-driven clock or chronometer.

- **Ships** can now find their position with pinpoint accuracy using the Global Positioning System or GPS. This works by electronically comparing signals from a ring of satellites.

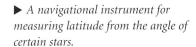

▶ *A navigational instrument for measuring latitude from the angle of certain stars.*

Stonehenge

- **Stonehenge** is an ancient stone monument in southern England made from circles of huge rough-cut stones.

- **The main circle of stones** or 'sarsens' is a ring of 30 huge upright stones, joined at the top by 30 lintels. Many of these sarsens have now fallen or been looted and used to make bridges and dams.

- **Inside the sarsen** ring are five 'doorways' called trilithons, each made with three gigantic stones, weighing up to 40 tonnes each.

- **In between** are rings of smaller bluestones.

- **The bluestones** come from the Preseli Hills in Wales, 240 km away. Archeologists puzzle over how they were carried here.

- **At the centre** is a single tall stone, called the Heel Stone.

- **Stonehenge was built** in three phases between 2950 BC and 1600 BC, starting with just a huge earth ring.

▼ *Experiments have shown a team of 150 people could haul the stones upright, but dragging them to the site on greased wooden sleds must have been a huge undertaking.*

▲ *The base of each upright stone was placed over a post-hole. Ropes and timber scaffolding were then used to raise the stones into an upright position.*

- **Archaeologists** believe it was a gathering place and a site for religious ceremonies for Bronze Age people.

- **Newman, Thom and Hawkins** have shown the layout of the stones ties in with astronomical events.

- **At sunrise on midsummer's day** (the solstice), the sun shines directly along the avenue to the Heel Stone.

469

The Colosseum

▲ *The Colosseum in Rome was one of the greatest buildings of the ancient world.*

- **The Colosseum** was a huge stone sports arena built in Ancient Rome.

- **It was 189 m long,** 156 m wide, and 52 m high.

- **It held** about 50,000 spectators who entered through 80 entrances.

- **The sports** included fights between gladiators with swords, nets and other weapons who fought to the death. They also fought against lions and other wild beasts.

- **Counterweighted** doors allowed 64 wild beasts to be released from their cages simultaneously.

- **It took just eight years** – from around AD 70 to AD 78 – to build the entire structure of the Colosseum.

- **To build** it the Romans brought almost a quarter of a million tonnes of stone by barge from quarries 20 km outside Rome.

- **During construction,** a cart carrying a tonne of stone would have left the riverside wharves every seven minutes on the 1.5 km journey to the site.

- **A huge awning** called a velarium, supported by 240 masts, protected the arena from bad weather.

- **Its opening was celebrated** by spectacular games lasting 100 days.

▼ *Romans admired gladiators for their strength, bravery and skill. However, their lives were short and their deaths were horrible.*

The Statue of Liberty

- **New York's Statue of Liberty** stands on Liberty Island off the tip of Manhattan.
- **The statue** was dedicated on 28 Oct 1886 by President Cleveland.
- **It was paid for** by the French people to celebrate their friendship with the USA.
- **Sculptor** Frédéric-Auguste Bartholdi began work on the statue in Paris in 1875.
- **It was built** from 452 copper sheets hammered into shape by hand and mounted on four huge steel supports designed by Eiffel and Viollet-le-Duc.
- **The 225 tonne statue** was shipped to New York in 1885.

▲ *The Statue of Liberty towers above Liberty Island at the entrance to New York Harbour.*

- **A pedestal** designed by Richard Hunt and paid for by 121,000 Americans brought it to a total height of 93 m.

- **The statue's full name** is *Liberty Enlightening the World*. The seven spikes in the crown stand for Liberty's light shining on the world's seven seas and continents. The tablet in Her left hand is America's Declaration of Independence.

- **Emma Lazarus's sonnet** *The New Colossus* on the pedestal ends: "Give me your tired poor, your huddled masses of your teeming shore. Send these, the homeless, tempest-tossed to me. I lift my lamp beside the golden door!"

◀ *New York's famous statue of Liberty in 1986 before it was restored and the flame covered in gold leaf.*

473

The Taj Mahal

- **The Taj Mahal** (said tarj m'harl) in Agra in India is perhaps the most beautiful tomb in the world.

- **Mughal Indian** ruler Shah Jehan ordered it to be built in honour of his favourite wife Mumtaz Mahal, who died giving birth to their 14th child.

- **Mumtaz** died in 1629, and the Taj was built over 22 years from 1632 to 1653.

- **The Taj** is set at the north end of a formal Persian garden with water courses and rows of cypress trees.

- **It is made of white** marble and sits on a platform of sandstone.

- **Inside the Taj Mahal,** behind an octagonal screen of alabaster marble tracery, lie the jewel-inlaid cenotaphs (tombs) of Mumtaz and Shah Jehan. The Shah was placed there when he died and his tomb is the only asymmetrical feature in the Taj.

- **20,000 worker**s worked in marble and sandstone, silver, gold, carnelian, jasper, moonstone, jade, lapis lazuli and coral to enhance the Taj's beauty.

- **At each corner** of the platform is a slender minaret 40.5 m tall.

- **In the centre** is a dome 21.3 m across and 36.6 m high.

- **The main architect** was Iranian Isa Khan, but the decorations were said to be by Austin of Bordeaux and Veroneo of Venice.

◀ *So perfect are the Taj's proportions that it was said to have been designed by giants and finished by jewellers.*

Skyscrapers

- **The first skyscrapers** were built in Chicago and New York in the 1880s.
- **A crucial step** in the development of skyscrapers was the invention of the first safety lift by US engineer Elisha Otis (1811–61) in 1857.
- **The Home Insurance Building** in Chicago, built in 1885, was one of the first skyscrapers.
- **In buildings** over 40 storeys high, the weight of the building is less important in terms of strength than the wind load (the force of the wind against the building).
- **The Empire State Building** built in New York in 1931, was for decades the world's tallest building at 381 m.

- **The tallest building** in America is the 442 m-high Sears Tower in Chicago, built in 1974.

- **The world's tallest building** is the 542 m Petronas twin towers in Kuala Lumpur, Malaysia.

- **A tower** now being built in Sao Paolo in Brazil may be the world's tallest single tower at 495 m.

- **If the Grollo Tower** is built in Melbourne, Australia, it will be 560 m high.

▼ *Chicago's skyline is dominated by spectacular skyscrapers, including America's tallest building, the Sears Tower (far left).*

...FASCINATING FACT...
Hong Kong's Landmark Tower, due to be completed in 2007, may be 574 m high.

Towers

- **Romans, Byzantines** and medieval Europeans built defensive towers in city walls and beside gates, giving them platforms for raining missiles on enemies.

- **Early churches** had square towers as landmarks to be seen from afar. From the 1100s, European cathedrals had towers called steeples, topped by a pointed spire.

- **Spires began** as pyramids on a tower, but got taller and were tapered to blend into the tower to make a steeple.

- **In the 17th and 18th centuries** church spires became simple and elegant, as in Park Street Church, Boston, USA.

- **The tallest unsupported tower** is Toronto's 553 m-high CN tower.

- **The tallest tower** supported by cables is the 629 m TV broadcast tower near Fargo and Blanchard in the USA.

◄ *The Leaning Tower of Pisa in Italy is a 55 m high belltower or 'campanile'. Building began in 1173, and it started to lean as the workers built the third storey. It is now 4.4 m out of true.*

- **The Tower of Babel** was a legendary tower built in ancient Babylon in the Near East. The Bible says God didn't want this high tower built, so he made the builders speak different languages to confuse them.

- **The Pharos** was a 135 m lighthouse built around 283 BC to guide ships into the harbour at Alexandria in Egypt.

- **The Tower of Winds** or Horologium, was built in Athens around 100 BC to hold a sundial, weather vane and water clock.

- **Big Ben** is the clock in St Stephen's Tower in London's Houses of Parliament. The tower once had a cell where 'rioters' like suffragette Emmeline Pankhurst were held.

▲ *Big Ben first tolled in 1859.*

479

Modern architecture

- **In the 1920s** many architects rejected old styles to experiment with simple shapes in materials like glass, steel and concrete.

- **The International Style** was pioneered by the Swiss architect Le Corbusier who built houses in smooth geometric shapes like boxes.

- **The Bauhaus** school in Germany believed buildings should look like the job they were meant to do.

- **Walter Gropius** and Mies van de Rohe took Bauhaus ideas to the USA and developed sleek, glass-walled, steel-framed skyscrapers like New York's Seagram Building.

◀ *Old and new in Hong Kong: the modern Hong Kong–Shanghai Bank dwarfs a 19th-century classical building.*

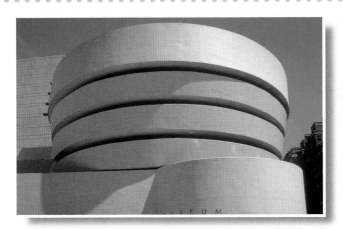

◄ The Guggenheim Museum, New York City. This unique circular building was designed by Frank Lloyd Wright.

- **American Frank Lloyd Wright** (1869–1959) was famous both for his low, prairie-style bungalows 'growing' from their site and his airy and elegant geometric buildings.

- **In the 1950s** architects like Kenzo Tange of Japan reacted against the 'blandness' of the International Style, introducing a rough concrete look called Brutalism.

- **In the 1960s** many critics reacted against the damage done by modern architecture to historic cities.

- **Post-modernists** were united in rejecting modern architecture, often reviving historical styles. American Robert Venturi added traditional decoration.

- **Richard Rogers**' Pompidou centre in Paris (1977) was a humorous joke on the Bauhaus idea, exposing the 'bones' of the building.

- **With shiny metal** and varied shapes the Guggenheim Gallery in Bilbao in Spain is a new masterpiece. It was designed by American architect Frank Gehry.

Golden Gate Bridge

- **The Golden Gate Bridge** spans San Francisco Bay in California, USA.
- **The Golden Gate Bridge** is one of the world's largest suspension bridges.
- **The total length** of the bridge is 2737 m.
- **The towers at either end** are 340 m high. The suspended span between the towers is 1280 m, one of the longest in the world.
- **The road** is 67 m above the water, although this varies according to the tide.

...FASCINATING FACT...
The tower's foundations are being
reinforced to withstand earthquakes.

- **The Golden Gate Bridge** was designed by Joseph Baerman Strauss and built for $35 million, a third of the original cost estimate.
- **The bridge was opened** to traffic on 27 May 1937.
- **The bridge carries** two six-lane highways and pedestrian paths.
- **Unusually, the bridge** is double-deck, carrying traffic one way on the upper deck and the other way on the lower deck.

▼ *The Golden Gate Bridge in San Francisco is one of the most beautiful – and busiest – bridges in the world.*

The Eiffel Tower

- **The Eiffel Tower** in Paris, France, was 312.2 m high when it was first built. An antenna brings it up to 318.7 m. There are 1665 steps up to the top.

- **On a clear day** you can see 80 km in all directions from the top. It is often sunny at the top when the weather in the Paris streets is cloudy.

- **The tower was made** from 18,038 pieces of iron, held together by 2,500,000 rivets.

- **It was built in 1889** for the exhibition celebrating the 100th anniversary of the French Revolution.

- **Gustave Eiffel** (1832–1923) was the most successful engineer of the day, building not only the Eiffel Tower but New York's Statue of Liberty as well.

▶ *Paris's Eiffel Tower is one of the world's most famous landmarks.*

- **The Eiffel Tower** was designed by Maurice Koechlin and Emile Nougier who calculated the effects of wind and gravity with amazing precision.

- **The Tower** was intended to show what could be done with cast iron.

- **During building work** Parisian artists, such as the composer Gounod and the poet Maupassant, protested against its ugliness. But when completed it was an instant success with ordinary people.

- **The cost of building** the Eiffel Tower was over $1 million. However, the fees from the visitors in the first year alone covered the construction costs.

- **When Paris was occupied** by the Nazis during the war, the lifts 'mysteriously' stopped working. They restarted the day Paris was liberated.

▶ *Approximately two million people visited the Eiffel Tower in the first year it was open.*

Index

A

A Brief History of Time,
Hawking 216
abdomen wall 244
absolute zero 43, 144, 146
absorption 280, *280*, *302*
absorption, light 87, 92,
93
acceleration **166–167**
engines *154*
laws of motion 164
vectors 172
acetic acid 28
acetylcholine 339
Achilles tendon 244, 245
acid soils 65
acids **28–29**
acids, digestion *281*
acoustics **102–103**
acquired immunity 403
actin *240*, 241
actinides *45*
active transport 300, 301
acute disease 408
additive colours 94, 95
adenine 365
adenoids 253, *279*, *398*
adenosine triphosphate
(ATP) *241*, 397
adipose tissue 291, 393
adolescence *373*
adrenal glands 287, 292,
368, 369
adrenaline,
exercise 390
glucose 287
hormones *368*, 369
mood 354
advanced gas reactors 138
aerials, television 124, *125*
aerobic exercise 390, *390*,
391
aerogels, density 180
aeroplane *443*
afterbirth 379
ageing **384–385**, 389
Agra, India 475
AIDS *398*, *410*, 411

air **52–53**
Airborne Early
Warning Systems 447
airways 252, *252*, 253
breathing *250*, 251, *251*
chemical reactions 34,
35
copper 71
density 180
diffusion 301
exercise 390
friction *184*, 185
heat 146
hydrogen 47
Lavoisier 188
light 199
lungs 256
music *101*
nitrogen 48, 49
oxygen 50, 51
particle movement *43*
pressure 43, 186
resistance 170, *170*
smell 322
sound 96, *96*, 97
states of matter 38
systems 249
temperature 312
vocal cords 254, *254*
warm 149
air sacs 256
aircraft 185
helicopters 453
jet engines *156*
missiles 449
take off 444, 445
airliners,
take off 445
Wright brothers 442
airship *47*
air-to-air missiles 449
airways **252–253**
cartilage 237
immune system 399
lungs 256, 257
tissue *393*
vocal cords 255
X-rays *413*
alchemy 37, 203
Alcock, John 450
alcohol 61, 283, *283*, 419
Alexandria, Egypt 479

algae 51
alimentary canal 280, 303
aliphatic organic
compounds 26
alkali metals 44, *45*
alkaline earth group *45*,
64
alkalis **28–29**, 31
alkanes 60
alkenes 26, 60, 61
allergies 275, *402*, 403
Allied shipping 458
alloys 67, 71
alpha radiation , 40, 41,
190, *191*
alternating current 108,
111
alternators 108
alto, music 100
alum powders 69
alumina 75
aluminium *15*, **68–69**
aluminium hydroxide 68
aluminium oxide 69, 75
alveoli 256, *256*, 257
Alvin submersible 456
amber 19
American Civil War 425
amino acids,
cell *397*
diet 295
genes 365
kidneys 306
urine 309
ammonia 21, 57, *211*
amniotic sac 379
amorphous carbon 54
amorphous solid 75
amplification 112, *132*,
134
amps 110
amygdala *349*
amylase 284, 302, 303
anaesthetics 416
analogue sound
recording 132
anatomy **386–387**
ancient Greece,
jet engines 156
ancient Rome,
Colosseum 470
androgens 370, 371

angular momentum 163
animal fats 31
animal oils 58
animal waste 52
animals,
carbon dioxide 52
genetic engineering 220
magnetism *104*
oxygen 52
ankle bones *223*
annulus 177
antacid 285
antiballistic missiles 449
antibiotics 418, *419*
antibodies **402–403**
blood cells 275
blood groups 277
immune system *398*
lymphocytes 400, *401*
systems 249
vaccination 404, 405
antigens 402, 403, *403*
anti-gravity 212
antimatter 194
anti-particles 194
antiquarks *197*
anus 280, 281, *281*
anvil 318, *319*
aorta *259*, *267*
Apollo mission 159
aponeuroses 244
appendicular skeleton
223
appendix *281*
arcades 470
archaeologists 229, 468,
469
Archimedes **204–205**
Archimedes' principle
182
architects,
Taj Mahal 475
architecture,
modern **480–481**
arenas 470
Argo-Jason submersible
456
argon,
air 52, *53*
heat 147
light 91
Periodic Table 44

490

diagnosis **406–407**
scans 414
X-rays *412*
diamonds 54, *54*, 55, *55*
diaphragm *250*, 251, *251*, 257
diastole 268, 269
diesel engines 458
diesel trains 154, **426–427**, 431
Diesel, Rudolf 426
diesel-electric locomotive *427*
diesel-hydraulic locomotive 427
diesel-mechanical locomotive 427
diet **294–295**
ageing *384*
exercise 391
vitamins 296
diffusion **300–301**
digestion 29, **280–281**
breathing 250
diet 295
enzymes 302, *303*
excretion 304
genes 365
liver 282, 283
pancreas 284
sleeping *353*
digestive juices 281
digestive system 248, *295*
digestive tract 280
digital data 119
digital images 126
digital sound recording 132
digital thermometer *144*
digital versatile disc 128, 133
dimensions 210, 212, 214, 215
diodes *111*, 112, 136
Diolkos 422
direct current 108, 111
discs, backbone 230, 237, *346*
disease **408–409**
antibodies 403
blood cells 275
fitness 389

germs 410, *411*
motor nerves 343
operations 416
vaccination 404, *404*, 405
vitamins 296
diseases 221
disks 128
dissolving 36
distance 166, 168, 175
distillation 58
diving 49
diving craft 456
dizzy, balance *321*
DNA 21, 24, 220, 221, *221*, 364, 365, 396, *396*
doctor,
diagnosis 406, *406*, 407, *407*
excretion *304*
operations 416
pulse 270, *270*
urine 309
X-rays 412
domains 104
domes,
Taj Mahal 475
dominant genes 367
doodlebugs 448
dopamine 339
double helix *364*, 365
down quark 196
drag *184*, 185
dreaming 352, 353
drinking 292, *292*, 293, *293*
driving wheels 425
drugs 83, **418–419**, *418*
operations 416
transplants *421*
ductile 71
Duryea Brothers 434
dyeing 69
dynamic friction 184, 185
dynamos 108, 207

E

ear canal *319*
eardrum 318, *319*
ears 249, **318–319**
ears 96, 98, 100
airways 252, 253

balance 320, 321, *321*
bones 223
cartilage 236, 237
co-ordination 329
ears *319*
muscles 238
sensory nerves 340, 341
Earth,
air 52, *52*
aluminium 68
calcium 64
carbon 55
centre 145
convection 149
diamonds 54
electromagnetic hydrogen *46*, 47
iron 66
laws of motion 165
magnetism 104
mass 180
oxygen 50
pressure 186
spectrum 116
telecommunications 122
temperature 144, *144*
water 56
weight 180
earthmover machines 169
earthquakes 483
eating 292, *292*
echoes **102–103**
eclipse *214*, 219
Eddington, Arthur 219
Edinburgh,
steam locomotives 425
Edison, Thomas Alva 91
effervescence 34
effort,
Archimedes 204
machines 168
turning forces 174, 175, *175*
egg cells,
chromosomes *363*
genes 365
pregnancy 378, *379*
reproductive system 374, 375, *375*, 376, *376*
hormones 370, 371
Egypt,

towers 479
Eiffel Tower **484–485**, *484*, *485*
Eiffel, Gustave 472, 485
Einstein, Albert **208–209**
black holes *216*
Hawking 217
laws of motion 164, 165
nuclear energy 140
quantum theory 200
relativity 218, 219
space *214*, 215
speed of light 89
time 210, 212
ejaculation 377
elastic limit 178, 179
elastic modulus 178, 179
elasticity 178
elastin 245, 385
elbow,
arms 242, 243
joints 234
pulse 270
transplants *420*
electric arc furnace 67
electric cars 439
electric circuits **110–111**, 112
electric current 110
computer 129
electromagnetism 114
Faraday 207
light 91
magnetism 104
power stations 108
electric light 84, 91, *91*
electric motor 207
electric power **108–109**
electric trains **428–429**
electrical cables 70, *70*
electrical charge 106, 107, 110
atoms 16, *16*
bonds 22
electrons 19
water 57
electrical energy *152*
electrical resistance *144*
electrical signals,
energy 153
sound recording 132, *132*

495

prisms 82, *83*, 93, *95*
products, chemical
    reaction 34
progesterone 369, 370,
    371, 372
prognosis 406
programmes,
    computer 128
propane 26, 60, *60*
propeller,
    helicopters *452*
    hovercraft *460*
    jet engines 157
    submersibles *457*
proprioreceptors 320,
    321, 329, 343
prostaglandin 418
prostate gland *377*
protease 302
proteins 21, 49, 220
    active transport 301
    antibodies 402
    blood 272, 273
    blood cells 274
    cells 396, *397*
    diet 294, *294*, 295
    enzymes 302
    fats 290
    genes *364*, 365
    immune system 399
    liver 282
    lymphocytes 401
    skin 331
    tissue 392
    urine 309
proteins,
protons
    atoms 16, *16*, 18, *18*, 19,
        19
    discovery 191
    hydrogen 46
    nuclear power 138
    Periodic Table 44
    quarks 196
    radioactivity 40
    scanners 127
    sub-atomic particles
        194
protozoa 411
puberty 332, **372–373**
pubic bone *377*
pubis 222

pulleys 168
pulling 170, **178–179**
pulmonary arteries 261,
    267
pulmonary circulation
    258, *259*
pulmonary veins 264, *267*
pulp, teeth *247*
pulse 242, 261, **270–271**
    fitness 388, 389
pump 204
pupils 314, *315*
pushing 170
pylons *109*
pyramids 478
Pythagoras 101

Q

quadraplegia 347
quantum effect 212
quantum theory
    200–201, 217
quarks 16, 194, **196–197**
quarries 471
quartz 24, 192
quicklime 64
quicksilver 62

R

rack and pinion gears *176*
radar *117*
Radar Absorbent
    Material 447
Radar Cross Section 447
radiation **80–81**
    Curies 192
    electromagnetic
        spectrum 82, 116, *116*
    heat 148, 149
    lasers 134
    nuclear explosions *141*
    quantum theory 200,
        201
    radioactivity 40
radial artery *243*, *259*,
    265, 270
radial nerve *335*
radio,
    navigation *466*
radio waves,
    electromagnetic
        scanners 127

spectrum 116, *117*
speed of light *89*
telecommunications
    122, *123*
electromagnetic
    television 124
radioactive decay 40
radioactive substances 80,
    126, 149, *149*
radioactive waste 138
radioactivity **40–41**
    Curies 192, *192*, 193
radio-isotopes 40
radium *41*
    Curies 193
    Periodic Table *45*
    radiation 40, 41, 80
radius *222*, 242, *243*
radon-223 41
RADOR warplanes 446,
    447, 447
rads 80
rails,
    electric trains 428
railways,
    first **422–423**
rain 149
rainbow colours *83*, 92,
    94, *95*
Rainhill speed trials,
    England *423*
ramjets 157
rapid eye movement
    (REM) sleep 353
rare earths *45*
rare metals 63
rarefactions 96
reactants 34
reactions,
    chemical **34–35**
    laws of motion 165
reactors 138
receivers 122
receptors,
    sensory nerves 340, 341
    smell 322
recessive genes 367, *367*
reciprocating engines 155
recording studio *133*
rectum *281*
recycling aluminium *15*,
    69

red blood cells 274, 274,
    275, 275, 396
red blood cells 396
    blood 272, 273
    capillaries 262
    circulation 258, *259*
    immune system 398
    liver 283
    marrow *227*
red marrow 226, 227, 232
Redeye missile 449
reduction reaction 34
reference beam 118
reflecting telescopes *203*
reflection,
    colour 92, 93, 93, 94, 95
    echo 102
    fibre optics 136
    holograms 118
    light 84, 84, 85
    sound 97
reflex action 311
reflex arc 311
reflexes **310–311**, *310*
    babies 383
refracting telescopes 203
refraction 82, *84*, 85, *85*
    Huygens 199
rejection, transplants 420,
    421
relativity **218–219**
    Einstein 208, 209
    laws of motion 165
    space 215, *215*
    time 210
Remote Operated Vehicle
    456
rems 80
renal artery *307*
renal vein *307*
Renault 434
reproductive system 249
    female **374–375**, *374*
    male **376–377**, *377*
resistance *91*, *110*, 111,
    144
resistors *111*
resonances 194
respiration 250, 301
respiration 50
respiratory disease 408
respiratory system 249